D1563738

Suny Series on Urban Public Policy
Mark Schneider and Richard Rich, Editors

PERSPECTIVES ON MANAGEMENT CAPACITY BUILDING

Edited by

Beth Walter Honadle

and

Arnold M. Howitt

State University of New York Press

Published by
State University of New York Press, Albany

© 1986 State University of New York

Printed in the United States of America

For information, address State University of New York
Press, State University Plaza, Albany, N.Y., 12246

Library of Congress Cataloging in Publication Data

Library of Congress Cataloging in Publication Data
Main entry under title:

Perspectives on management capacity building.

    (SUNY series on urban public policy)
    Includes bibliographies and index.
    1. Municipal government—United States—Addresses,
essays, lectures. 2. Local government—United States—
Addresses, essays, lectures. I. Honadle, Beth Walter, 1954–
II. Howitt, Arnold M., 1947–   . III. Series.
JS331.P44 1986   352'.0072'0973   85-8010
ISBN 0-88706-130-3
ISBN 0-88706-132-X (pbk.)

10 9 8 7 6 5 4 3 2 1

Contents

v

Acknowledgments

As the "mid-wives" of a collaborative research project, we understand well that this book rests on the hard work of many people. Most of all, we owe thanks to the authors of these essays for putting up with our prodding, short-term demands, and occasional long silences; they deserve full credit for the quality of work produced under sometimes trying conditions. Mark Schneider and Richard Rich, as series editors, have provided us with helpful advice and feedback at several stages of this project. Judith Block, Michelle Martin and Susan Suarez have provided assistance, too, from their vantage point at SUNY Press.

Each of the editors received kind support and encouragement from her/his institution while this project was taking shape. Without that help, particularly from J. Norman Reid at the U.S. Department of Agriculture and H. James Brown at the John F. Kennedy School of Government's State, Local, and Intergovernmental Center at Harvard University, this book would not have seen the light of day. At Harvard, Carol Scanlon solved many production problems with her usual intelligence, speed, and enthusiasm.

To all of these people, we offer sincere thanks.

Beth Walter Honadle
Arnold M. Howitt

Contributors

ROBERT W. BAILEY is Visiting Assistant Professor of Political Science at Columbia University, on leave from Baruch College of the City University of New York. He is the author of *The Crisis Regime: the MAC, the EFCB and the Political Impact of the New York City Financial Crisis* (1984).

WALTER D. BROADNAX is Lecturer in Public Management and Public Policy, John F. Kennedy School of Government, Harvard University. His interests include state and local government, human resource management, public policy, and organization behavior and theory. He has served in executive capacities in both the federal and state governments.

JONATHAN BROCK is Associate Professor in the Graduate School of Public Affairs at the University of Washington. He also serves as a principal in a consulting firm specializing in public sector issues, and works as a neutral in public labor-management relations. He is the author of *Managing People in Public Agencies* and *Bargaining Beyond Impasse*, which was named one of the "Outstanding Books in Industrial Relations and Labor Economics" for 1983 by Princeton University's Industrial Relations section. His public sector work experience includes management and policy positions in several federal agencies.

BEVERLY A. CIGLER is Associate Professor, Department of Political Science and Public Administration, North Carolina State University. Her writings on capacity building, growth management, local energy policy and management, state policy effectiveness, state-local policy coordination, and planning consultants have appeared in a variety of social science journals and books. Dr. Cigler recently completed research as co-principal investigator on an NSF-funded grant assessing the effectiveness of state programs for flood hazard mitigation.

SHELDON S. COHEN is Associate Director of Field Services for the Massachusetts Municipal Association. He has consulted with more than 35 local governments, school districts and other organizations in planning for, acquiring, implementing and managing computer technology. He holds an M.P.A. from Cornell University.

RICHARD G. HIGGINS, JR. is an Assistant Professor of Government and Public Administration at The American University. He received both a Ph.D. and an M.P.A. from the Maxwell School, Syracuse University. His teaching and research interests include public budgeting and financial management, state and local government, and intergovernmental relations.

BETH W. HONADLE is National Program Leader for Economic Development in the Extension Service of the U.S. Department of Agriculture. Her interests include economic development, public finance, intergovernmental relations, capacity building, and public sector labor relations.

ARNOLD M. HOWITT is Associate Director of the State, Local, and Intergovernmental Center at Harvard University's John F. Kennedy School of Government. He has taught at Harvard, Brown, and the State University of New York at Albany. Author of *Managing Federalism*, his research focuses on issues in state and local government management and intergovernmental relations.

ROBERT B. HUDSON is Professor of Social Policy, School of Social Work, Boston University. He has written widely on the politics of aging, health and aging policy, and social services implementation. He is the editor of *The Aging in Politics*.

BRUCE JACOBS is Associate Professor, Department of Political Science at the University of Rochester, where he teaches in the Department of Political Science and the Public Policy Analysis Program. He is author of *The Political Economy of Organizational Change* and co-author of *Old Folks at*

Home. His research interests include organizational behavior and policies for the aging and the poor. He has done studies for governmental agencies at the federal, state, and local levels.

DONALD F. KETTL is Assistant Professor of Government and Foreign Affairs at the University of Virginia. He is the author of *The Regulation of American Federalism*, as well as numerous articles on intergovernmental relations and public administration. He has also written a forthcoming book on the bureaucratic development of the Federal Reserve System.

RICHARD M. KOBAYASHI is Deputy Assistant Secretary of the Executive Office of Communities and Development, Commonwealth of Massachusetts, where among other duties he directs technical assistance services to local governments. His interests include public finance, institutional capacity building, and training.

TIMOTHY D. MEAD is Coordinator, Master of Urban Administration Program, University of North Carolina at Charlotte. His interests include urban management and politics, public choice theory, and capacity building.

J. NORMAN REID is Chief, Rural Business and Government Branch, Economic Research Service, U.S. Department of Agriculture. His work has focused on the availability, quality, and financing of public infrastructure in rural areas, the allocation of federal funds, substate regionalism in the United States, and the programs and finances of governments in rural areas. He recently completed an analysis of the implications of renewed rural development for public management in OECD member nations.

PETER F. ROUSMANIERE is Project Director, New England Medical Center. Previously he was President of Rousmaniere Management Associates, Inc., consultants on financial planning and computer technology to state and local governments, higher education, and voluntary associations. He serves on the finance committee of Brookline, Massachusetts. He holds an M.B.A. from Harvard University, and has taught and written on municipal management.

MARK SCHNEIDER is Associate Professor of Political Science, State University of New York at Stony Brook. His interests include suburban growth, services, and management.

GRAHAM S. TOFT is Associate Professor of Technology and Public Policy, Institute for Interdisciplinary Engineering Studies, Purdue University. His interests include strategic planning in the public sector, local governance, public/private partnerships, user fees and infrastructure, high technology industrial development, state technology policy, and technology transfer.

JOSEPH P. VITERITTI is Visiting Associate Professor of Public Administration at the Nelson A. Rockefeller College of Public Affairs and Policy, State University of New York at Albany, specializing in the areas of management and organizational development. He is the author of *Across the River: Politics and Education in the City* (1983); *Bureaucracy and Social Justice* (1979); *Police, Politics and Pluralism in New York City* (1973).

CHARLES R. WARREN is an adjunct faculty member and Ph.D. student at Indiana University. He was previously Senior Research Associate, National Academy of Public Administration.

KATHLEEN D. WARREN is a consultant with interests in public management, productivity improvement, and capacity building.

DAVID LEO WEIMER is Associate Professor of Political Science and Deputy Director, Public Policy Analysis Program, University of Rochester. He has conducted research in the areas of energy policy, criminal justice, and regulation. He is currently investigating the way courts and regulatory agencies deal with concepts of probability and statistics.

Introduction

BETH WALTER HONADLE AND ARNOLD M. HOWITT

State and local governments are caught between two political eras. Decades of expansion since World War II—reflected in expenditures, staffing, and number and complexity of governmental functions—were the direct result of public recognition of serious socioeconomic problems in the United States and a determination to "solve" them through government action. But the ability of the public sector to handle its affairs efficiently and effectively has been challenged repeatedly since the middle 1970s, and state and local governments have received a large share of the criticism. Harsh political campaign rhetoric, tax and expenditure limitations, cutbacks in federal aid, and the effects of national recession have all placed difficult pressures on municipalities around the country. Yet the responsibilities and citizen expectations that local government bears have changed relatively little.

Unquestionably, as anyone who has worked with local governments knows, there are dedicated, hard-working, and able men and women managing public services in most communities. Yet the quality of performance, just as unquestionably, is disappointing in many localities. Local government has not been able to keep pace with the demands placed upon it. Not at all exceptional is the small-city manager who reports that his department heads are unfamiliar with long-range planning and that he is speaking a "foreign language" when he brings up capital budgeting.[1]

If local government is to ride out the economic and political pressures of the 1980s, it will have to make large strides in improving its capacity to manage. "Management capacity" in this context means the ability to identify problems; develop policies to deal with these problems; devise programs to implement the policies; attract and absorb financial, human, information, and capital resources effectively to operate the programs; manage those resources well; and evaluate program outcomes to guide future program activities. Specifically, local governments need to know whether they are doing the "right" thing programmatically, whether they are doing it "well," and whether they are doing "enough" or "too much" of it.[2]

Capacity building is not a new activity. The federal government has tried to facilitate the transfer of successful management techniques from one local government to others that can use them. States, public interest groups, and universities have sponsored training and technical assistance programs to help local officials improve the way they manage. Large cities[3] and rural and small cities[4] have received assistance to help them improve their ability to plan, manage, and measure performance. Sometimes these efforts have made a difference, but sometimes they have not.

The challenge for all who care about the quality of government is to refine and improve understanding of management capacity and how to build it, to use scarce capacity-building resources wisely, and to evaluate the impact of capacity-building programs so that the next generation can be more effective. The authors of the essays in *Perspectives on Management Capacity Building* have attempted to cast light on these issues.

The Organization of This Volume

This volume consists of six sections. The first, "The Concept of Management Capacity," explores the meaning of that term. In her essay, "Defining Capacity Building," Beth Walter Honadle examines a number of other authors' works to show the range of definitions and approaches taken toward the subject of improving local management. She then offers a synthesis of this literature, identifying the essential elements of management capacity. In counterpoint, Timothy D. Mead's "Issues in Defining Local Management Capacity" argues that the meaning of management capacity depends critically on context, that no single definition appropriately describes capacity in all settings. Mead suggests that several variable factors affect one's sense of government capacity:

role perspectives, scale of government, resources available, form of government, and the functions it performs. At root, he insists, our views about these are *political* judgments, not technical determinations.

The book's second section, "Capacity-Building Needs in Different Settings," explores how substantive needs for management capacity vary over time and among different types of local government. Donald F. Kettl's essay, "Managing the Burdens of Modern Government," argues that management needs constantly evolve in response to socioeconomic and political conditions. He then surveys how contemporary pressures affect local governments' tasks of managing direct services, contract services, and regulatory programs. Kettl concludes with a discussion of how political accountability has become a more elusive problem as government's tasks have become more complex.

The other three papers in this section examine in detail how management needs vary depending on the scale of government. In "Building Capacity in Rural Places," J. Norman Reid identifies distinct management capacity needs in rural areas and then describes how these needs have evolved over the past two decades. Reid reports rural public administrators' own assessments of their management needs and concludes with a forecast about how these needs will change in the future. Mark Schneider's paper, "Capacity Problems of Suburban Governments," explores how suburban governments have been affected by changing demographic and economic conditions, the intergovernmental environment, and citizens' changing demands and expectations. He then assesses the consequences of these forces for contemporary municipal management. Finally, Joseph P. Viteritti and Robert W. Bailey examine a different scale of problem in "Capacity Building and Big-City Governance." They are concerned with the interaction between capacity and "governability," which they see as a matter of political expectations and conflicting constituency demands. Viteritti and Bailey examine several developing trends in big-city governments—better financial planning, improved management information systems, greater control over quasi-public corporations, innovations in personnel policy—and conclude by expressing concern over a possible new crisis in legitimacy for big-city governments.

The book's third section deals with "The Organizational Context of Capacity Building." Arnold M. Howitt and Richard M. Kobayashi address "Organizational Incentives in Technical Assistance Relationships." They first assess how variation in the interests of different types of assistance *providers*—private consulting firms, "mission" and "helping" agencies, nonprofit organizations, associations of governments, and volunteers—affects their behavior in assistance relationships. The authors then reverse perspective and inquire how the organizational politics of aid _recipients_ affects their responses to the aid providers' initiatives. In the next essay, "Inducing Capacity Building: The Role of the External Change Agent," Bruce Jacobs and David Leo Weimer compare the potential effectiveness of a variety of strategies of assistance, emphasizing the organizational context in which they are implemented. Among the strategies considered are targeted financial subsidies, information, and technical assistance.

In the next section of this volume, "Improving Management Control Systems," two essays consider computers and financial management. Peter F. Rousmaniere and Sheldon S. Cohen discuss in "Harnessing the Computer" how municipal managers can gain control of burgeoning municipal expenditures for computers and data processing. They trace the growth of computer use in local government, both in general and with a detailed look at the city of Boston. Then they discuss how public officials can establish a process to determine the municipality's computer needs, select an appropriate computer system, and work with a vendor to purchase, install and use it. In the other essay in this section, "Developing Financial Management Capacity: Integration at the Local Government Level," Richard G. Higgins, Jr., assesses the need for comprehensive financial control systems, including not only the traditional function of budgeting but also accounting, performance management, auditing, capital facilities planning, and cash management.

The fifth section of this book deals with human resource problems in municipal government. Jonathan Brock explores the difficulties of "Capacity Building in Municipal Labor-Management Relations," stressing not only contract negotiations but the entire range of cooperation and conflict between public employee unions and municipal management. In "Improving Local Governmental Competence," Walter Broadnax asks about the advantages and disadvantages of different points of intervention to improve the skills of managers in municipal government. He compares federal, state, state-local, local-private, and local strategies of human resources development. In the last essay in this section, Graham S. Toft focuses on "Building Capacity to Govern." His concern is the skills of municipal legislators, not management personnel.

"Federal Effects on Municipal Management Capacity" is the topic of the sixth and last section of this volume. The initial two essays are concerned with efforts by the federal government to promote improved local management in two critical areas: financial management and energy. In "The Federal Role in Capacity Building," Charles R. Warren and Kathleen D. Warren summarize the findings of their evaluations of both programs, which they conducted for the sponsoring federal agencies. Beverly A. Cigler then examines "Capacity Building Policy for Local Energy Management" from the perspective of municipal managers and develops recommendations that might have made the federal assistance program more effective. Finally, in his essay "Capacity Building in an Intergovernmental Context: The Case of the Aging Network," Robert B. Hudson looks at the management capacity problems of particular grant-supported institutions—the area agencies for the aging—and considers why the stresses they face in the future make improvements imperative.

Taken together, these papers offer provocative perspectives on the need for management capacity building in local government, the methods available, and the problems encountered in making it happen. While no comprehensive policy recommendations emerge, the lively viewpoints expressed should stimulate the thinking of all concerned with these topics.

Notes

1. Michael Murphy, "Profile of a Small City Manager," *Public Management*, 55 (November 1973): 2-6

2. See Beth Walter Honadle, "Defining and Doing Capacity Building," in this volume.

3. See *Urban Affairs Papers*, ed. Chester A. Newland, 3 (Winter 1981), for an entire issue on capacity building.

4. See Arnold M. Howitt, "Improving Public Management in Small Communities," *Southern Review of Public Administration* (December 1978): 325-344

I
The Concept of Management Capacity

1

Defining and Doing Capacity Building: Perspectives and Experiences

BETH WALTER HONADLE

A necessary assumption which underlies programs aimed at building management capacity is that there is a definable, measurable phenomenon, "management capacity," which can be purposefully changed. There is a need to arrive at a consensus definition of this concept.

—Council of State Community Affairs Agencies

Defining Capacity

A lot of organizations and individuals purport to be doing something they call "capacity building." These so-called capacity-builders go about this activity in a variety of ways—through demonstrations, grants, community development, consulting, training and development, technical assistance, and circuit riding, to name a few. Capacity building usually addresses specialized management problems—financial management, organization development, grantsmanship, personnel management, and services integration, for example—depending upon the purview and interests of the capacity-builders.

Although these characteristics of capacity building are not necessarily bad, too often capacity building is thought of as the application of a particular approach to every management problem or it concentrates on the improvement of a single area of management equated with organizational capacity. Such an approach is too narrow in that it fails to address the interrelatedness of management functions by focusing on discrete managerial areas.

This chapter[1] begins by reviewing some of the more common conceptions of capacity and emphasizes a need to arrive at a more comprehensive concept of the term. The second part of the chapter is devoted to the activity called "capacity building."

The Concept of Capacity

There have been numerous attempts in research and in government reports to define "capacity." A review of representative examples of these definitions illustrates the range of views on capacity building.

SURVIVAL. The most common definition of "capacity" is the ability of an organization to survive, that is, to be self-sustaining. Perhaps this definition is useful for some private enterprises. However, for public organizations, it ignores the fact that they are created to serve the public. Thus, to survive is not enough.

Over two decades ago, George A. Graham asked: "How Can Capacity to Govern Be Measured?" He began by rejecting survival as an index of capacity:

> The simplest and oldest test of capacity to govern ... survival ... has limitations. Its chief definitive reading is negative, for it does not measure degrees of success or differences of capacity. Survival is an index which can be read only in retrospect. It is a clock which tells what time it was—never what time it is. The fact that a state has survived does not indicate that it will continue to.[2]

The fact that survival is not an indicator of the quality of an organization's contribution to society makes it a questionable criterion for assessing the capacity of public sector organizations.

EMPOWERMENT. Another conception of capacity is empowerment; that is, an organization has capacity if it has the power to achieve social goals. Consider the following definition:

> There is a federal system with Congress at its center, and older Americans (among other Americans) at its periphery.
> If any element of the system does anything that causes an element "farther out" in the system to become more competent in the use of

its powers and resources to accomplish social purposes, that's *capacity-building.*[3]

Thus, according to some definitions, capacity building has to do with providing disadvantaged groups with the political clout necessary to achieve representation in questions of resource allocation.

INSTITUTIONAL DEVELOPMENT. Another focus of capacity is on the creation of institutions for performing various tasks. It is similar to the survival school in that it emphasizes the development and maintenance of organizations.

Robert Hawkins defines capacity in institutional terms:

> Capacity building is a concept that encompasses a broad range of activities that are aimed at increasing the ability of citizens and their governments to produce more responsive and efficient public goods and services. At its core capacity building is concerned with the selection and development of institutional arrangements; both political and administrative.[4]

Another institution-building view of capacity is put forth by the Tennessee Municipal League, which defines "true capacity" as

> "know how" that is built into the organizational structure on a continuing basis and which will be operating effectively regardless of changes in policy direction or political leadership.[5]

SYSTEMS DEVELOPMENT. Some see the need to build the capacity of local governments as systems for converting inputs into socially desirable outputs. Judah Drob's definition of capacity building is to

> build capacity of state and local governments to determine needs; seek solutions; process information; change priorities, programs, and procedures; provide feedback; and modify behavior on the basis of evaluation.[6]

Similarly, Arnold Howitt refers to the "management capacity" of a local government as "its ability to identify problems, develop and evaluate policy alternatives for dealing with them, and operate government programs."[7]

The major difference between these two definitions is that Howitt's does not require any kind of feedback mechanism, while Drob's does.

Such systems perspectives are relatively helpful because they get away from some of the more common definitions, which focus solely on the inputs side of systems. For example, two community development experts wrote that "the general intent [of capacity building] is to help the community build internal resources to carry on its developmental plans with a minimum of outside assistance."[8]

INNER- VERSUS OTHER-DIRECTEDNESS. An issue in defining capacity building is whether capacity building helps communities achieve their own goals or outsiders' goals. Some differing views will illustrate this question.

Christopher Lindley states that the function of capacity building is "to enhance the capability of local governments to perform intelligently and efficiently under their own direction. [9] Likewise, an Office of Management and Budget report on providing technical assistance defines TA as

> aid provided by a source, upon request, to a recipient, which is oriented toward solving problems which are identified by the recipient but beyond its immediate capacity to resolve.[10]

In a similar vein, the following definition is contained in proceedings from a national conference on capacity building: "to help local governments to improve delivery of services to their constituents. In other words, help local governments to become more self-sufficient."[11]

In a report on providing technical assistance, the General Accounting Office refers to "the ability of state and local governments to plan and direct programs on a long-term basis for the needs of their particular jurisdictions."[12]

Moreover, Anthony Brown writes of capacity building:

> The primary goal of this approach is to develop the capacity of ... jurisdictions ... to manage their own affairs, and to more effectively protect and promote their interests and decrease their vulnerability to disruptive changes coming from without.[13]

Such definitions are most compatible with the empowerment approach to capacity building discussed earlier. However, there are many who argue that the purpose of capacity building is to assist communities in meeting externally imposed goals and criteria. For example, a Tennessee Municipal League report states:

> When we use this term [capacity-building] we are referring to any and all efforts directed toward helping municipal governments to

plan and manage their affairs more effectively, and *in accordance with national policy and recognized standards of professional competence.*[14] (emphasis added)

Edward Anthony Lehan expands this view of capacity writing that "worries about the capability of local governments to produce . . . nationally desirable outputs are legitimate, based on the record.[15] The issue, then, is who is to decide whether a local government is peforming capably—the local government or an independent source? It is this author's opinion that there should be some minimal standards expected of local government management and that external support should be used to help all communities meet them. Beyond that, though, communities should have a lot of discretion in the types and amounts of changes they make.

On the question of standards setting, it is important to realize that how such criteria are phrased has profound implications for how we evaluate local institutions. This problem was well stated by Irwin Feller:

> It is one thing to say that Alabama's legislature should perform as well as, say the average of the 50 states; it is another to say that all state legislatures should achieve some minimum level of perfor-mance . . . and yet another to say that California's . . . legislature should *fully* be the co-equal of the executive branch . . . [16]

Capacity, in short, is a difficult concept to capture. It is probably safe to say that, at a minimum, it has something to do with all of the elements discussed above: survival, power, institutions, systems, and conforming to local expectations and external standards. It is not likely that there will ever be the kind of consensus definition of capacity called for by the Council of State Community Affairs Agencies.

A Capacity-Building Framework

The following operational definition is the author's attempt to identify some of the essential actions performed by organizations having so-called capacity. It includes elements of power, institution development, and maintenance, and is a variant of the systems approach to capacity building.

Capacity is defined by the ability to do the following (depicted in figure 1):

> anticipate change
> make informed decisions about policy

Figure 1. A Capacity-Building Framework

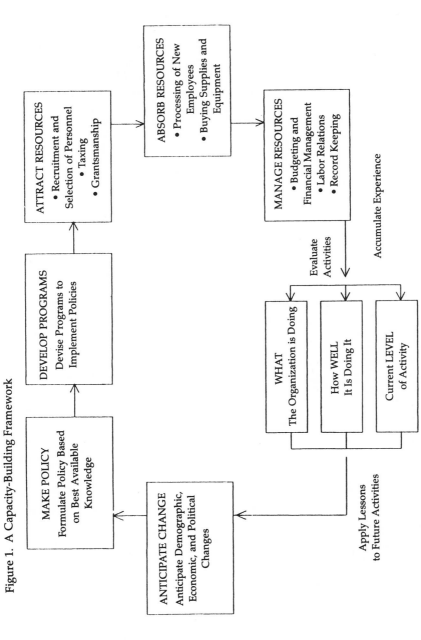

Source: Beth Walter Honadle, "A Capacity-Building Framework: A Search for Concept and Purpose," *Public Administration Review*, V. 41 (Sept.–Oct. 1981): 578.

develop programs to implement policies
attract and absorb resources
manage resources
evaluate performance to guide future actions.

ANTICIPATE CHANGE. The purpose of capacity building is to help communities handle their environments rather than have their environments control them. In some cases, communities cannot help being controlled by their physical environments, as when a natural disaster occurs. However, ordinarily, communities know that they will have fires, medical emergencies, crime, and certain weather conditions common to their locales. They need to be prepared for such exigencies when they occur.

There are other types of influences on local communities which they must anticipate and to which they must respond. For example, the discovery of natural gas in the region should alert a community to a potential for growth and development. A decline in the birth rate should tell community decision makers where to invest scarce resources. The closing of a major employer's plant (assuming that could not have been anticipated and/or prevented) should occasion community level decisions to avert the economic, social, and psychological hardships such an event is likely to have on local people. Monitoring macroeconomic trends can also help communities anticipate local needs.

Anticipating change also means keeping abreast of legislation pending in state and national capitals. A community needs to understand how changes in regulations, grants-in-aid, and its authority to raise needed revenue will affect it. If possible, the community should get involved in such decisions to make sure that its interests are adequately represented. Communities can do this through their representatives in the capital and through public interest groups representing similar communities.

In sum, the ability to anticipate change is an essential part of a community's capacity. Advance knowledge contributes to a community's power to deal with problems. Anticipating change is directly related to a community's ability to adapt effectively to a constantly shifting environment. It may require the development of specialized institutions to scan for particular types of changes likely to affect future decisions.

MAKE INFORMED DECISIONS ABOUT POLICY. Confronted with a local problem, a community needs to develop appropriate policy based on the best information available. For instance, if a boom-town suddenly finds itself coping with a large influx of new residents and the community is having to pay all of the costs of extending new facilities to residential developments, the community may decide that it is in its interest to force new residents to bear the true cost of extending community facilities to them. This requires accurate information about costs and methods by which they can be fairly shared. One task of capacity building is to collect information and help localities know how to use it for decision making.

If a community is suddenly forced by voter referendum to limit its reliance on the local property tax, it will have to decide whether to cut services and by how much or to shift to alternate, perhaps new, sources of revenue. The community will need comprehensive information on the actual cost of providing a service, what its options are, and how alternative decisions will affect the area.

These are political decisions involving the distribution of costs and benefits between current residents and newcomers and between taxpayers and service recipients (which are not always the same groups). They involve subjective determinations of equity, efficacy, and fairness as well as objective analysis of outcomes.

DEVELOP PROGRAMS TO IMPLEMENT POLICY. Programs can be conceived very broadly to mean simply ways of carrying out policies. A program is not necessarily directed from a department in city hall, staffed with civil servants, and financed out of general revenues. The defintion of program used here accepts the role of "arranger" (rather than provider) of service, which a community may also play.[17]

The community can exercise some choice in how it implements its policies and may even combine types of programs for delivering a particular service. For instance, user fees are becoming more and more common as government budgets are squeezed and more services demanded by citizens. However, the fact that a community charges people a fee for using a service does not preclude the community from subsidizing the service for lower-income residents. Other alternatives include contracting out a service to the private sector, to nonprofit or neighborhood groups, or to other governments. A nutrition program could consist of distributing vouchers to needy people or providing meals directly to eligibles. In other words, a policy may be implemented in various programmatic ways.

ATTRACT AND ABSORB RESOURCES. Another element of capacity is the ability of an organization to attract resources. Resource availability is information that should be taken into account in policy-making deliberations. Resources may be in the form of citizen participation in decision making, tax revenues, intergovernmental transfers, information, volunteers, rulings, and other inputs used in the "production" of community goods.

Not only must a community be able to draw resources from its environment, it also needs the capacity to absorb those resources. This is especially important from the point of view of the capacity-builder. Sometimes aid is granted to a community without taking into account the community's ability to effectively use the aid within a specified period of time, such as a fiscal year. Or a community may view volunteers as free goods without taking into account its ability to absorb them. If the community has no workplace for the volunteers, no one to manage them, and no resources to support them, the community is not in a position to effectively absorb the resources even though it may have the capacity to attract them.

In another sense, a community may not be able to absorb resources. If a management innovation was designed for systems of a certain minimum size, then smaller communities may not be able to use the technology. Thus, the capacity of communities to attract and absorb resources is an important variable for capacity builders to consider.

MANAGE RESOURCES. Assuming that a community does have the capacity to absorb additional resources, it needs to manage them. Without effective management of personnel, finances, time, information, and the other resources assigned to an organization, such resources will be dwindled away, and personnel will become demoralized by the lack of organization and direction. Thus, capacity building should involve the development of appropriate budgeting, personnel, and other administrative operations.

EVALUATE CURRENT ACTIVITIES TO GUIDE FUTURE DECISIONS. One of the most critical elements of capacity is for an organization to understand its ongoing activities in order to improve on them in the future. This goes back to its ability to anticipate change; that is, by knowing what the organization is currently doing, it can avoid repeating its mistakes in the future.

Evaluation has three distinct purposes in this definition. It means assessing: (1) what the organization is currently doing, (2) how well it is doing what it does, and (3) the level of current activity.

In other words, it matters little how well an organization is performing a function if it is performing the wrong function. Nor is it ideal for the community to be doing the right thing but be doing it so ineffectively that it cannot achieve its objectives. Likewise, if a community is doing too much or too little of a desirable activity, it is either wasting resources or falling short of achieving the objectives it has set for itself. Thus, the three functions of evaluation I have delineated provide important information for policy-makers to use in making decisions about the future.

Doing Capacity Building

Knowing what capacity is and knowing how to build it are separate, but related, issues. Based on knowledge of capacity building it is possible to identify some of the desirable features of successful capacity-building programs. To summarize, the most successful capacity-building programs have some of the following characteristics:

> Recipient has confidence in the technical-assistance provider;
> Funding is provided by a combination of sources;
> Implemented change is rewarded;
> Local-level officials are actively involved;
> Management practices advanced can be utilized most effectively by the size and character of government receiving the assistance;
> Provider alleviates perceived risk or threat to the recipient; and
> Effort builds on established resources of the recipient.

These factors contribute to the successful management of capacity-building programs by making it possible for local governments to take risks, by tailoring efforts to local needs and preferences, and by creating incentives for local managers to make the programs work. Several of these characteristics are closely related, but I separate them below for explanatory purposes.

Trust

It is essential for the recipients of technical assistance to have rapport with the provider. Good working relationships are based on mutual trust between the parties. This confidence is affected, in part, by the source of the assistance itself. For example, a small town official is likely to be skeptical of assistance from a "Fed" because the federal government is perceived as being remote, condescending, and intrusive. By comparison, a retired city manager or a state extension worker may be regarded as a more trustworthy source of assistance.

I have witnessed some very good working relationships between local officials and state extension workers who had a genuine interest in improving the community. Some local officials may be "turned off" by university professors because the officials fear that the scholar is more interested in studying them, collecting data, and publishing the results in professional journals than in helping the community manage itself better. Moreover, some local officials question whether a professor is practical enough to provide anything useful to them.

Combined Funding

Some of the most successful capacity building occurs when the costs of the program are shared by all the parties. This is because each of the participants has a stake in making the program succeed. The willingness of local governments to pay is also a way of judging the true interest of the local government in the program. If the community sees the assistance as a free good, it has no reason to reject it, but may use it without enthusiasm or real commitment. Likewise, the community will have little incentive to give the program much priority among its other activities.

Another reason for funding capacity building from multiple sources is simply that some local communities do not have the resources to afford it. Moreover, since society as a whole benefits from good management at the local level, sharing responsibility for capacity building is justifiable on equity grounds.

Rewards

It is important to reward local governments, work groups, and individuals who succeed in building their managerial capacity. This means rewarding the specific behavior one wants performed. In the words of Donaldson and Bell: "If the goal is implemented change, implemented change is what should be rewarded—not plans for change or plans to build unused capacity, but implemented change."[18]

For example, individuals' promotions, raises, and responsibilities can be tied to improving their performance in specified areas. Likewise, federal or state financial assistance can be tied to particular management improvements on the part of recipients.

Local-Level Officials Involved

The involvement of local officials should go further than merely funding the program. Local officials should be involved from the outset in identifying needs, developing solutions, scheduling, coordinating, and so on. One lesson learned from a number of programs is that a capacity-building program cannot succeed without the commitment of top-level local officials. It is also not likely to serve local purposes without it. The reason is that public employees will work harder on a project when they perceive the activity as a high priority of top management.

Appropriate Assistance

For capacity building to work, the techniques offered by the capacity-builders should be appropriate for the recipient. In other words, trying to get a very small town to adopt budgeting practices designed for big cities will frustrate the local government and make the capacity-builder look foolish. More generally, whatever solutions are proffered must take into account local needs, practices, and structures. Otherwise, the capacity building is merely a transfer agent pushing standardized management practices from a source to all localities. One way of ensuring that assistance is appropriate is to involve the people who are going to have to change their behaviors in the design of the program.

To make assistance appropriate, it may be necessary to have one-on-one consulting to gear solutions to the local situation. Although it is not always the case, one potential problem with the demonstration method is that it assumes transferability of the solution to other settings.

Risk Alleviation

Perhaps the main reason why there is a need for using outside help in the first place is that local (elected) officials cannot afford politically to take the necessary risks by themselves. Introducing new productivity-enhancing procedures, reorganizing, and other management innovations are always expensive. If they fail to achieve desired results, it is easier for an official to explain to her or his constituents that it was not entirely a "local" mistake. Therefore, to get officials to try something new, it is necessary to alleviate some of the risk involved.

One way of alleviating risk for local officials is through demonstrations. With demonstrations, capacity-builders can show officials who are afraid to take the plunge that the solution they are being offered has a proven record. Again, however, the solution needs to fit the local situation.

Use of Established Resources

Capacity-builders should assess the current situation before trying to improve it. Otherwise, capacity building runs a very big risk of throwing the baby out with the bath water. In other words, build upon what the community is doing right rather than discard all of the old procedures and substitute new ones. The latter is counterproductive, and it adds to the perception of risk on the part of local actors.

Conclusion

Over the years there have been a lot of attempts to build the capacity of local governments in the United States. Most of the time little thought appears to have been given to the goals of capacity building and to the most effective methods for generating lasting and appropriate change.

In this chapter, I have reviewed a number of definitions of capacity. Clearly, the definition of capacity chosen has a profound effect on the receptivity of localities to attempts at building their capacity and on the approaches a community will take in trying to do capacity building. I tried to make the point that some common definitions of capacity are lopsided, emphasizing one function of organizations at the expense of all the others. For example, although an organization has to survive to be capable, mere survival does not signify capacity. Likewise, all organizations need inputs to perform their functions, but the impartation of inputs by itself is not capacity building.

I developed a framework of capacity for local governments, which included the ability to: anticipate and influence change, make informed policies, develop programs, attract and absorb resources, manage resources, and evaluate current activities to guide future action. This definition was intended to be flexible enough to cover a wide range of settings, but sufficiently specific to facilitate the analysis of individual organizations.

Finally, I delineated some of the factors that make capacity-building efforts successful. In general, these had to do with tailoring solutions to local needs, alleviating the risks associated with innovation on the part of local officials, and providing incentives for recipients of assistance to make desired changes.

Notes

1. The two main sections of this chapter are adapted (with permission) from previously published articles by the author. The section on defining capacity is taken from: "A Capacity-Building Framework: A Search for Concept and Purpose," *Public Administration Review*, 41, 5, (September-October 1981); 575-580. The section on doing capacity building is taken from: "Managing Capacity-Building: Problems and Approaches," *Journal of the Community Development Society*, 13, 2 (1982): 65-73.

2. George A. Graham, *America's Capacity to Govern: Some Preliminary Thoughts for Prospective Administrators*. (University: University of Alabama Press, 1960) 52.

3. E.H. White and Co., *Capacity-Building and Decentralization (Session E)*. AoA *Staff Program Materials*. Prepared for U.S. Department of Health, Education, and Welfare, Administration on Aging. SHR-0000620. (Washington, DC, Oct. 1975).

4. Robert B. Hawkins, Jr., *Extension Project: Capacity-Building for Small Units of Rural Government*. Prepared for U.S. Department of Agriculture, Extension Service, Unpublished and final draft (1980) 2.

5. Tennessee Municipal League, *Community Development Assistance for Tennessee Cities*. Vol. 1: *Final Report and Appendices A-E*. Prepared for U.S. Department of Housing and Urban Development, Office of Policy Development and Research. Contract number H-2184R. (Washington, DC, June 1976).

6. Judah Drob, "Targets of the Program," *Report of the OMB Study Committee on Policy Management Assistance*, Vol. 3: *Background Papers and Resource Materials*. (Washington, DC: National Science Foundation, June 1975) 1014.

7. Arnold M. Howitt, "Improving Public Management in Small Communities," *Southern Review of Public Administration*, 2 (December 1978): 325.

8. Larry Gamm and Frederick Fisher. "The Technical Assistance Approach," *Community Development in America*, ed. James A. Christenson and Jerry W. Robinson, Jr. (Ames: The Iowa State University Press, 1980) 55.

9. Christopher Lindley, "Changing Policy Management Responsibilities of Local Legislative Bodies," *Public Administration Review*, 35, Special Issue (December 1975): 797.

10. U.S. Office of Management and Budget, "The New Federalism—Report on Technical Assistance," Internal Document (written by Ann C. Macaluso), (November 1973) 1.

11. Commonwealth of Pennsylvania, Department of Community Affairs, *Report of National Conference: States' Role in Strengthening Local Government Capabilities*. (Harrisburg, Pa., May 1975) v.

12. U.S. General Accounting Office, General Government Division, *State and Local Governments' Views on Technical Assistance.* GGD-78-58 (July 12, 1978) 1.

13. Anthony Brown, "Technical Assistance to Rural Communities: Stopgap or Capacity Building?" *Public Administration Review*, 40, 1 (January/February 1980): 21.

14. Tennessee Municipal League, 11.

15. Edward Anthony Lehan, "The Capability of Local Governments: A Search for the Determinants of Effectiveness," *Connecticut Government*, 28, 3 (Spring 1975): 2.

16. Irwin Feller, "Issues in the Design of Federal Programs to Improve the Policy Management Capabilities of State Legislatures," *Public Administration Review*, 35, Special Issue (December 1975): 783.

17. See: Martha A. Shulman, *Alternative Approaches to Delivering Public Services,* Urban Data Service Reports, 14, 10 (Washington, DC: International City Management Association, October 1982).

18. W. Donaldson and C. Bell, "Can You Make a Man Drink?" *Report of the OMB Study Committee on Policy Management Assistance. Vol. III: Background Papers and Resource Materials.* (Washington, DC: National Science Foundation, 1975).

2

Issues In Defining Local Management Capacity

TIMOTHY D. MEAD

Local governments in the United States provide a bewildering array of management practices and public services. There are over 3,000 counties, 35,000 general purpose local governments, and 53,000 special districts (including school districts) in the U.S. Each of these units is somehow distinct from its neighbors, including differences in management practices.

As a consequence, management capacity is typically discussed either in very abstract descriptive terms,[1] or in terms of a case study[2] or a small number of carefully selected cases.[3] Upon reading these studies, management capacity is rather likely to be recognized by its absence. Thus, after the fact, we can all readily explain why the financial management practices of New York, Cleveland, or Wayne County got those jurisdictions in trouble.[4]

How widespread is this difficulty? A recent annotated bibliography of 162 titles—mostly U.S. government documents—that considered state and local government capacity building showed that only 41, or 25.3 percent, included an explicit definition of management capacity and that only 36, or 22.2 percent, included an implicit definition.[5] Moreover, those definitions were very general, referring to "enhanced performance" or "improved processes" or "greater capability."

If, as scholars trying to understand management capacity or practitioners trying to improve it, we are to have an impact on local management capacity other than in a sporadic and localized fashion, a more systematic understanding of local management capacity is required. A major reason why this has not been accomplished in the last decade is that there are unresolved and largely unaddressed issues in the discussion. This paper will address five, viz., the issues of perspective, scale, resources, form, and function.

Preventing a common understanding of what constitutes a local government with management capacity are context-free expectations of what local governments should be doing and how they should be doing it. The five issues discussed in this paper show how contextual factors impinge on local capacity. The rub, of course, is that local governments themselves are not context-free. They are appropriately parochial because they are the only unit of government whose authority corresponds uniquely to the area, functions, and resources available. What constitutes a satisfactory level of capacity, therefore, need not be externally validated, but locally acceptable. As Gargan has observed, "Simply put, a local government's capacity is its ability to do what it wants to do."[6] That definition of capacity is used here.

The Issue Of Perspective

What constitutes an adequate level of local government capacity, then, varies by the perspective of individuals and their determination of what it is that they want local government to do. Among the most important differences of perspective are the level of government with which an individual is associated, the role of the individual vis-a-vis local government, and the particular local government with which an individual is affiliated within units of government at the same level. These different perspectives often imply conflicting values. Frequently, therefore, admonitions for improving local management capacity fall on deaf ears; both the admonisher and the admonished agree on what the proposed capacity building would do, but disagree on its desirability.

An important aspect of the recent wave of voter-mandated cuts in local revenue capacities—the sons and daughters of Proposition 13—is the assumption by many that reducing local revenues will not have a corresponding effect on municipal activities, at least in part because there is lots of "fat" in municipal budgets caused by "lazy bureaucrats" and mismanagement. The upshot has been to augment an impression that "even in the provision of their traditional services, city bureaucracies looked 'flabby' and 'inefficient' in comparison to private bureaucracies."[7]

The difference in perspective as it varies from one level of government to another was highlighted in the 1975 report of the Office of Management and Budget's Study Committee on Policy Management Assistance (SCOPMA), *Strengthening Public Management in the Intergovernmental System*. The nub of the study committee argument is summarized under the heading "The Managerial Backlog." The study committee contended that antiquated state and local management structures designed for smaller and more rural environments frustrated the ability of officials to provide public services.[8] The perspective that emerges from the study committee work is that local governments are just a little behind the times in terms of structures, staffed by persons not familiar with the techniques of "the modern age," and indifferent to advances in public management.

In the past fifteen years that perspective has characterized portions of the national government. One sign that it is not diminishing is the rapid growth of mandates to local governments. Almost "84 percent of the federal and nearly 90 percent of state mandates are 'how to' mandates stipulating the activities which must be performed in connection with the provision of programs and kinds and working conditions of personnel who must do them."[9] Indeed, a major impact of the various mandates has been to erode local autonomy and independence of judgment.[10] Mandates are thus a means of control, control that seems appropriate from the perspective of those adopting the mandates, whether through legislation or regulation, because of the unreliability of those being mandated. Doubtless in many areas of national concern, civil rights for example, local governments would not have pursued national ends in the absence of mandates. Nonetheless, as Lovell and Tobin demonstrate, the overwhelming preponderance of mandates are procedural rather than substantive.

Though the perspective of some federal officials that state and local governments leave a great deal to be desired is of long standing, the Advisory Commission on Intergovernmental Relations recently concluded "that the sensitivity of national policymakers to the role and needs of subnational governments is less now than it was a generation ago . . . "[11] As the ACIR points out, the irony of this circumstance is that subnational governments have vastly expanded their representational efforts at the national level during this same time.

Perspective on what constitutes management capacity also varies by the role of the observer. Citizens are likely to have a less sophisticated view than specialized observers like public officials and their peers, academic observers, consultants and others whose business it is to think about things like "local management capacity." Gargan classifies this factor as "community expectations."[12]

In some jurisdictions, citizens expect the municipality to pick up trash along the curb, whereas in others rear-of-the-house pickup is expected. Charlotte, North Carolina's city council, for example, refused to continue an experimental program of curbside trash pickup despite evidence of reduced cost and user satisfaction among those actually receiving such service. In other areas of the city, however, opposition to curb pickup was vociferous. Political expectations, rather than management capacity issues, were the major factor in the city council's decision.[13] The city manager and the professional staff of the Operations Department perceived their role as requiring them to seek out and implement means to enhance productivity, particularly in this case reducing cost. But the city council perceived its role to require that controversy be minimized. Consequently, what constituted an acceptable level of management capacity varied here by role and the city council was willing to accept the less productive alternative by trading cost effectiveness for political support. This does not mean that the city council made a "bad" decision. But it does illustrate how the role of participants in the capacity determining process varies.

Yet another example of the way in which perspective by role affects suitable levels of management capacity is the contrast between how citizens and officials perceive the role of local officials in a disaster. In a study of perceptions of citizens and public officials in the Wyoming Valley of Pennsylvania just after the 1972 flooding that resulted from Hurricane Agnes, Wolensky and Miller discovered substantial variation between the two groups.[14] Before the disaster struck, both citizens and local officials had congruent perceptions of what local officials should be doing, what role they should play. Both groups perceived this role in custodial terms. In the aftermath of the disaster, however, discontinuities developed between the two perceptions. Public officials continued to hold to a custodial view of their function. In both the short-run and long-run disaster period, public officials were concerned with cleaning the streets, repairing the storm sewers, and other comparable tasks. In contrast, leaders of citizen groups expected innovative leadership, planning for long-range economic and social recovery, and facility in generating resources from beyond the area.

But such leadership was not forthcoming. Wolensky and Miller contend that the shared citizen-office holder perspective which the office holders brought to office was an important constraint preventing them from adopting a more active role after the disaster.[15] Clearly, then, perception of role was an important consideration in evaluations of the conflicting assessments of the management capacity brought to bear on post-disaster recovery.

Additional data from case studies indicates the importance of role perceptions of individual mayors who have illustrated a capacity to manage local affairs.[16] Yet others have focused attention on mayors whose perception of their political role did not include political entrepreneurship, with the result that the level of management capacity suffered.[17]

Role constraints, then, play an important part in determining whether an individual observer of local governments believes that an adequate level of management capacity is present. These role perspectives are intimately tied to what the observer wants a local government to accomplish, i.e., what values the local government should promote. And since values differ among individuals, so too do notions of what constitutes desirable management capacity levels.

The Issue Of Scale

Local governments are frequently judged wanting in management capacity because of their size, usually because they are too small. Size is rarely defined rigorously, though population is often used as a surrogate.

The issue of scale is most often found in arguments that small units of government are inherently subject to diseconomies of scale. In 1976 the Advisory Commission on Intergovernmental Relations wrote:

> The traditional assignment patterns [of service responsiblities] often result in service inefficiencies when local or areawide governments perform services which could be less expensively provided by another level or unit of government for reasons of economies of scale.[18]

Though ACIR asserted that economies of scale were available, no evidence was given to demonstrate that this was the case. Indeed, the only assistance offered to someone who wanted to identify which services could be provided with greater "economic efficiency" was that functional assignments should be made to jurisdictions "that are large enough to realize economies of scale and small enough not to incur diseconomies of scale."[19] More recently the ACIR has reasserted the same proposition, viz., that aggregating service arrangements resulted in economies of scale, but again without any specific evidence of the kinds of services or the appropriate cutpoints where such economies came into effect.[20]

The "economy of scale" argument is not limited to the capacity of local governments to supply services. It applies to the broader area of policy management as well. Fitch has argued that "informed decisions about expenditure and investment priorities require sophisticated planning and budgeting processes which lend themselves to the economies of scale which are impossible in small jurisdictions."[21] The OMB Study Committee wrote, "Policy management is the performance on an integrated, cross-cutting basis of the needs assessment, goal setting, and evaluation functions of management."[22] Here words like "integrated" and "cross-cutting" suggest that effective policy management may not occur in smaller jurisdictions where such characteristics of the policy process may not be required. An additional element of the "bigger is better" school of local management capacity is the argument that the scale of problems often outstrips the scale of the institutional capacity to handle them.[23] A conclusion often reached from such analysis is that jurisdictional boundaries, because of the "production characteristics" of public policies, "should be coterminous with the metropolitan area,"[24] and that small local governments lack the management capacity to deal with such problems.

Yet, it is not clear that economies of scale always result from the consolidation of services. A study of waste collection in St. Louis County, Missouri, found that of fifty-three suburban municipalities, diseconomies of scale were present only among municipalities that had fewer than 1000 collection units. Variations in cost were related to factors other than scale.[25] Another study of the 799 largest cities in the country compared the size of the population with the size of the bureaucracy, controlling for region and services. It found evidence of "diseconomy of scale" among the cities and concluded "that whole-sale consolidation or enlargement of local government jurisdictions is unlikely to achieve economy and efficiency in municipal services."[26]

Capacity to provide desired public services in a productive fashion is related to scale, but a single relationship is not common to all services. Some services require a large scale and some a modest scale. After reviewing the literature on the relationship between the size of police departments and their operation, Gordon Whitaker concluded that larger departments could more efficiently supply their own support services while smaller ones could more efficiently provide patrol services.[27]

How can we determine the scale at which services can be provided with maximum capacity? Some have suggested that the critical feature is whether the service is consumed directly by citizens, and thus labor-intensive, or whether it is indirectly consumed and capital-intensive. The most efficacious scale for services consumed directly—like police patrol, fire protection, and education—is small. In contrast, more capital-intensive services like pollution control, water and sewer services, and public transportation are more capably provided on a larger scale.[28]

Nonetheless, the research suggests that there is a minimum size of local government that constitutes a threshold of capacity. This is not to say that all local governments above the threshold demonstrate management capacity. Nor does it argue that no government below the minimum population can demonstrate capacity in selected activities. Rather, it suggests that it is more difficult for a local government below the threshold to develop an adequate level of capacity. Herrington Bryce has concluded that there are special problems affecting the capacity of cities between 25,000 and 50,000 population to do planning. In addition to the problems of adequate staff and data, Bryce found the quality of local leadership in small jurisdictions to be a major impediment to planning and the implementation of planning. Bryce does not argue that these factors do not affect large cities, but that the effect on smaller cities is more debilitating. [29] B.J. Reed and Roy Green studied the capacity of small cities, those with population under 50,000, to manage federal grants. They found that officials in cities of less than 10,000 population were more likely to report that they lacked the staff capacity to apply for federal grants than were the larger cities. They found that officials were willing to postpone developing capacity, to apply for grants or to manage them should they be awarded, in order to deal with short-term problems.[30] It appears, then, that there is some threshold of scale that serves as a boundary for high levels of management capacity, though it is not clear from the research where this boundary is.

Frequently this issue can be reduced to a difference of opinion over the desirability of an externally validated standard of capacity rather than one that meets local expectations. HUD, the International City Management Association, state departments of community affairs, all suggest to local governments "the way" that capacity issues should be resolved.

In political terms, however, it may be that residents of the smaller jurisdictions choose not to develop the administrative mechanisms and practices that would make for management capacity. As is so often true, there are trade-offs; small jurisdiction local officials choose to deal with more immediate problems with their scarce resources. Some persons may prefer the feeling of community that exists, indeed, may have sought to live in such a community, rather than to live where the local government demonstrates high levels of management capacity.

Or it may be that local officials do not see greater management capacity as something that is needed. A study of the attitudes toward administrative innovation of Mississippi county officials—Mississippi counties are among the smaller jurisdictions in the country—found that these officials were not convinced of a need for administrative innovation, usually cited as a hallmark of a jurisdiction with a high level of capacity. Rather, "what all of this points to is that most [Mississippi] county officials do not consider county procedures as administratively developed, nor do they necessarily feel that there is a need for revision."[31]

What explanation can there be for such a benighted perception that modern and innovative administrative practices ought not be adopted? Rosenthal has suggested that "the capacity of an operating system [must] be sufficient to meet the demand for its services."[32] And therein lies the answer. The demand for similar levels of management capacity for different-scale local jurisdictions is based on the assumption that local governments are or should be pretty much alike. Values other than state-of-the-art local management are desired by local citizens.

But as the studies above have suggested, small jurisdiction local officials prefer to meet other demands than the need to develop high levels of management capacity, including the demand to hold taxes down and to provide minimal public services. There are political trade-offs in small-scale jurisdictions that inhibit the development of levels of management capacity that are required in larger-scale jurisdictions. Steps likely to result in greater economies of scale are rejected because to adopt them would be to accept values smaller communities choose to reject. For small-scale jurisdictions, capacity building may be counter-productive in the sense of the trade-offs required. Even though local officials may perceive that a lack of management capacity inhibits some choices, they accept the inability rather than incur the costs of enhanced capacity.[33]

The Issue Of Resources

Resources are intimately linked to levels of management capacity among local governments. Obviously the level of resources—their adequacy in assuring that a given local government is able to do what it wants to do—is critical. Other ways in which resources are linked to local management capacity include the discretion to determine how resources shall be committed and to what, the significance of political choice in resource commitment, and the relationship between resources and management operations.

The issue of resources is rarely overlooked but often misstated. Frequently capacity-builders assume that satisfactory levels of resources can be obtained by local governments in rather straightforward fashion, that there are few political constraints or trade-offs. In doing so, the richness of local tradition and the choices of which resources to consume for what ends is missed.

In order to sustain high levels of management capacity adequate resources must be available. A threshold of resources is a necessary, but not sufficient condition for local management capacity.

In terms of management capacity, no resource is more crucial than competent personnel resources. Quality personnel, both elected and professional, make the wheels of local government go round best. In order to develop high levels of management capacity, local governments must be willing to hire quality personnel. This approach is not so readily agreed upon as might be suspected. During the field work for a HUD capacity-building project undertaken several years ago by the Academy for Contemporary Problems, a personnel official from a local jurisdiction told the research team that its policy was to hire persons with local origins who got Cs in college; if they were local they would not be likely to look for jobs elsewhere, and if they were "average" students they would be glad to have the job and not filled with new ideas about the way things should be run. That jurisdiction was selected for study because of its reputation for poor management.[34]

In addition to professional employees, the level of elected officials is important to management capacity. But what constitutes excellence among the large volunteer corps of elected American local officials and what occasions it remains largely unknown.[35] Particularly important in the linkage between financial resources and management capacity is the extent of local discretion in determining how resources are committed and to what uses.

Restrictions on local financial resources, either by national or state governments, are important factors affecting local management capacity. Such restrictions may inhibit capacity by limiting the availability of resources. Certainly this is not to argue that states, in particular, have no responsibility to oversee the financial management of local governments or that Congress and agencies acting pursuant to the Congressional will have no valid purpose in assuring that sufficient management control is exercised in channeling federal funds to the federal purpose. From the perspective of local management capacity, however, regulations of the processes of financial management are much more efficacious than limits on revenues or expenditures. These latter may reduce the amounts available to local governments or inhibit their flexibility in meeting citizens' demands.

For some activities of local governments, a lack of financial resources may translate directly into a lack of capacity, planning and analysis capacity in particular.[36] Indeed, there is evidence to suggest that the "least productive" public agenices are unable to generate sufficient slack resources to provide the sorts of policy analysis prerequisite to utilization of productivity programs. The General Accounting Office has noted that local governments were much more likely to respond to fiscal constraints with "belt tightening" than with efforts to increase productivity.[37] Levine characterizes the relationship between adequate resources and the capacity to engage in analysis useful for management purposes *"the management science paradox."* Organizations with slack resources can devote some of them to analysis while others can be directed toward political support. But when resources are in scarce supply, analytic capacity is sacrificed. Levine concludes that "the management science paradox means that when you have analytic capacity you do not need it; when you do need it, you do not have it and *cannot* use it anyway."[38]

Resource restrictions also reduce the flexibility, and thus the capacity to adapt, of local governments. Such restrictions on the use of resources affect not only financial flexibility but organizational flexibility as well. Despite early assurances by federal officials that Community Development Block Grants and Comprehensive Employment and Training Act programs would be administered with fewer restrictions than earlier generations of grants, these programs soon developed the sorts of devices that federal officials thought would enhance federal control. One example of the impact of these regulations on administration is provided by Richmond, Virginia. In order to adapt to federal requirements for accountability, Richmond has developed a series of ad hoc administrative arrangements that include private providers of services and complex intergovernmental agreements with other local and regional units of government.[39] Such ad hoc arrangements inhibit local governments' ability to devise context-specific solutions to organizational problems. This process, however, is not limited to federal grants. In the now classic *Urban Outcomes*, Levy and his associates document the way in which acceptance of state gas tax revenues by the city of Oakland determines which streets will be constructed and maintained within the city.[40]

An additional aspect of local management capacity is the ability of a local government to make choices. Local governments lose some of their independent capacity when they give up functions to other levels of government, are forced through resource inadequacy to discontinue services provided at an earlier time, or become more reliant on outside funding sources. This latter was experienced by local governments in California when the state provided additional monies in the wake of Proposition 13. It is very hard to exercise independent judgment when someone else is paying the bills. Problems of local independence from other levels of government, even in those that demonstrate apparent capacity in responding to resource scarcity, seem to be exacerbated when resources become more scarce.[41]

In part, the impact of resource scarcity on local discretion depends on what local governments have done with external monies in the past. Such funds have been made available to get local governments to do something that they would not have done at all or would not have done as rigorously in the absence of external funds. For governments with both adequate self-generated resources and high levels of management capacity, the recent cuts in federal funds and the apparent unwillingness or inability of states to make up for the federal cuts has had little impact on providing basic services. For one thing, local governments with high levels of management capacity seem to have been very judicious in allocating federal funds. Savannah, Georgia, for example, has had a long-standing policy of applying for federal funds only to accomplish purposes that Savannah officials have determined that they want to accomplish. They have not sought federal money simply because it was there.[42] In doing so Savannah has avoided letting the federal government set its priorities.

In addition, if they could afford to do so, well-managed local governments have avoided using federal funds for the operation of traditional local services. External funds have been used to support "extra" things. And though some of those activities have generated local bureaucracies supported by "soft money," local governments that have kept the two types of projects separate have been able to absorb reductions more easily without cutting out programs that local officials thought were of top priority, like police and fire. Both Jacksonville and Pensacola, Florida, for example, anticipated which programs would require funding by local sources in the event that federal funds were cut and what obligations the jurisdictions might wish to assume. In addition, external funds were frequently used to purchase equipment or meet other one-time needs. These cities were "fiscally conservative" in their approach to federal funds. This approach to federal funding has made it easier for these cities to absorb cutbacks than for cities that used federal funds to fund on-going operational costs.[43]

Certainly absorbing federal cutbacks, as Jacksonville and Pensacola have done, is easier when there are adequate local sources of revenue to accomplish the basic requirements of local public service.

Finally, resources are linked to local capacity through the need to manage day-to-day operations. Often when discussion turns to management capacity what appears to be meant is "excess capacity" or "slack resources." Stephen Rosenthal, for example, has written of "the value of excess capacity." His argument is based on the need to allow "the production system to meet unplanned contingencies, such as plant shutdowns, or to accommodate future growth."[44] Rosenthal's examples and approach originate in operations management. They are apolitical. From a different perspective, Bryan Jones also talks of excess capacity. Jones contends that service quality and quantity are inversely related and that without some excess capacity the ability of an urban service distributor to provide both good and frequent service will decline.[45] Jones found that some agencies or parts of agencies in Detroit were better able to provide services because they have otherwise unused resources to deal with them.

Clearly, then, the issue of resources is closely linked to local government capacity. But which or how many of the available resources should be brought to bear is a political question subject to the choice of local officials. They choose what community resources will be converted to deal with which problems. It may be that one or another local government does not meet our expectations of what resources local government should command. But that does not mean that it lacks capacity.

The Issue Of Form

Another recurrent issue in the discussion of local management capacity concerns the form of local government: what institutional pattern best meets the needs of management capacity? The history of political science and public administration, extending at least back to

Plato and Aristotle's debate over the most desirable form of the polity, has been dominated by such analysis. At some levels of this debate, empirical considerations are appropriate while at others values are; the upshot is that frequently the protagonists debate past one another. This concern for institutional form is closely linked to perceptions of the extent of local management capacity. The assumption has been that needed institutional changes will result in greater levels of local management capacity.

Despite the long search for the ideal form of local government, one that would assure high levels of management capacity, a particular form of local government is no guarantee. Rather local governments with acceptable management capacity come in a variety of guises. Efforts to find a single model have been unsuccessful because there are too many suitable alternatives.

In the United States the wave of reform that swept local government in the early part of this century accepted the assumption that a particular form of local government would assure management capacity, in itself a major goal of the reformers. The solution to municipal corruption was to create institutions that would frustrate it, in particular manager-council governments, nonpartisan elections, at-large elections of local legislatures, civil service reform, and the application of business techniques to local government. Form often affects the processes of local government, channeling citizen preferences in one direction rather than another. An example appears to be the impact of district rather than at-large election of local city council members. District systems alter the behavior of council members in ways that give citizens more direct access to council members, but they do not appear to have much impact on the content of policy or on the processes of management.[46]

Though the specific suggestions for reform have changed during the last fifty years, the current goals of the capacity-builders, or reformers, remain comparable. They still wish to make local government more standardized, more rational, less political. Most commonly this means some form of consolidated government. Professor Zimmerman has characterized fragmented local government as one pole of a continuum with rationalization at the other pole.[47] Following the same line, the Advisory Commission on Intergovernmental Relations argued that "fragmented governmental structure in metropolitan areas" is a critical problem and that states must take the lead in "civilizing the local government jungle" and to "tidy up the local government landscape."[48]

The basic assumption of the consolidation element of the capacity argument is that effective decisions cannot be made where governmental lines do not correspond to economic and social lines. Twenty-five years ago Robert Wood argued, "[t]he metropolitan dilemma is defined as the existence of many local governments within a common economic and social framework."[49]

This argument assumes that there is a unitary public interest across the metropolitan region. It also assumes that the only reason this public interest is not paramount is because it is "beset" by multiple governmental units that cannot cooperate.[50] Certainly there are political disputes among jurisdictions in metropolitan areas that inhibit resolution of pending issues. Anyone who has observed the quarrels in the regions surrounding New York, Philadelphia, and Washington concerning the local share funding for mass transit knows this. But the orthodox position seems to be that this is the common legacy of all metropolitan areas.

For at least fifty years consolidation of local governments has been a common theme among those who have sought to reform or enhance their capacity. Why, then, have there been so few successful consolidation referenda? Doubtless there are as many reasons, or more, than there have been referenda. An illustrative example, however, is found in the 1982 defeat of city-county consolidation in the Louisville-Jefferson County referendum. Political and community influentials argued that consolidation would create greater efficiency and effectiveness. Business leaders agreed. Newspapers heartily endorsed the plan. But it failed narrowly. The public administration argument for efficiency and effectiveness was not as powerful as the political argument for the status quo.[51] In other words, if the local governments seem to the citizens to meet their needs, a level of capacity exists that will prevail politically.

Indeed, the rare instances where such referenda pass suggest that political factors are significant in determining their outcome. An example is the 1982 consolidation of Battle Creek, Michigan, with Battle Creek Township. W.K. Kellogg Company, the cereal manufacturer, announced that it would leave Michigan unless citizens voted to consolidate the two local governments. After a bitter campaign, consolidation was approved. In most other recent successful referenda, there has been some external political consideration that tipped the balance in favor.

A related institutional issue in identifying management capacity concerns the use of special districts. Generally speaking, special districts are presumed to reduce the management capacity of local governments because districts cannot be held publicly accountable in the same fashion as general purpose governments. In the words of the OMB Study Committee, such "fractionalization of power limits the effective control of general purpose policymakers and locally-elected officials."[52] Over the years, the Advisory Commission on Intergovernmental Relations has also been critical of special districts.

At the same time the ACIR has been critical of special districts, it has been the most rapidly growing form of government in America in the last few decades. Indeed, in the recent ACIR general study of state and local governments, *State and Local Roles in the Federal System*, special districts are discussed at two separate points in much more sympathetic terms than the commission has usually applied to such units of government. In particular, ACIR notes that special districts are often the result of political pressures to provide a service that cannot or will not be provided by a general purpose unit of government. Nonetheless, ACIR contends that such units are inherently lacking in political accountability. Their number is simply too great for citizens to monitor the activities of the districts that are likely to exist in a given area.[53]

It may not be necessary, however, for citizens to monitor the activities of special districts for them to be accountable. That they were created in response to an otherwise unmet need suggests a degree of accountability that was absent among the general purpose units. Hawkins has argued that special districts are neither more nor less likely to be unresponsive than are other units of government.[54] Indeed, it may be that citizens can more easily assess the quality of a specific service, or at most two or three related services, than a service provided by a single department of a general purpose government. The literature of general purpose government service delivery is replete with the impact of agency decision rules on service provision, decision rules that often serve to isolate service providers from accountability to elected officials.[55] Thus, special districts are not necessarily less responsive than general purpose governments. They are simply responsive to more particular interests.

What difference, then, does form of government make? Have centuries of debate been wasted? At the very least, among American local governments form seems to have little to do with management capacity. Examples of adequate and inadequate management capacity among local governments can be found in virtually all forms of local government. Other factors are better predictors of the presence of management capacity. Particularly through the processes of federal grants management, too much attention has been paid to getting local governments to adopt common administrative practices. Though these devices enhance federal control, they do not guarantee management success. What appears to be a "rational" form of government to some seems "irrational" to others. In adopting a form of government, complete with its accumulated idiosyncracies, local citizens have exercised choices. What choices they make more frequently reflect the values of the local political culture than empirical analysis. Implicitly they have chosen the level of management capacity they want. It is not "irrational" for them to have done so.

The Issue Of Function

A critical means of understanding local governments is to understand what they do, what functions they provide. Most commonly, we develop some rather comprehensive laundry list of common "municipal functions." Subsequently we use our list to describe and even evaluate the management capacity of local governments based on their functional comprehensiveness. Those local governments that "do more" are assumed to exhibit greater management capacity.

Management capacity for local governments, however, is not synonymous with functional comprehensiveness. Indeed, "City governments in modern American are often organized to *exclude* most community problems from their agenda."[56] Some public functions are done by municipal corporations, some by counties, some by special districts, some not at all. To include or exclude a particular functional responsibility is a choice made by individual local governments and supported by the local political culture.

There are patterns to the functional responsibilities of local governments. Some local jurisdictions are more functionally comprehensive than others; that is, they provide nearly a full range of common public services. Liebert offers three factors that explain this variance: local political culture and institutional forms, bureaucratic interdependencies among units and levels of government, and growth of the urban population.[57] The functionally comprehensive local governments are more likely to be center city rather than suburban, northeastern rather than western, older rather than newer, larger rather than smaller, "unreformed" rather than "reformed." Age of the city, defined as the time it reached a population of 50,000, was the best predictor of functional comprehensiveness. Indeed, "Apparently the explanation of comprehensive versus specialized municipal governments lies in the history of municipal government in America."[58]

Political responsiveness, certainly a form of local government capacity, has been linked to functional comprehensiveness of local units. Corroborating the analysis of Lineberry and Fowler a decade earlier,[59] Dye and Garcia argue that functionally comprehensive cities are more politically sensitive to the interests of socially and ethnically diverse populations, i.e., total taxes and spending were greater in these cities than in functionally specialized cities.[60] This suggests that a different functional pattern among local governments indicates a different system of political responsiveness, though clearly these two systems are responsive to different types of communities. Both un-reformed and reformed cities have adopted a form of government that reflects the type of management capacity required. The reformed manager-council cities are better able to handle the less vigorous conflict of a more homogenous population that requires a narrower or more specialized range of services.[61]

Aggregate analysis suggests that local cultural factors, particularly history, critically affect the functional scope of local governments. History, in this sense, is not an accident or series of accidents. Rather it reflects choice, though it may be choice of past city officials and ought, therefore, to be subject to scrutiny by present city officials. Local government capacity is often assumed to be reflected in the scope of functions, particularly whether local governments provide the full range of services. A better assumption is that local governments may choose not to provide a given service or function and that in doing so they exercise political capacity to determine the extent of management capacity they will support with scarce resources.

Conclusion

The major thrust of this discussion is that definitions of local capacity fail to account for the rich variety of local government practices in the United States. This paper has identified five issues—perspective, scale, resources, form and function—commonly neglected in analyses or prescriptions of local capacity and has suggested some of the impact these issues appear to have on local capacity, defined as the ability of a local government to accomplish what it wants to do.

Much of the literature of capacity building hangs on pejorative expectations, as demonstrated by reliance on words like "improve," "enhance," or other generalities. Among those who wish local governments well, who seek "enhanced capacity," there is little agreement about what constitutes enhancement. The contrast is greatest, perhaps, between the pleas for "excess capacity" required to handle unexpected problems[62] and the analyses of "cutback management" suggesting that the greatest capacity exists where effective ways are found to reduce or eliminate idle capacity.[63]

The difficulties in reaching agreement on what constitutes local capacity are endemic to theory building. The greater the degree of abstraction in a theory, the less it applies to any individual case. But without the theory the cases must be treated as unique. This paper suggests that the five issues raised here be treated specifically and that consideration be given to capacity as constrained by them. Some useful work has been done in this regard, particularly in distinguishing between governments of very small scale, usually rural, and all others. For local governments to apply capacity building efforts, these efforts must be based on a theory that is sufficiently context-specific.

The theoretical foundation for such a theory of local government capacity already exists in the work of the public choice school. Though there are implications of the public choice school that are unsatisfactory, particularly the way in which some taxpayers are able to "export" their burdens of taxation, there are two elements of public choice theory that are well adapted to the sort of conceptualization of capacity I have in mind.

One of these is that variety in local practices is not a threat to capacity but a manifestation of it. This means that multiple jurisdictions in a metropolitan area, the use of special districts to handle particular functional responsibilities, varied local accounting and financial management practices, as examples, are not prima facie evidences of a lack of local capacity. Rather, they must be evaluated in the context in which they are found. Even though the local pattern of governance grew in an incremental, rather than a comprehensive, fashion, there are reasons for that particular pattern. What are those reasons? Why were the responses to problems chosen? Those reasons made sense to the persons making the choice. And in making the choice, they demonstrated capacity even though the choice may not reflect state-of-the-art thinking about resolution of the problem or problems faced by the local unit of government.

A second element of the public choice school that is appropriate for an understanding of local capacity suggests that whatever level of capacity exists, it must have political support. Local citizens must support the level of resources; norms of institutional patterns of local cultures must be observed; state regulations must be followed. Capacity in some abstract sense may not fit. Under changed circumstances (e.g., natural disasters or changes in the availability of resources), the level of capacity required by political systems may change. What constitutes capacity at one time or place may not suffice in another. Consequently, conceptions of what constitutes capacity must be dynamic, that is, subject to political choice about appropriate change in the context of each local government.

Notes

1. John J. Gargan, "Consideration of Local Government Capacity," *Public Administration Review*, 41 (November/December, 1981), 649-658.

2. Robert A. Dahl, *Who Governs? Democracy and Power in an American City* (New Haven: Yale University Press, 1961); Fredrick M. Wirt, *Power in the City: Decision-Making in San Francisco* (Berkeley: University of California Press, 1974).

3. Timothy D. Mead, "Identifying Management Capacity Among Local Governments," *Urban Affairs Papers,* 3 (Winter, 1981), 1-12.

4. There are, of course, some who were able to predict from aggregate data such difficulties, though they are typically seen as Cassandras and disregarded. See David T. Stanley, *Cities in Trouble* (Columbus, Ohio: The Academy for Contemporary Problems, 1976).

5. Beth Walter Honadle, *Capacity-Building (Management Improvement) for Local Governments: An Annotated Bibliography* (Washington, D.C.: U.S. Department of Agriculture, 1981).

6. Gargan, "Consideration of Local Government Capacity," 652.

7. John J. Harrigan, *Political Change in the Metropolis,* 2nd ed. (Boston: Little, Brown and Company, Inc., 1981), 197.

8. Study Committee on Policy Management Assistance, *Strengthening Public Management in the Intergovernmental System* (Washington, D.C.: U.S. Government Printing Office, 1975), 4.

9. Catherine Lovell and Charles Tobin, "The Mandate Issue," *Public Administration Review,* 41 (May/June, 1981), 320.

10. Lovell and Tobin, "The Mandate Issue," 325.

11. Advisory Commission on Intergovernmental Relations, *An Agenda for American Federalism: Restoring Confidence and Competence* (Washington, D.C., U.S Government Printing Office, June, 1981) (Report A-86), 144.

12. John J. Gargan, "Consideration of Local Government Capacity," 652. Emphasis in the original.

13. Laura L. Carnes, "The Roll-Out Experiment in Charlotte," Unpublished Master of Urban Administration Thesis, The University of North Carolina at Charlotte, 1979, Chapter 5.

14. Robert P. Wolensky and Edward J. Miller, "The Everyday Versus the Disaster Role of Local Officials: Citizen and Official Definitions," *Urban Affairs Quarterly*, 16 (June, 1981), 483-504.

15. Wolensky and Miller, "The Everyday Versus the Disaster Role . . . ," 495.

16. Edward C. Banfield, *Political Influence: A New Theory of Urban Politics* (New York: The Free Press, 1961); Robert A. Dahl, *Who Governs? Democracy and Power in an American City* (New Haven: Yale University Press, 1961); Ann L. Greer, *The Mayor's Mandate: Municipal Statecraft and Political Trust* (Cambridge, Mass.: Schenkman Publishing Company, 1974).

17. Jeffrey L. Pressman, "Preconditions of Mayoral Leadership," *American Political Science Review*, 66 (June, 1972), 511-524.

18. Advisory Commission on Intergovernmental Relations, *Improving Urban America: A Challenge to Federalism* (Washington, D.C.: U.S. Government Printing Office, 1976), 111.

19. Ibid. 115

20. Advisory Commission on Intergovernmental Relations, *State and Local Roles in the Federal System* (Washington, D.C.: U.S. Government Printing Office, 1982), 327-330.

21. Lyle C. Fitch, "Fiscal and Productive Efficiency in Urban Government Systems," in Amos H. Hawley and Vincent P. Rock, eds. *Metropolitan America in Contemporary Perspective* (Beverly Hills: Sage Publications, distributed by Halsted Press, a division of John Wiley and Sons, New York 1975), 409.

22. Study Committee, *Strengthening Public Management*, 4.

23. Advisory Commission on Intergovernmental Relations, *State and Local Roles*, 245.

24. Fitch, "Fiscal and Productive Efficiency in Urban Government Systems," 414.

25. John N. Collins and Bryan T. Downes, "The Effects of Size on the Provision of Public Services: The Case of Solid Waste Collection in Smaller Cities," in Robert L. Lineberry, ed. *The Politics and Economics of Urban Services* (Beverly Hills: Sage, 1978), 71-85.

26. John D. Hutcheson, Jr., and James E. Prather, "Economy of Scale or Bureaucratic Entropy? Implications for Metropolitan Governmental Reorgani-

zations," *Urban Affairs Quarterly*, 15 (December 1979): 164-182. Quote from page 179.

27. Gordon P. Whitaker, "Police Department Size and the Quality and Cost of Police Service," Unpublished manuscript, (January 1982), 13.

28. Elinor Ostrom, "Metropolitan Reform: Propositions Derived from Two Traditions," *Social Science Quarterly*, 53 (December 1972), 482, 488 et passim.

29. Herrington J. Bryce, *Planning Smaller Cities* (Lexington, Mass.: Lexington Books, 1979), passim, esp. 9 and 172-174.

30. B.J. Reed and Roy Green, "A Perspective on Small City Development: Local Assessments of Grants Management Capacity," *Urban Affairs Papers*, 2 (Summer 1980), 23-36, esp. 28-33.

31. William A. Giles, Gerald T. Grabis, and Dale A. Krane, "Dynamics in Rural Policy Development: The Uniqueness of County Government," *Public Administration Review*, 40 (January/February 1980), 25.

32. Stephen R. Rosenthal, *Managing Government Operations* (Glenview, Illinois: Scott, Foresman and Company, 1982), 82.

33. Reed and Green, "A Perspective on Small City Development," 31 and passim.

34. Timothy D. Mead, *Measuring the Management Capacity of Local Governments* (Columbus, Ohio: Academy for Contemporary Problems, 1979).

35. Kenneth Prewitt, "Political Ambitions, Volunteerism, and Electoral Accountability," *American Political Science Review*, 64 (March, 1970), 5-17.

36. Bryce, *Planning Smaller Cities*, esp. 47, 65-66.

37. General Accounting Office, *State and Local Government Productivity Improvement: What Is the Federal Role?* (Washington, D.C.: U.S. Government Printing Office, December 6, 1978), 19.

38. Charles H. Levine, "More on Cutback Management: Hard Questions for Hard Times," in Charles H. Levine, ed., *Managing Fiscal Stress: The Crisis in the Public Sector* (Chatham, New Jersey: Chatham House Publishers, Inc., 1980), 307. Emphasis in the original.

39. Donald F. Kettl, "The Fourth Face of Federalism," *Public Administration Review*, (May/June 1981), 370. Observation of other cities and the way in which they have administered CETA and CD Programs suggest, at least to me, that Kettl's findings are not unique.

40. Frank S. Levy, Arnold J. Meltsner, and Aaron Wildavsky, *Urban Outcomes: Schools, Streets, Libraries*, (Berkeley, California: University of California Press, 1974), 102-103.

41. Charles H. Levine, Irene S. Rubin, and George G. Wolohojian, "Resource Scarcity and the Reform Model: The Management of Retrenchment in Cincinnati and Oakland," *Public Administration Review,* 41 (November/December 1981), 626 et passim.

42. Timothy D. Mead, *Measuring the Mangement Capacity of Local Governments,* 42.

43. Robert K. Whelan and Larry Walker, "Intergovernmental Assistance and Cutback Management: A Preliminary View from Two Florida Cities," Paper presented at the American Political Science Association (New York, September, 1981).

44. Stephen R. Rosenthal, *Managing Government Operations,* 70.

45. Bryan D. Jones, in association with Saadia Greenberg and Joseph Drew, *Service Delivery in the City: Citizen Demand and Bureaucratic Rules* (New York: Long, 1980), 95.

46. Robert J. Mundt and Peggy Heilig, "Impacts of the Change to District Representation in Urban Government," Paper presented to the Midwest Political Science Association (Chicago, April 1980).

47. Joseph F. Zimmerman, "Metropolitan Reform in the U.S.: An Overview," *Public Administration Review,* 30 (September/October 1970), 531-543.

48. Advisory Commission on Intergovernmental Relations, *Improving Urban America,* 157

49. Robert C. Wood, "Metropolitan Government, 1975: An Extrapolation of Trends: The New Metropolis: Green Belts, Grass Roots or Gargantua?" *American Politcal Science Review,* 52 (March 1958), 111.

50. Robert L. Bish and Vincent Ostrom, *Understanding Urban Government: Metropolitan Reform Reconsidered* (Washington, D.C.: American Enterprise Institute, 1973), 72.

51. D. A. Gilbert, "Reorganization: The Ultimate Local Government Evaluation," Paper presented at the American Society for Public Administration, Region V and VI Annual Conference (November 1982) 1-2.

52. Study Committee, *Strengthening Public Management,* 23.

53. Advisory Commission on Intergovernmental Relations, *State and Local Roles,* 358-360.

54. Robert B. Hawkins, Jr., "Special Districts and Urban Services," in Elinor Ostrom, ed., *The Delivery of Urban Services: Outcomes of Change* (Beverly Hills, Cal.: Sage, 1976), 185.

55. Frank S. Levy, Arnold J. Meltsner, and Aaron Wildavsky, *Urban Outcomes*; Bryan D. Jones, *Service Delivery in the City.*

56. Roland J. Liebert, *Disintegration and Political Action: The Changing Functions of City Governments in America* (New York: Academic Press, 1976), 15.

57. Roland J. Liebert, *Disintegration and Political Action*, 15.

58. Thomas R. Dye and John A. Garcia, "Structure, Function, and Policy in American Cities," *Urban Affairs Quarterly*, 14 (September 1978): 103-122. See Also Liebert, *Disintegration and Political Action*, 110.

59. Robert L. Lineberry and Edmund P. Fowler, "Reformism and Public Policy in American Cities," *American Political Science Review*, 61 (September 1967), 701-716.

60. Dye and Garcia, "Structure, Function, and Policy," 112-117.

61. Dye and Garcia, "Structure, Function, and Policy," 112. Liebert, *Disintegration and Political Action*, 95-113. For an earlier analysis that makes a comparable case see Duane Lockard, *The Politics of State and Local Government*, 2d ed. (New York: MacMillan, 1969), 399-416.

62. Stephen R. Rosenthal, *Managing Government Operations*, ch. 4.

63. See references to the work of Charles Levine and his associates cited above.

II
Capacity-Building Needs in Different Settings

3

Managing the Burdens of Modern Government

DONALD F. KETTL

One of Ronald Reagan's most remarkable achievements in his first two years in office was to bring debate about American federalism to the front pages of the nation's newspapers. Issues that had long been the almost exclusive province of a small band of academics and constitutional aficionados became the object of much public debate. If they had thought little about the question previously, citizens soon discovered that they cared deeply about the principles of local self-government. The Reagan proposals tapped deep public sentiment that the federal government had grown too large and that many of the jobs done by the federal government might better be performed by states and cities.

Nearly everyone favored giving state and local governments as much to do as they could handle. The problem came in deciding just what state and local governments *could* handle and in fact what it means to "handle" government problems. One dimension of "handling," or capacity, is fiscal: do state and local governments have adequate financial resources, both in tax base and willingness to tax that base, to pay for the services citizens desire? A second dimension is administrative: can state and local governments effectively and efficiently carry out the programs they begin? The third dimension is political: who gets the benefits of these services? Are they distributed fairly, or do state and local decisions tend to benefit some groups at the expense of others?

Answers to these questions vary widely. Some students of state and local operations argue that the governments are well meaning and well structured and that trust in their decisions is well placed. Others argue that state and local governments have characteristic flaws that demand federal intervention to protect the rights of minorities. State and local governments have capacity, the arguments go, or they don't. Mayors and governors and county executives (and city councils and state legislatures and county boards) are responsible or they tend to leave some citizens out in the cold. The differing answers are shaped by two centuries of local self-government tradition and by one century of progressive critiques of patronage, inefficiency, and corruption.

The answers, in any case, tend to be firmly held and statically defined. Capacity—fiscal, administrative, or political—is usually held either to exist or not to exist, and it is usually assumed to be a constant. Arguments about state and local governments' capacity are typically ideological. Liberals who favor an expansive government role (usually an expansive *federal* government role) typically contend that trust in state and local governments is not well placed. Conservatives stress the strength of state and local governments as a way of countering the growing power of the federal government. Rarely is this debate over capacity based on an informed understanding of the burdens that modern state and local governments must carry. Capacity is not a state of being but a process. And it is a process that depends not only on adequate resources but also, more importantly, on the job to be done.

The first year of the Reagan block grants proved an instructive example. Numerous critics had argued that state and local governments could not possibly be trusted with the responsibilities that the block grants required because they simply lacked the capacity to meet them. On the other hand, proponents of the programs contended that the block grants made great sense precisely because state and local governments did have the capacity, and therefore there was no sense in having the federal government do a job that the states and cities could do for themselves. The General Accounting Office's 1982 survey of state governments' administration of the new block grants showed that most of them had managed the chore well. The main reason, GAO discovered, was that the new programs called on them to continue doing what they had been doing in previous programs. GAO worried about how the governments would react to future programs that made different demands.[1] The crucial element of state and local capacity is relating the skills required to the job to be done.

That job, especially since World War II, has grown enormously. Even after allowing for inflation, state and local expenditures have nearly quintupled since 1950, substantially more than the quadrupling of federal spending. State and local spending has grown most rapidly for interest on state and local debt, for health services, for parks and recreation, for education, for police, and for hospitals. (See Table 1.) The federal government, furthermore, has added its own demands on state and local governments through federal grants. These grants have mushroomed from 132 in 1960 to 539 in 1981, just before the Reagan block grants; they have grown from 16.8 to 29.5 percent of state and local revenue from their own sources.[2] To tackle these chores, state and local government employment has grown far more rapidly than the federal workforce. The number of federal civilian employees increased very modestly from 1950 to 1980, by 37 percent. State and local employment, however, mushroomed by 211 percent. (See Table 2.) Despite the popular picture of a huge and every-growing federal bureaucracy, state and local governments have outstripped federal growth.

State and local governments have tended to use four general strategies for these functions. First, to a limited degree, they employ transfer payments for administering income redistribution programs. This strategy is more a state than a local strategy, for as Edward K. Hamilton points out, state governments characteristically operate

Table 1. Fastest Growing State And Local Expenditures 1950–1980

	*Percent increase after inflation**
Interest on the debt	842.8
Health	574.3
Parks and recreation	527.3
Education	443.3
Police	409.2
Hospitals	403.0
All expenditures	371.9

*Increases are adjusted for inflation by using the consumer price index.

Source: U.S. Bureau of the Census, *Statistical Abstract of th United States: 1982–83* (Washington, D.C.: 1982), 281, 452; and *Historical Statistics of the United States, Colonial Times to 1970* (Washington, D.C.: 1975), 1127–28.

Table 2. Government Employment

Thousands of employees

	1950	1965	1980	Percent change
Total	6,402	10,589	16,213	+153
Federal civilian	2,117	2,588	2,898	+37
State and local	4,285	8,001	13,315	+211
Percent of total	66.9	75.6	82.1	

Source: U.S. Bureau of the Census, *Statistical Abstract of the United States: 1982–83* (Washington, D.C.: 1982), 303.

indirectly as "banker governments."[3] Some recipients of the checks are on welfare or unemployment, while others hold state debt. Second, they directly provide some services. They educate children, put out fires, maintain public safety, run public transportation systems, and try criminals, among many other things. Third, they contract with private and nonprofit organizations for a growing array of services. From construction of new highways to rehabilitation of urban housing, from social services to garbage collection, state and local governments sign contracts with outside organizations to supply public services. Fourth, to a degree to which budget figures only hint, state and local governments engage in substantial regulation. Housing codes, professional licensing, and land use are areas where state and local governments extensively regulate their citizens.

There are general administrative approaches, as Gulick pointed out long ago, that are of great value for all problems: planning, organizing, staffing, directing, coordinating, reporting, and budgeting. These famous POSDCORB skills form the core of all executive jobs. [4] The increasing demands on state and local government, however, have made uniform application of these POSDCORB skills impossible. Each administrative strategy raises peculiar problems that demand special skills finely honed to its unique challenge. Each strategy has different politics, different players (both within and outside of the government), and each player has different incentives to play the game. Capacity in modern state and local government demands tailoring special administrative approaches to the different strategies that state and local governments use.

The debate over whether capacity exists or not is thus a bark up the wrong tree. The real question is what capacity is needed for the job at hand. More elegantly, capacity is a process by which governments fit the functions they perform with the strategies they use. We need, as Lester M. Salamon has pointed out, to concentrate "on the generic tools of administration,"[5] to uncover the general administrative tools that government can use and to link them with the functions on which they are most effective. For state and local governments, that means managing direct services, contract services, and regulation.

Managing Direct Services

State governments provide relatively few direct services. State officials run the courts and the jails. They patch and plow state highways (although they rarely build the highways themselves). They run extensive systems of higher education, although few educators at state universities think of themselves as bureaucrats.

Local governments, by contrast, are service oriented. Local governments provide most basic government services—police and fire protection, education, sanitation, recreation. But when it comes to problems like defective traffic lights or loose dogs or potholes, citizens tend to turn first to county, township, and city governments. The politics of these direct services, naturally, revolve around who receives their benefits: the politics of distribution.

Some of these services, like police and fire, are provided by street-level bureaucrats who share two characteristics: they tend to act with a high degree of discretion, and they enjoy relative autonomy from organizational authority.[6] Police officers patrol alone or in pairs, and what goes on in most classrooms is known only by the teacher and his or her pupils. The quality of most local services, therefore, depends ultimately on how these street-level bureaucrats behave. Such services are inherently very difficult to manage or control because their goals are fuzzy, numerous, and conflicting. Police officers feel pressure to be sensitive not only to the citizens they serve but to the department for which they work. They have a mission to enforce the law and are promoted by the number of good arrests they make, but citizens often expect service related neither to law enforcement nor to making arrests. The very nature of police work—and most other urban services—leads to multiple and often-conflicting goals.

If it is hard to define a street-level bureaucrat's goals, it is even harder to measure the bureaucrat's performance. It is hard to decide which goal to measure, and most goals do not lend themselves easily to any measurement at all. The natural tendency is to retreat to quantitative standards like the number of arrests. But not all arrests hold up in court. Furthermore, how should a supervisor weigh a stack of burglary arrests against a bust in an important murder case? In other areas like teaching, fire fighting, or garbage collection, the problem is no easier. In fact, the relative autonomy that governs the actions of most street-level bureaucrats means that even if a suitable measure of performance could be found, there would be no one to view directly the bureaucrat's work and to do the measuring.

For other services state and local governments directly provide— like health, hospitals, and waste disposal—technologically skilled professionals often dominate. Physicians dislike political meddling in medical decisions, and careful waste disposal requires meeting engineering standards. For these services, there is a different kind of autonomy, an autonomy spurred by professionalism. Professionally trained bureaucrats believe they alone should determine goals and that makes measurement of performance difficult. But for state and, especially, local officials, the administrative challenge is the same: balancing the inevitable (and, indeed, desirable) autonomy of the servers with the need to make them accountable to the served.

As Douglas Yates points out, the administrative system with which local officials try to manage these problems is both too centralized and too decentralized to provide adequate control of the services. It is too centralized because the relationship between the system's managers and its clients is too distant to judge how well the system is working. It is too decentralized because the managers have little control over the workers ultimately providing the service.[7] The result is a tendency to defer to the workers' expertise and autonomy,[8] and that further weakens managerial control.

The world of direct government services, then, is increasingly a world of great discretion for front-line officials and weak control for both top administrators and elected officials. It is a world where coordination of related services is difficult and where the tendency of other governments to pile on more services further complicates the system. Direct services thus pose a sharp challenge to state and local capacity: the task of ensuring adequate administrative control over front-line workers without robbing the flexibility their jobs require. Careful management of these services requires the ability to specify in advance what each of them should seek to achieve. More important, it requires the ability to measure results: what services they actually produce; how well those services meet the expectations of political officials; and ultimately, how citizens feel about the services for which they pay.

Managing Contract Services

During the 1960s and 1970s, both state and local governments contracted out for a growing share of the services they provided, even for traditional functions. State governments have for years contracted with private companies to build state roads, but E.S. Savas found that by the late 1970s, 21 percent of the U.S. cities contracted for garbage collection.[9] The *New York Times* reported in 1979 that 18 of 30 cities its reporter examined had expanded their contracting in the previous five years, [10] while Savas discovered that state and local governments could contract for sixty-six different services, ranging from fire protection to libraries. [11]

Federal grants fueled even more of the growth in contracting. The grants paid for new services like health screening centers, day care, housing rehabilitation, and downtown redevelopment, among many others. For many of these new programs, state and local governments relied on private corporations for construction of new facilities; nonprofit neighborhood associations and social service agencies for services ranging from job training to lead paint screening; and quasi-public organizations like redevelopment authorities for local reconstruction. The reasons were diverse. Many governments did not want to set up large, new bureaucracies to run the programs, since there was no guarantee that the federal money would continue to flow. Neighborhood associations were often interest groups demanding a share of the grant dollars, and contracting with them was an important way of satisfying powerful local constituencies. Sometimes state and local governments believed that contracting would be cheaper, and some federal programs like urban renewal demanded special organizational arrangements.

As more grant programs during the 1970s guaranteed more communities more money, contracting vastly expanded. In 1971, Lester M. Salamon and Alan J. Abramson estimated, 25 percent of the federal social service grants eventually folded into Title XX block grants were contracted out. By 1982, contracting out reached 70 to 80 percent in some jurisdictions.[12] In Richmond, Virginia, city officials contracted with noncity organizations for 63 percent of the city's Community Development Block Grant funds and 64 percent of the CETA manpower training grant.[13] Contracting proved an easy way simultaneously to satisfy neighborhoods' demands for a share of the funds, to avoid the delays that building new agencies would cause, and to insulate the city budget from the uncertain flow of federal funds.

Demands for a wide variety of background studies and reports, furthermore, created a whole new contract industry. Consultants prepared the environmental impact statements that many federal programs required, because most governments did not have enough environmental review business to keep a good analyst busy. Other firms conducted market research for new projects like downtown revitalization programs or convention centers. Expansion of policy analysis led state and local governments to contract for benefit-cost studies and evaluations. And in an increasingly litigious society, state and local governments protected their legal flanks by contracting for background reports before venturing into new projects. In some cases, these jobs were sufficiently technical and intermittent that contracting simply made economic sense. In other cases, the outside studies could have been—and in fact often were—done in-house; the outside reports gave added legitimacy to the plans that state and local officials made.

The increase in contracting created its own demand. Contractors naturally wanted to keep the flow of government money coming. Some contractors, especially neighborhood groups receiving a share of federal grants, viewed contracts as a political right; others simply viewed them as an economic good. But in all cases, state and local governments faced a central challenge in managing those contracts: pursuing their own goals through nongovernmental agents. This was a job that required using the contract to ensure some match between the motivations of the contractor (typically for procedural flexibility and adminstrative autonomy) with the goals of the government and its officials (typically for distribution of services first and control of services second). The problem, as Bruce L.R. Smith recognized, is a dual one: "the problem of enforcing accountability, while not destroying the contractor's independence."[14]

Most theories of government management assume that governments operate by delivering services themselves, but managing contracts is not like the direct provision of services. The people ultimately responsible for providing the services are not public employees and the organizations themselves have only a paper tie—the contract itself—to the citizens paying for the service. Contract management demands skills in negotiating, writing, and monitoring legal documents, and that is much different from supervising officers on the beat or teachers in the classroom. That in turn demands the ability to set goals, define them clearly enough to meet the demands of a legal document, monitoring the performance of the contract, and help contractors who might not have adequate management skills meet the terms of the agreements they sign.

In the public sector, these steps are far more complicated than in the private sector. The central goal of private sector contracting is efficiency, and this leads to the award of contracts to the lowest bidder who agrees to meet the contract's terms. (There are exceptions to this, needless to say. Some private sector contracts are awarded on grounds other than efficiency, for politics is scarcely a public sector phenomenon.) But in the public sector, the award of the contract itself is a political good. Neighborhoods demand their fair share of grants awarded to cities, as do different regions of the state for grants that come to state capitals. Highway contracts are also goods in themselves, prizes over whose distribution state legislators fiercely struggle. The distribution of public funds, in short, has a symbolic importance apart from the goods and services that the funds buy. The symbolic and distributional elements of public sector contracting are part of its very raison d'etre.

Public sector contracting also differs from the private sector because government typically is far less able to specify the outputs it desires. Most government programs have multiple, mushy goals, especially intergovernmental grant programs that simultaneously seek federal, state and local objectives. It is one thing to specify the tolerances for a machine tool or even for a new highway. It is quite another to contractually list the objectives for garbage collection or day care. A contract might state that garbage should be collected three times a week, but it is more difficult to ensure that garbage trucks do not make excessive noise or that their workers do not leave more garbage on the street than in the truck. In job training programs, if contractors are measured by the share of their trainees they place in permanent jobs, their incentives will be to select for training the workers who need training the least. And if they select workers who need training the most (and who therefore will be the hardest to place), how should their success be measured? The programs themselves make goals hard to define, while legislative bargaining often muddies program goals still further.

Closely related to this central problem is the task of monitoring the contractor's compliance with the contract's objectives. It is naturally hard to measure performance where the goals are vague and varied, and even with clear objectives it is usually very hard to get good data. Many government programs do not lay still like a highway for careful measurement of their quality and durability. Instead, they are constantly changing and geographically scattered, and their results are therefore hard to measure.

As a result, governments must often rely on information provided by the contractors themselves. Are neighborhood organizations actually supplying quality job training for the workers in their care? Is garbage collection thorough? Contractors often dislike filling out paperwork to report on their performance, and if required by contract to do so they can scarcely be expected to report enthusiastically on their problems. The natural alternative is for state and local governments to conduct their own evaluations, but this is expensive if it is to be done well. Few organizations are willing to pay to have bad news brought to them, and most state and local governments are not anxious to hear that a program, even a contracted program, is not going well.

The problem of specifying objectives in advance and evaluating their achievement sometimes leads to a regulatory pathology: attempts to control contracted programs by procedural rules. If the quality of health care defies definition, it is usually easier to set rules about who is eligible for service, what services can be performed, and what records must be kept on each visit. The mountain of paper produced as a result at least creates the illusion of accountability, but it does not guarantee that a program will work well.

Thus, despite its many attractions, the contracting process raises critical problems for state and local managers. It is very difficult to write good contracts and to evaluate how well contractors live up to their terms. It is hard to resist the tendency to replace program evaluation with procedural regulation. It is hard to coordinate government services provided through such an extended chain. Contracting simply substitutes one set of admininstrative problems for another, and the biggest problem is setting the goals of the contract. We (whether as citizens, legislators, or administrators) often do not know what services we want until we see what we get. Program goals are constantly changing with citizens' and politicians' expectations. This is a special problem for contracting, which requires that the terms be laid out in advance for bidding and negotiation. Such a process cannot proceed very easily if program goals continually change; in fact, this problem sometimes leads to sole-source contracts—noncompetitive contracts with a single organization—that undermine the very cost savings that contracting promises.

Objectives for government programs are evolutionary, not static. Contract management thus requires a way to fine-tune goals as programs change and a way of finding out what results the contracts are producing. It demands finding a way to combine the goals of government officials and the incentives of the contractor, without trampling on the contractor's operating flexibility or sacrificing the government's goals. These are problems that demand a skilled cadre of lawyers, substantive experts, accountants, monitors, and contract managers, a cadre much different from the individuals required to administer direct services.

Managing Regulation

Although regulation seems in the public mind to be a distinctively federal strategy, state and local governments have proved to be important regulators as well. State governments have long regulated entry to the professions as well as the supply and cost of services provided by public utilities. Local governments regulate the use of land and the structures built on it. And just as the federal government's regulatory activity has increased, so has the volume and importance of state and local regulation.

At the state level, independent regulatory commissions have traditionally reviewed the utility rate structure for customers and the investment returns for stockholders. The rapid advance of technology, galloping federal deregulation, and increasing uncertainty of foreign energy supplies, however, have taken state regulators into occasionally esoteric and always difficult questions: should an electric company be allowed to build a nuclear power plant? Who pays the enormous capital cost during construction? And who bears the financial costs if a project is cancelled or—worse yet—an accident occurs? How should the costs of local and long-distance telephone service be balanced? State regulators have found themselves trying to tackle a new breed of challenging problems for which past practice provides little guidance. State regulators have also faced the continuing problems of regulating entry to the professions and trades. Doctors, lawyers architects, and dentists have for years been certified by state boards. Trades like repairman, harbor pilots, and hearing aid dealers have enjoyed the protection against competition that limited entry has given.

The states have for decades delegated to local governments substantial regulatory responsibilities, none more important than land use and building standard regulation. These areas proved a field of substantial regulatory growth during the 1970s. Local governments wrote energy conservation and environmental standards. They more strictly controlled growth, and they tightened rules on rent control and condominium conversion. Encouraged by federal grants for housing rehabilitation that mandated uniform standards, they also tightened the terms and enforcement of building codes. Local governments controlled not only how property owners could use their land, but also the size, height, area, breadth, location, content, construction, and appearance of any structures they built on it.

Both state and local regulation flowed from a basic source: the perception, by citizens and elected officials, of the failure of the market to provide services in adequate supply and quality and at an acceptable price. For the utilities, state regulation originated in the problem of ensuring that all citizens, regardless of where they lived, could receive the benefits of electrical power and telephone service without having to pay unacceptably high rates. That often meant that all citizens shared the large costs of stringing lines to out-of-the-way places, but it did guarantee a minimum level of service. For the professions, it meant that the states tried to protect citizens from quacks masquerading as doctors and television repairmen who did not know a transistor from a resistor. At the local level, regulation protected parks and public places from unsightly contamination, and it ensured that all homes would be safe and be equipped with basic amenities.

These regulations, however, also created a politics of protection in which the stakes were high. Beauticians, painting a horrid picture of unskilled workers destroying the hair of the women of Virginia, fought back a recent attempt to deregulate their business. Behind their complaints was a simple point: loosening entry to the field would make it easier for more persons to become beauticians and that would lower the wages for all of them. "The great truth is never spoken directly," one state regulator said, "but anybody in the field with two bourbons in them will tell you . . . that these boards work primarily to protect the practioners and have little to do with protecting the public."[15]

At the local level, exclusionary zoning set minimum standards for house and lot size, as well as limitations on the density and location of subdivisions and multifamily developments. Agricultural protection rules sought to preserve existing farmland from development. Strict restrictions on manufactured housing, often including new prefabricated homes as well as more traditional mobile homes, protected the jobs of local craftsmen but limited productivity improvements in home construction. Such rules, the President's Commission on Housing reported in 1982, benefited many existing property owners but hurt prospective owners by limiting their choices and raising their costs. In some cases, the commission reported, these regulations increased the selling cost of homes by as much as 25 percent.[16] There were good reasons for most of these regulations, but the regulations did not come without political and economic costs.

The administrative chores in managing these regulations are large. State and local officials faced the job of defining what goals they sought to protect through regulation, defining those goals through standards that would stand up to legal challenge, and monitoring compliance with those standards to prevent broad deviations from regulatory policy. Just as important, these officials faced a more subtle administrative challenge: preventing the vicious cycle of regulation in which problems beget regulation; where regulations leave loopholes that crafty persons and organizations exploit; and where governments seek to eliminate the loopholes by tightening the regulations which, in turn, impose higher regulatory costs on all.

The problem of managing regulation, thus, is not only writing and enforcing rules but doing so in a way that ensures a regulation's costs do not exceed its benefits, broadly construed, to society. These problems demand the skills of lawyers to draft clear rules that can withstand judicial challenge; of monitors who can measure compliance with the rules; and sophisticated administrators and politicians who can weigh the costs of noncompliance with the burdens that tighter rules would create.

At the core of these regulations was an inherent conflict: balancing the vested interests of those benefiting from the regulations with those who might gain from relaxing them. The case is strong for at least some government interference with the market. Public utilities might engage in overly ambitious public investment that would hurt ratepayers but not stockholders. Untrained persons masquerading as lawyers or doctors could do great harm, and unsound buildings can collapse with devastating effects. Furthermore, some rules protect a community's aesthetic values—the beauty of its parks or the character of its business district.

The administrative politics of regulatory enterprise, however, is significantly different from other strategies of state and local activity. Effective regulatory management requires skills in drafting clear rules, in litigating their meaning, in monitoring and inspecting the regulated, and enforcing the regulations' provisions. These are skills different from managing contracts and direct services, and the incentives of the regulated are different as well. The politics of this regulation, furthermore, tends to be different. A subsystem composed principally of those writing and those benefiting from the rules tends to dominate decisions. That subsystem creates a politics much different from—and often much more closed than—the often-heated but more public battles over the distribution of direct services or the award of contracts.

The Search For Accountability

The administrative strategies used by state and local governments pose important problems for the accountability of government services. In direct services, the problem arises because of the great autonomy under which street-level bureaucrats operate. In contracted services, it is because the contractors are not under direct government control and because the contracts are difficult to write and supervise well. In regulation, it is because technical rules and subsystem politics often preclude broad participation. In each of these strategies, the problems are similar: fragmentation of the process by function and a gap between those who make basic decisions and the people who ultimately deliver government services. The managerial demands are also fundamentally alike: defining the goals of government services, balancing the government's goals with the incentives of those who deliver the services, and monitoring the results of the process. The strategies that state and local governments have come to use, however, make the application of similar approaches to all strategies impossible. Each one presents special problems that demand special technical training and sophisticated understanding of the incentives of those involved, both within and outside of government. Although general management skills are useful, they are not automatically transferable to the detailed managerial problems that each strategy of modern state and local government presents.

The strategies of state and local governments have ultimately made the "how" of accountability the most difficult to answer, for managerial control operates differently in each of them. Each strategy requires special administrative skills. In direct provision of services, the chain of command is weak. And because there is often substantial distance—physical, psychological, and technical—between manager and front-line bureaucrat, the manager must often rely on the professionalism of that bureaucrat for the quality of service delivery. In contracting, managerial control tends to work through negotiated, legal agreements. Because a contractor is outside the governmental body, reliance on that body's norms is no guarantee of accountability; a legal agreement thus is the rock on which accountability must rest. In regulation, control comes through authoritative commands that must be clearly given and carefully supervised.

In such a world, the meaning of state and local government "capacity" grows fuzzier. Capacity to do what? Given the increasingly indirect nature of state and local government activities, capacity means developing the ability to supervise functions that are not under direct government control. Capacity also means producing better information about state and local government services. Administration is far less a process of carrying out orders through a chain of command than of developing good information about what widely disparate elements of the administrative structure—public, private, and nonprofit—are doing. Two techniques—marketing and monitoring—offer some hope in improving this information.

Marketing gives promise, both as an analytical device and as a way of thinking about government. Marketing for most people is demand creation, and indeed government has in the past few years turned to advertising for functions as diverse as armed forces recruiting and tourism. But marketing can also serve as demand measurement to improve government's ability to link citizens' wants with the services governments (and their contractors) offer. [17] It can help state and local governments define their goals more clearly. In New Jersey, the Turnpike Authority changed its basic food service after surveying travelers about the food they desired. And in New York City, a poll of community boards revealed that citizens valued good streets and parks highest, even though these are the services that budget cutters often attack first.[18]

When governments charge for public services, marketing can help determine how much citizens would be willing to pay. Variable pricing plans can also help prevent overuse of systems like mass transit during peak periods of the day. Marketing can help determine where to make cuts when budget cuts are needed. It can help measure the demand for services used (as opposed to services distributed): what actually happens as a result of government spending instead of who wants government money spent in his neighborhood. By thus helping to measure demand for outputs instead of inputs, marketing can help state and local officials manage their services better.

There are, to be sure, important problems with marketing. It can be blind to questions of equity or externalities. But it may be most useful in helping state and local officials, and their contractors, see citizens as clients to be served. Many citizens are irritated by their perception of an unresponsive government. The increasing tendency of state and local governments to rely on indirect mechanisms only worsens responsiveness, for it becomes harder to determine whose job a given function is.

Public sector marketing encourages government officials to think of government as a service organization, and this may be a useful way of making street-level bureaucrats more accountable. It is a way of better defining the goals of contracts, and citizen satisfaction with contractors is one important way of measuring results. Finally, marketing, with its consumer orientation, may be the most effective tool for prying open the regulatory subsystems that capture state and local rule making.

Monitoring, furthermore, can help in determining the final result of the galaxy of indirect state and local services. Most evaluative approaches are ambitious attempts to compare program goals with results, and just deciding what goals ought to be measured can stop an evaluation dead in its tracks. However, more reliance on monitoring—simply measuring program results without comparing them with program goals—can be an important management aid. In direct service delivery, monitoring provides important feedback to top managers about the interaction on the street between street-level bureaucrats and citizens. It tells contract managers about how well contractors are performing, and it helps measure compliance with and the effects of regulations. By building feedback into the system, more and better monitoring can provide important political and bureaucratic leverage for managing the world of indirect services.

Despite these alternatives, however, the ultimate irony is that governments presumed "closest to the people" are increasingly using administrative strategies that impose large separations between policymakers and the citizens being served. Because they are "closer" to the people, they may indeed know best what people want. But they have a hard time making accountable the administrative system that delivers those services. They have an equally hard time knowing what results that system produces. Dealing with these problems, and developing the different skills needed to manage such very different strategies, is the real challenge to state and local government capacity.

Notes

1. U.S. Comptroller General, *Early Observations on Block Grant Implementation* (Washington, D.C.: U.S. General Accounting Office, August 24, 1982), Report GGD-82-79.

2. U.S. Advisory Commission on Intergovernmental Relations, *Significant Features of Fiscal Federalism, 1980-81* (Washington, D.C.: U.S. Government Printing Office, 1981), 58.

3. Edward K. Hamilton, "On Nonconstitutional Management of a Constitutional Problem," *Daedalus* 107 (Winter 1978): 122.

4. Luther Gulick, "Notes on the Theory of Organization," in Luther H. Gulick and L. Urwick, eds., *Papers on the Science of Administration* (New York: Columbia University, Institute of Public Administration, 1937), 13.

5. See Lester M. Salamon, "Rethinking Public Management: Third-Party Government and the Changing Forms of Government Action," *Public Policy* 29 (Summer 1981): 256.

6. See Douglas Yates, *The Ungovernable City* (Cambridge, MA: MIT Press, 1977); and Michael Lipsky, *Street-Level Bureaucrats* (New York: Russell Sage Foundation, 1980), 13.

7. Yates, *The Ungovernable City*, 166.

8. Lipsky, *Street-Level Bureaucrats*, 43.

9. E.S. Savas, *Privatizing the Public Sector* (Chatham, NJ: Chatham House, 1982), 62.

10. *New York Times*, 23 November, 1979, B-17.

11. Savas, *Privatizing the Public Sector*, 62.

12. Lester M. Salamon and Alan J. Abramson, "The Nonprofit Sector," in John L. Palmer and Isabel V. Sawhill, eds., *The Reagan Experiment* (Washington, D.C.: Urban Institute Press, 1982), 231.

13. Donald F. Kettl, "The Fourth Face of Federalism," *Public Administration Review* 41 (May/June 1981): 367.

14. Bruce L.R. Smith, "Accountability and Independence in the Contract State," in Bruce L.R. Smith and D.C. Hague, eds., *The Dilemma of Accountability in Modern Government: Independence versus Control* (New York: St. Martin's Press, 1971), 13.

15. *Washington Post*, 7 February, 1983, A-10.

16. *The Report of the President's Commission on Housing* (Washington, D.C.: U.S. Government Printing Office, 1982), 181.

17. See, for example, Philip Kotler, *Marketing for Nonprofit Organizations*, 2d ed. (Englewood Cliffs, NJ: Prentice-Hall, 1982).

18. James R. Cleaveland, "Marketing and Local Government Service Delivery," *Public Management* 62 (May 1980): 12.

4

Building Capacity In Rural Places: Local Views On Needs

J. Norman Reid

Most recent studies of governmental capacity address the topic in general terms, without distinguishing the individual requirements of particular classes of governments. This is a natural tendency given the focus of much of the capacity-building literature on essential functions that capable governments must perform.[1] Still, governments vary widely in the challenges that confront them and in the effectiveness with which they carry out their duties. It is reasonable to conclude that capacity-building needs vary as well.

The purpose of this chapter is to explore the special capacity-building needs of one such class—rural local governments. I begin by considering differences that set rural governments apart from larger, urban jurisdictions. I next consider some recent changes that pose new challenges for rural governments. I then report on the views of rural local officials regarding their own capacity-building needs, and conclude with some thoughts on the outlook for building rural governments' capacities in the future.

Why Treat Rural Areas Separately?

Rural governments differ from urban governments in ways that produce special capacity-building needs. In the first place, there are important institutional differences between urban and rural areas. Counties, which handle over 50 percent of local revenues, are the most prominent form of general purpose government in rural areas.[2] Municipalities, by contrast, collect just over 40 percent of local dollars, while townships account for under 10 percent. This contrasts sharply with the image of the municipality as the predominant local service provider, an accurate picture among metropolitan area governments, where municipalities handle 65 percent of local revenues, compared with 30 percent for counties and only five percent for townships.

These structural differences reflect fundamentally distinct settlement patterns between urban and rural areas. Characteristically, fewer rural residents live in population concentrations, and thus a much smaller proportion (48 percent) are served by municipalities than metropolitan area residents (70 percent).

Rural governments are typically quite small. Among rural general purpose governments, counties are the largest, with average full-time staffs of over 200 and average annual budgets of $4.5 million (Table 1). Rural municipalities and townships are far smaller. The average rural city has only twenty-five full-time employees and less than $750,000 in annual revenues. Eighty percent of rural cities have populations under 2,500, however, and among them, the scale of operations is smaller still. Cities in the 1,000 to 2,500 population range—about 20 percent of all rural cities—have an average of twelve full-time employees, while fully 50 percent of all rural cities have fewer than four full-time employees! Township governments are tinier yet: half have no full-time employees and annual revenues totalling less than $50,000.

Because their smaller size will not support much structural differentiation, rural governments tend to be less sophisticated organizationally. Key functions—such as budgeting, personnel management, and evaluation—are less likely to be institutionalized or even explicitly recognized as distinct public functions.[3] Few rural governments employ professional administrators, and elected rural officials are believed to be untrained in such skills. Similarly, the *political* will and skills of rural leaders are often less well developed,[4] due partly to lower levels of interaction between rural officials and other government leaders. Partly, too, it is because rural officials have different career ladders from urban officials, and they often enter public office with neither an apprenticeship at a lower level nor aspirations to a higher position. As a result the public careers of rural leaders tend to be shorter.[5] Their level of acquired leadership skills tends to be lower[6] and their "institutional memory" more prone to failure. This may have subtle but ultimately

Table 1. Employment and Revenues of Nonmetropolitan Governments, 1977

	Average number of employees 1977		Average total revenues 1977 (thousands)
Type of government	Full-time	Full-time equivalent	
Counties	210.5	225.2	$4,532
Municipalities	24.9	29.8	725
Townships	3.5	4.4	120

Source: Computed from U.S. Census Bureau, *1977 Census of Governments,* Computer tapes for finances and employment.

harmful effects, including inattention to long-range planning issues and a failure to follow through on implementing earlier policy decisions.[7]

An often-noted benefit of small communities is the likelihood that community leaders will be personally familiar with community issues and actors.[8] Rural conditions are often far less complex than those in major urban areas. Where the social structure has been stable over many years, an intuitive grasp of events may well suffice. But despite the value of such familiarity, it can also lull officials into believing they have no need for factual information and analysis about community trends and problems. This, perhaps, explains the reluctance of many rural leaders to seek information and outside advice. At a time when most rural communities are growing, some rapidly, this attitude can lead to unfortunate and avoidable mistakes.

The intergovernmental context in which rural governments operate presents other problems. State laws and constitutions frequently place stricter limits on the taxing and service delivery powers of smaller governments, and rural governments many times find their hands tied when it comes to developing programs or designing financing options.

The physical features of rural communities affect their methods of delivering public services.[9] Rural places are seldom contiguous and are usually separated by at least a few miles, often many more. Separation reduces both the opportunities and need for cooperation, and historically rural governments have shown little interest in intergovernmental relations.[10] But in the last decade, the general revenue-sharing program and a host of other federal and state actions have impinged heavily on all governments, and both small and large have had to cope with the growing number and complexity of intergovernmental events. Not surprisingly, the smaller governments find it hardest to keep up.

Almost by definition, rural communities have much lower population densities than urban areas. For some services, such as public water supply, higher production costs may result if the service must be transported over greater distances (through more miles of pipe, for instance). Costs may also be higher if diseconomies of size exist for the service. Often rural governments cannot afford to maintain the specialized facilities and services that could improve their overall performance.[11] As a cost-saving measure, they often contract with other public or private service providers. While this may hold costs in check and keep the stream of services flowing, it adds little to the community's accumulated stock of management capacity.[12]

For all of these reasons, rural governments are much more fragile than their larger urban cousins. Their small size means that even small changes in outside forces, such as population movements or reductions in financial aid, can have relatively large effects. A change that is tiny by urban standards may produce an important shock to a rural community.[13] Their small size means rural communities have less productive plant capacity and a reduced level of management capacity, making it more difficult to respond to, and manage, these exogenous events. Their smaller management staffs are less able to effectively process the rising flow of communications from other governments, and they may even be less able to absorb technical assistance that is extended to help them cope with other challenges that face them.

While it would be wrong to assume that all rural governments are alike, it is clear that the capacity of the smaller jurisdictions that populate the rural landscape differs substantially from that of larger, urban jurisdictions. An approach to capacity-building programs that reflects these differences is therefore warranted.

Recent Trends and Challenges

To better appreciate the capacity-building needs of rural governments, it is also helpful to understand the context in which they presently operate. In this section, I review some of the principal trends affecting them and some challenges they face in the mid-eighties.

Two Decades Of Change.

The past twenty years have been a time of great change for rural governments. Between 1962 and 1977, the last year for which data are available, the per capita general revenues of nonmetropolitan local governments grew to $635, more than three and a half times the 1962 level of $175. While the rapid inflation that characterized the seventies was a major factor in the spending growth, in real terms total revenues increased by 47 percent, reflecting a major increase in the duties borne by rural governments. Most of the increased spending went for public health and safety programs, rather than to education and highways, though these remain the major objects of local expenditures.[14]

Increasingly, governments have become integrated into the intergovernmental system. The change in the federal system since the early sixties has been dramatic, affecting both urban and rural governments. At its heart is the rapid growth of intergovernmental aid. From 1962 to 1977, per capita federal and state aid to nonmetro local governments grew by 75 percent in real terms and by 1977 rural governments relied on these higher level governments for 48 percent of their revenues, much more than they now receive from property taxes, long the mainstay of local finances.

The aid increases took many forms. The massive expansion of federal aid in the sixties led to increased direct aid in some cases, though it was not until general revenue sharing was adopted in 1972 that most rural governments received their first funds directly from Washington. Historically, most federal aid to smaller governments has "passed through" state agencies and despite increased federal-local contact this basic fact continues to hold. Federal dollars by no means account for all the increases, however, and many states adopted their own revenue-sharing programs in the sixties and seventies.

The increasing rural involvement with federal and state programs has had several effects. Many have added to the difficulty of governing the modern age. In exchange for aid dollars, rural governments have had to face up to increased complexity in the intergovernmental system, along with new regulations, standards, and increased paperwork that added frustrations to the jobs of harried local officials. The need for closer communication between local governments and other institutions, government and nongovernment, has added to the complications facing all parties in the intergovernmental system. In addition, local governments have picked up new responsibilities, such as conforming to federal environmental protection regulations and to state mandates.

But there have been benefits as well. To qualify for funding, rural governments have often added new skills in writing applications, accounting for expenditures, and other management practices.[15] And the expanded funding has helped many rural governments to improve their public services, sometimes dramatically.

A crude but useful indication of improvements in local government performance can be derived from trends in spending. Between 1962 and 1977, real spending per person by nonmetro governments rose by 39 percent. This increase reflects both improvements in service quality and a broadening of local programs to more nearly match the range of amenities available in urban areas. Still, rural governments in 1977 spent 25 percent less per capita than urban governments, with most of the difference resulting from lower spending for noneducational programs in such areas as welfare, public safety, environmental protection, and housing.

Federal aid—especially remedial programs—is a major reason for this progress, of course. But local tax bases have strengthened as well, and rising income levels have allowed locally raised revenues to increase in per capita terms but still decline slightly in relation to local income. As a result there has been an overall improvement in rural fiscal conditions—higher levels of local services and mild relief in local revenue efforts.

Not all localities have participated equally in these service improvements, however. While a recent study found a significant reduction between 1962 and 1977 in the number of county areas below a "government services poverty line,"[16] a substantial number of counties remain below minimum national standards for per capita local expenditures. Most of these are nonmetropolitan, relatively poor, predominantly black, and concentrated in the South.

In addition, some areas have experienced rapidly rising local revenue efforts. Between 1972 and 1977, local revenue raising efforts increased in many nonmetro areas, with rapid increases concentrated in the most highly rural counties.[17]

Local governments have also experienced a number of important structural changes during the past two decades. Possibly the most dramatic is the formation of a national network of substate regional agencies. The creation of these bodies in the sixties and seventies introduced a new layer of government serving larger areas than traditional local governments. While they seldom exercise full governmental powers, substate agencies have considerable local planning and coordinating duties and are an important source of technical services and assistance to their member governments. As such, they provide a means for smaller jurisdictions to obtain needed expertise that they cannot afford on their own.

Though underway for two decades in many urban areas, the regional approach was slower to be established in rural areas and was just getting started when federal budget cuts forced the termination of most programs supporting these agencies.[18] Exact figures are not available, but since 1980 a number of regional agencies have gone out of business while many others have had to curtail their programs. Informal evidence suggests that rural areas may have been hit the hardest.[19]

Local governments have made improvements in their internal organization as well. Rural leaders—more likely to be part-time, citizen officials—have made use of the greater number of training opportunities available through the Cooperative Extension Service, state community affairs agencies, associations of governments, community colleges, and the like. These have led to general improvements in the capacity of rural governments to anticipate, influence, and direct change in their communities through more effective policy development and program administration. Federal funds have provided incentives to hire professional managers, and many communities have done so, sometimes on a shared basis with other communities.

Coming Challenges

The evolution in the governmental system has left rural governments in a much better position than they were in just twenty years ago, but that evolution has not stopped. The change goes on, and rural governments will face important challenges in the eighties.

The population growth experienced by rural communities in the seventies will present important challenges for many. While most rural counties lost population in the sixties due to out-migration, the impressive population "turnaround" in the seventies caused most rural communities to gain population, many for the first time in decades.[20] For some communities this growth has been very rapid, but not all have grown; in some areas—especially in the Great Plains region—populations have been stable or even declining. Despite some signs that the rates of increase may be abating,[21] population growth will be an important factor in the future of many rural places.

Growth puts enormous pressures on rural communities and their governments. New populations demand more public services—water, waste disposal, police protection, education—which must be provided by raising expenditures to higher levels.[22] The result may be considerable fiscal stress if the added costs must be met before the new residents and businesses begin to pay their share of taxes. Growth forces important community choices and poses the risk of costly mistakes if local leaders fail to plan carefully. And the influx of new residents may upset a community's social structure, adding community conflict over goals to the inevitable financial challenges.

The expected restructuring of the federal system also promises to shake up the world of rural governments. Recent reductions in aid levels and the proposed decentralization of those programs promise an intergovernmental system that is significantly different from the present.[23] As one observer has noted, "the nation is approaching, but has yet to cross, an historic threshold in the continuing evolution of federalism."[24] Even if the proposals of the Reagan administration should fail to be adopted, observers are agreed that major changes are on the horizon. The levels of financial aid to state and local governments peaked in 1978, two years before the Reagan Administration took office, demonstrating that the current reductions are part of a long-term trend and not just the result of a particular political philosophy.[25]

Just how the system will change, and how much, remain to be seen, but an enlarged role for states seems likely to be a major factor in the rest of the eighties and in the nineties. Should this come to pass, two consequences are probable. First, the center of decision making on many critical intergovernmental issues will be shifted away from the Congress and into the halls of state legislatures. And second, for this reason, a greater variety in intergovernmental policies is likely as each state defines its state-local programs in its own way.

Their expanded participation in the federal system has left rural governments more vulnerable to such changes than they were just ten short years ago. Under the old system, rural governments often labored under rules designed for much larger governments with greater fiscal and management capacity and a greater ability to respond to federal program requirements. Much care will be needed during the transition if rural communities are to receive fair and effective treatment in the new federal system.

Many experts expect the rest of the eighties to be a time of fiscal austerity for all governments—especially those at the local level—which will make the job of meeting growing service needs all the more difficult. While population growth will put more pressure on local budgets, it is the cutbacks in aid that will ultimately force the tough choices between raising taxes or cutting services. Inflation, which plagued local governments throughout the seventies, now seems to be abating, and this may provide some relief to local governments. Still, rational choices about where to cut services—if cuts are needed—will not come easily.

Rural Officials' Perspectives

It is one thing to postulate the capacity-building needs of rural officials from a model of ideal local government performance. However, the responsibility for matching actual performance with the ideal rests for the most part with rural government officials themselves. Whether they recognize these same needs, and what priority they attach to them, is clearly important.

In this section I report on capacity-building needs as perceived by rural officials themselves. The observations are drawn from the National Rural Symposium held in March 1982, which brought together sixty leading officials and scholars for intensive discussions on the problems and prospects of rural governments.[26] The attendees included local government officials holding national leadership positions in their representative associations; members of national and state public interest groups representing counties, development districts, regional councils, and towns and townships; federal and state officials concerned with rural policy issues; students of rural governments; and representatives of nongovernmental rural community institutions. The two-day symposium concentrated on the major challenges facing rural governments and the problems and opportunities they present for the future. Some of the principal conclusions from these discussions are summarized below.

Training and Information

The fundamental conclusion of the symposium deliberations was the continued need for training. The prime concern, however, was not that there is a lack of training opportunities, but rather that it is difficult to match them with officials who need the training. Lack of motivation appears to be a key: the officials who most need skill development are often the hardest to motivate, and many stay away from training.

There are limits to what additional training can do to improve local government performance, of course. Because rural officials come and go from office with regularity, the benefits to the community from skill development are likely to be lost after a few years. Still, the prevalence of citizen leaders in rural areas means that even superficial training can noticeably improve governmental performance, since it is these officials, rather than a trained and paid civil service, who bear the responsibility to develop and implement local policies.

Local officials cite a variety of specific training needs ranging from technical skills to general orientation to the job of governing. Among the highest priority topics are:

(1) budgeting and financial management, including capital budgeting, accounting, and handling fiscal shortages;

(2) revenue administration and planning, including forecasting methods and assessment of the productivity and equity effects of new revenue alternatives;

(3) decision-making techniques, such as problem solving, goal setting, needs assessment, and the use of data;

(4) personnel management and labor relations;

(5) management and leadership skills, including planning, managing meetings, parliamentary procedure, conflict resolution, working with consultants, and the use of computers; and

(6) orientation to the job of governing, including legal background, roles and responsibilities of office, and introduction to relevant organizations and agencies that affect the community.

To improve the effectiveness of this training, however, local officials see several obstacles to be overcome. Not only do many officials believe training is unnecessary, but some have been left with a bad aftertaste from training they have already experienced. Among the frequent complaints are that:

(1) training is often inaccessible, due to the distance that must be traveled or the times when it is held;

(2) instructors often have little experience in common with students and thus are unable to communicate effectively;

(3) inexperienced instructors may teach subjects that are not relevant (or perceived as relevant) to local officials; and

(4) local officials themselves may be unconvinced of the need for training and often will not attend events labelled "training" or support training for their paid staff.

Training needs are not limited to local officials and their staffs. Educating the public about important community issues has the potential to facilitate public involvement and increase acceptance of community decisions. Especially during a time when service cuts are expected, public education about the trade-offs between the cost, quantity, and quality of services can help lead to appropriate choices.

In some cases, designing appropriate training programs is hindered by the lack of basic knowledge. Advice about the efficiency and effectiveness of alternative policies is in great demand, for example, but scholars seldom feel they are in a position to provide it. Still, local officials need reliable benefit-cost information about particular institutional arrangements, such as contracting for services, and the trade-offs involved in policy choices, such as repairing versus reconstructing local roads. Meeting these information needs may first require directed research to fill critical knowledge gaps.

Training is only one form of capacity building, of course, and the potential exists for improvements in local performance through technical assistance, demonstrations, and other approaches as well. The value of these, too, was recognized by local officials, though principal attention was addressed to issues related to training opportunities.

Good Leadership

Many local officials complain about the difficulty of attracting and retaining good leadership in their communities. To a large extent, the problem is perennial. Finding capable persons who are willing to expend time and money running for public office and then carry out their duties once they have attained it is seldom easy, especially considering the low pay and long hours that come with the job. Some local officials argue that many who do stand for and reach office are motivated by narrow economic and political interests, which then become the focus of their attention, to the detriment of their other responsibilities.

The often dramatic population change facing most rural governments compounds leadership problems. Managing a growing community is much more complex and confusing than presiding during a time of relative stability. At the same time the current squeeze on revenues means that many incumbents must preside over program cuts, always a thankless task. The growing complexity of government adds to the burden of responding to these challenges. As a result, many rural leaders, whose chief reward of office is pride in their accomplishments, now face demoralization and burnout. Rekindling the spirit of public officials is seen as an important and continuing issue, but one for which few solutions are offered.

Human Resources

Capable governments must have adequate levels of resources to complete the tasks that confront them. Most public attention fixes on financial resources, and local officials devote considerable time examining their revenue options. But increasingly, local leaders are coming to regard the human resource potential in their communities as an equally significant resource base, and they are looking for ways to use it better.

Volunteers have long been important to rural communities. In the best of times, ample numbers of volunteers were available and it was unnecessary to worry about their proper use. Now, in a time of resource shortage, local leaders wonder how to find enough rewards to reinforce the civic-mindedness said to characterize rural populations. And they question how they can find ways to better manage and coordinate their volunteers.

Rural communities need ways to attract additional volunteers as well. One strategy focuses on breaking down barriers to voluntarism, such as legal liability issues. Another seeks positive ways of finding new resources and attracting them to public service. Among the innovative approaches being tried are establishing networks among community organizations to invite their involvement in public programs and creating special programs—such as town meetings and talent searches on university campuses—to identify and recruit individuals with leadership potential.

Of course, many skills needed by rural communities must be bought, and paid employees are important in delivering rural services. The demands on local employees are greater than ever before, and many service areas—such as law enforcement, wastewater treatment, and finance—now require considerable training and skills. As the skills of these local employees have improved, the dilemmas facing rural governments have increased as well. Rural governments are now in a more competitive and costly job market for their most highly skilled employees. Increasingly, small places have become training grounds for employees who, once trained, are lost to larger communities where they can find higher salaries and more challenging assignments.[27]

Rural officials recognize that good leadership is needed if local governments are to get and use human resources effectively. The ability to communicate a sense of mission and relate it to community goals can help attract people and assist them in matching their interests and talents with community needs. But just as important is the need to manage these resources with the same care given to dollars. An organized approach to human resource management is called for, though it is lacking in many communities. Building such a program, and sticking to it, also requires leadership and administrative skill.

Organization

Local officials regard several organizational changes as necessary if they are to maximize their capacity to govern. But rather than arguing for particular internal forms of organization, they look outward toward the lifting of constraints on their flexibility of operations, such as their taxing and spending authority, use of regulatory powers, and authority to undertake cooperative operations. In particular, they would like to see legal and administrative barriers to the use of innovative service delivery arrangements lifted.

These rural officials turned some attention to their own responsibilities as well. Rural government officials generally give themselves low marks on their dealings with federal and state officials, whom they have failed to "educate" about rural conditions and the special needs of small communities. The enactment of federal and state programs inappropriate for rural places is one product of this failure to organize. Policies designed with urban areas in mind are often applied to small, rural communities where they do not work well. This "one size fits all" approach to governing rankles rural officials and results in policies that are inefficient or ineffective in small town settings. Rural governments must, they conclude, devote much more effort to organizing and representing their views in statehouses and the halls of Congress.

The Outlook for the Eighties

It would be difficult enough to address these rural capacity needs if the target were a stationary one. But of course it is not. Changes in the rural socioeconomic environment, the federal system, and in the content of the leading policy issues will supplement the challenges of the past with new issues requiring different responses by capacity-builders.

The importance of population change should not be underestimated. The "turnaround" in population movements between urban and rural areas is one of the truly impressive demographic trends of the twentieth century, and on a smaller scale it will pose challenges for communities that, while individually small, may be just as dramatic in local eyes. Many places that had become accustomed to the easy, if painful, pace of slow, steady decline are now faced with the task of assimilating new populations and meeting their needs. At a minimum, public services must be expanded to meet increased demands. This may require not only building new facilities, but also finding new service production methods that are efficient at the expanded scale of operation. So that the costs of responding to the needs of new businesses and new residents do not fall disproportionately on long-time residents, public officials in growing towns will be seeking new ways to finance expanded services equitably. Strains on local revenue and service delivery systems, along with the inevitable upsets to the social structure, may produce tensions within the community; these too become the responsibility of the public official. Meeting rural needs for advice and information about coping with these problems will remain an important objective for capacity-builders.

The major changes in the intergovernmental system during the past twenty years have led to many improvements in rural services. The expansion of federal aid for rural governments helped them finance enhanced services, while the spread of regional councils into rural hinterlands offered technical assistance to many rural governments that previously had "gone it alone."

Recent proposed changes in the system threaten to upset these new relationships. Since federal aid to state and local governments peaked in the late seventies,[28] local governments have been seeking new ways to finance services; further proposed reductions in aid will intensify the need to find new revenue sources or to make cuts in services to match lost dollars.

Perhaps just as unsettling to many rural governments is the prospect of altered relations among levels of government. As the decentralization of federal programs proceeds, the need to build new relationships with state agencies—who are often just as unfamiliar with rural problems as their federal counterparts—grows.[29] Local officials are especially fearful of the policy nightmares that may be created as each state now decides from the beginning how it will administer block grant programs. As they face these changes, rural governments will be in special need of adequate representation at the state level. Capacity-builders will find new roles in helping rural communities to deal with these new policies.

The range of issues that rural communities face also seems destined to change as we proceed into the last half of the eighties. The decentralization of federal programs and the cutback of federal support for nonprofit agencies will create new pressures for rural governments to take on social programs that have traditionally been handled elsewhere. Though some may resist successfully, many rural governments will devote themselves to the unfamiliar tasks of ministering to the social, as well as the physical, needs of their citizens. Doing so concerns many local officials. Not only are the issues new to them, but rural officials perceive social policy issues as being overlaid with sophisticated techniques and problems and complicated by service delivery areas that spill over traditional boundaries and an extraordinary amount of litigation. Rural officials take on these tasks willingly, but with some trepidation: here too they will need the capacity-builder's aid.

The continuing technical revolution will add other complex issues to the rural official's agenda. Some, like the disposal of hazardous wastes, become predominantly rural problems, for it is in remote settings that disposal sites are usually sought. Technical advice that clarifies options can help localities choose their destinies wisely and help the nation to resolve the troubling issue of how it is to live with the byproducts of its success.

Technology can also be part of the solution, but even then it may add issues to local agendas. Microcomputer technology has advanced to the point that electronic data processing is now within the financial ability of all but the very smallest governments. Still, what hardware to purchase and how best to put it to use are difficult, if more promising, questions. Advice on the selection of appropriate software and on ways to best integrate these technological advances with governmental processes will be welcomed.[30]

Conclusion

Despite advances in the training available to rural government officials and the development that has occurred in many small towns, the essential conditions that make rural areas rural will, of course, continue to exist. High rates of turnover in rural leadership will create continued demand for training programs that provide basic skills and convey essential knowledge and information. Coupled with this, technological changes and alterations in the governmental system will create new issues and challenges requiring special information and novel solutions. Addressing these needs in ways that speak to the special circumstances of rural communities will provide many challenging opportunities for rural capacity-builders in the future.

Notes

1. One of the best definitions is Honadle's; see chapter 1. For an excellent review of the capacity-building literature, Beth Walter Honadle, *Capacity-Building (Management Improvement) for Local Governments: An Annotated Biblio-*

graphy. RDRR. No. 28. (Washington: U.S. Department of Agriculture, Economic Research Service, March 1981). Also see her *Improving Public Management Through Capacity-Building: A Review of the Literature.* CPL Bibliography No. 69. (Chicago: Council of Planning Librarians, December 1981). For a discussion of various capacity-building methods, see her "Managing Capacity-Building: Problems and Approaches," *Journal of the Community Development Society,* vol. 13, no. 2 (1982): 65-73.

2. In this chapter, "rural" is taken to mean all communities located outside a Standard Metropolitan Statistical Area (SMSA). An SMSA is a county or group of contiguous counties (towns and cities in New England) that contains at least one city of 50,000 inhabitants or more, or twin cities with a combined population of at least 50,000. Contiguous counties are included in an SMSA if, according to Census Bureau criteria, they are socially and economically integrated with the central city or county. General purpose governments are counties, municipalities, and townships. Other types are school districts and special purpose districts.

3. One study finds the process of budget formulation to be much less differentiated in small communities than in larger ones where the executive budget model prevails. See Alvin D. Sokolow and Beth Walter Honadle, "How Rural Local Governments Budget: The Alternatives to Executive Preparation," *Public Administration Review,* 44 (September/October 1984): 373–83.

4. Alvin D. Sokolow, "Local Governments: Capacity and Will," in *Non-metropolitan America in Transition,* ed. Amos H. Hawley and Sara Mills Mazie. (Chapel Hill: University of North Carolina Press, 1981), 704-35.

5. In a study of a rural community in the Southeastern United States, Nix and associates found a high rate of turnover among rural community leaders. While the study did not focus on elected leadership, a high degree of overlap exists between formal and informal leadership positions and similar rates of turnover can probably be expected. See Harold L. Nix, Paula L. Dressel, and Frederick L. Bates, "Changing Leaders and Leadership Structure: A Longitudinal Study," *Rural Sociology,* 42 (Spring 1977): 22-41.

6. Anthony Brown, "Technical Assistance to Rural Communities: Stopgap or Capacity Building?" *Public Administration Review,* 40 (January/February 1980): 19.

7. Arnold M. Howitt, "Improving Public Management in Small Communities," *Southern Review of Public Administration,* 2 (December 1978): 330-31.

8. Alvin D. Sokolow, "The Local Dimension: Finding and Using Community Resources for Rural Governments," in *Background Papers for the National Rural Symposium* (Washington: National Association of Towns and Townships, 1982), 86-87. Familiarity has a negative side as well and may raise concerns

about the objectivity of local leaders or their ability to keep sensitive matters confidential. See Beth Walter Honadle, *Public Administration in Rural Areas and Small Jurisdictions: A Guide to the Literature.* (New York: Garland Publishing Company, 1983), chapter one.

9. Honadle has identified a number of rural community characteristics that affect local administration. See her *Public Administration in Rural Areas and Small Jurisdictions.*

10. J. Norman Reid, "Distinguishing Among Rural Communities: The Differences Really Matter," *Municipal Management,* 5 (Autumn 1982): 83-89.

11. William F. Fox, "Can There Be Size Economies in Providing Government Services?" *Rural Development Perspectives,* 4 (Washington: U.S. Department of Agriculture, Economic Research Service, September 1981): 33-36.

12. Brown, "Technical Assistance to Rural Communities," 20-21.

13. Stephen P. Coelen, "Public Service Delivery in Rural Places," *Rural Development Perspectives,* 4 (Washington: U.S. Department of Agriculture, Economic Research Service, September 1981): 20-23.

14. For a good review of recent fiscal trends affecting rural governments, see Thomas F. Stinson, "Fiscal Status of Local Governments," in *Nonmetropolitan America in Transition,* ed. Amos H. Hawley and Sara Mills Mazie. (Chapel Hill, N.C.: The University of North Carolina Press, 1981), 736-766.

15. Roy E. Green and Burton J. Reed, "Small Cities Need Grants Management Capacity," *Rural Development Perspectives,* 4 (Washington: U.S. Department of Agriculture, Economic Research Service, September 1981), 28-30.

16. Thomas F. Stinson, "Public Services in Rural Areas," in *Outlook '83: Proceedings of the 59th Annual Agricultural Outlook Conference.* (Washington: U.S. Department of Agriculture, 1982), 591-604.

17. Richard J. Reeder, *Rural Governments: Raising Revenues and Feeling the Pressure,* RDRR-51 (Washington: U.S. Department of Agriculture, Economic Research Service, 1985).

18. J. Norman Reid and Jerome M. Stam, "Funding Cuts Hit Substate Regions," *Public Administration Times,* 5 (15 January, 1982), 3; Bruce D. McDowell, "The Future of Local Development Districts in Appalachia," Presentation before the Appalachian Local Development District Conference (Washington, D.C., 10 May, 1983).

19. A special survey of regional organizations to follow up the Census Bureau's 1977 survey was undertaken by a consortium of organizations, and answers to some of these questions should be available by the end of 1985.

20. For example, see Calvin L. Beale and Glenn V. Fuguitt, "The New Pattern of Nonmetropolitan Population Change," in *Social Demography*, Karl E. Taeuber et al., eds. (New York: Academic Press, 1978), 157-177.

21. Herman Bluestone, *Employment Growth in Metro and Nonmetro America: A Change in the Pattern?* AER No. 492. U.S. Department of Agriculture, Economic Research Service (1982).

22. Thomas F. Stinson, "Overcoming Impacts of Growth on Local Government Finance," *Rural Development Perspectives*, 4 (Washington: U.S. Department of Agriculture, Economic Research Service, September 1981): 12-19.

23. Deil S. Wright, "New Federalism: Recent Varieties of an Older Species," *American Review of Public Administration*, 16 (Spring 1982): 56-74.

24. William G. Coleman, "An Overview of the American Federal System: Entering an Era of Constraint," in *American Federalism in the 1980s: Changes and Consequences*. Lincoln Institute Monograph 81-7. (Cambridge, Mass.: Lincoln Institute of Land Policy, 1981), 23.

25. John M. DeGrove and Nancy E. Stroud, "Local and Regional Governance in the Changing Federalism of the 1980s," in *American Federalism in the 1980s: Changes and Consequences*, 45.

26. The National Rural Symposium was held on 29-31 March, 1982 at the Wingspread Conference Center, Racine, Wisconsin. The theme was "Rural Governments in a Time of Change: Challenges and Opportunities." Two reports containing the findings of the symposium, *Background Papers* and *Symposium Highlights*, were published by the National Association of Towns and Townships, 1522 K Street, N.W., Suite 730, Washington, D.C. 20005.

27. Alvin D. Sokolow, "The Local Dimension: Finding and Using Community Resources for Rural Governments," in *Background Papers of the National Rural Symposium*, (Washington: National Association of Towns and Townships, 1982), 87-88; Howitt, "Improving Public Management in Small Communities," 335.

28. William E. Bivens III, "Rural Government in the Eighties: Adapting to Change," in *Background Papers for the National Rural Symposium*. (Washington: National Association of Towns and Townships, 1982), 20-22.

29. Howitt, "Improving Public Management in Small Communities," 339-42.

30. Curtis Braschler, *County Government Computer Utilization and Application in Four North Central States*. (Ames, Iowa: Iowa State University, North Central Regional Center for Rural Development, January 1983).

5

Capacity Problems
of Suburban Governments

MARK SCHNEIDER

The United States is now a suburban society: the 1970 census was the first to show that more people live in suburbia than in central cities or rural areas. Despite arguments about demographic countertrends, suburban population growth continues to outpace any central city expansion. With this population growth has come new problems of government. However, as the problems facing suburbs mount, the enduring image of suburbia as a trouble-free retreat from the problems of urban government remains. As a result of the continuing stagnation of the American economy, of significant changes in the rate and composition of suburban growth, and of the relatively wide gyrations in the system of intergovernmental aid, suburban communities face complex problems. Their capacity to respond to this turbulent environment is uncertain.

In this analysis we conceive of the term capacity broadly, referring to the ability of governments to anticipate problems emerging in their environment and to mobilize sufficient resources to meet these challenges. We investigate three types of changes in the suburban policy environment that seem most likely to challenge the capacity of local government: the changing demographic and economic conditions of suburbia, the changing intergovernmental environment in which suburbs operate, and, finally, the changing expectations and demands on suburban service delivery systems. In the second half of the chapter, we tie these environmental changes more specifically to demands on suburban government capacity. We also show how the fragmented structure of suburban government and the unequal distribution of local resources affect the ability of different suburbs to meet these challenges.

Background Issues: The Changing Suburban Environment

In a moment of big-city chauvinism, New York's Mayor Ed Koch uttered probably the single most devastating remark of his political career by calling suburbs "sterile." Perhaps, like many of his contemporaries, he was influenced by a television diet of "I Married Joan" and "Leave it to Beaver." Suburbia was probably never the idyllic escape from the demands of urban life these situation comedies portrayed. Certainly it is not today. But some stereotypes die hard, and the image of suburbia as a set of homogeneous middle-class white residential communities is one of the most enduring images in American society.

Yet, of the multitude of communities in suburbia, many clearly do not meet the stereotype. In some suburbs, needs far exceed local resources, and problems that were previously thought confined to central cities are clearly evident. On the other hand, some suburbs approach the stereotype—resources are in excess of needs and a relatively benign environment still is found. This unequal distribution of needs and resources is one of the most fundamental characteristics of suburbia and one that profoundly affects management capacities.[1]

Suburban Fragmentation

The major source of the unequal distribution of needs and resources is the basic structure of suburban government in the U.S., in particular its fragmentation into a number of autonomous units. This governmental fragmentation overlaps with patterns of land development to create inequalities.

Suburban areas are divided into multiple government jurisdictions (such as towns, villages, and school districts), each of which is responsible for raising revenues, for providing a range of local services, and for regulating growth and development within its borders. Fragmentation creates the conditions for wide disparities among suburban governments by drawing government boundaries—"invisible walls"—around specialized land use areas.[2] Such boundaries and the tradition of local service provision reduce the possibilities of inter-jurisdictional transfers of resources, making the allocation of services and taxes unequal across communities.

Fragmentation also induces local governments to use growth and budget policies to create even more specialized growth patterns. Exclusionary growth policies may be motivated by the desire to preserve a homogeneous settlement pattern, especially by barring low-income people perceived to have a lifestyle different from the existing upper-income population; by the desire to preserve the level of community fiscal wealth by barring poor people who would demand services but could not pay for them; or by the desire to preserve a community's tax base by attracting taxable business development. As some suburbs succeed in these competitive growth strategies, others inevitably fail. The rising burden of property taxes and escalating service costs has further increased the stakes in exclusionary growth policies.

Suburban Diversity: Population Changes

Two demographic trends reinforce fiscal disparities among sub-urban communities. First, more blacks now reside in suburbia than ever before. But as blacks have breached the color barrier between central city and suburbs, similar barriers have developed among suburban communities. While this new black suburbanization includes a signifi-cant number of middle-income black families, most blacks have lower incomes than whites. Furthermore, racial prejudice and the dual housing market still severely limit the residential choices of black families to only a small number of suburban communities.

Suburbs open to blacks can be categorized as two major types. First, there are "traditional" black suburbs often with long histories of black population concentration. Second, there are many older suburbs, usually close to or contiguous with the central city, being abandoned by whites, and in which racial succession is evident. But these types of suburbs are often the least attractive communities in a region. As a result, blacks are concentrated in suburbs that often resemble central cities: black suburbs have low socioeconomic status, high density, an aging housing stock, and high service needs combined with a weak local fiscal base.[3] In the 1970s, black suburbs managed their fiscal situation through high dependency on intergovernmental transfers, high debt, and high taxes.[4]

At present, suburbanization also includes a wider range of income groups than in the past. But the segregation of social classes in suburbia is extensive. Similar to black suburbs, suburbs with a large low-income population in the 1970s had high service expenditures, especially for social services such as housing, health, and hospitals. These costs were paid for through reliance on transfer payments and high levels of debt.[5]

The Changing Economy of Suburbia

Radical changes in the economy of suburbia are taking place, often exacerbating problems caused by its changing demography. The decentralization of manufacturing from cities to outlying areas dates to the beginning of this century as changes in transportation technology, energy usage, and manufacturing processes reduced dramatically the rewards for locating in the central city.[6] The shift of manufacturing out of the cities into the suburbs, and beyond, has continued unabated throughout this century. In the past, suburbs often resisted such industrial growth. However, the shift to lighter, cleaner industries with less adverse environmental impact has made industrial growth less onerous to suburban communities. With these technological changes came a growing recognition by suburbs of the fiscal benefits that accrue to communities with a manufacturing tax base. These changes have caused suburbs radically to redefine their attitudes toward business: many suburbs now actively court development.

Paralleling the continued deconcentration of manufacturing, more and more retail sales are now suburban. In most metropolitan areas, well over half of the retail sales were generated in suburban communities. Indeed, regional shopping malls, anchored by several large department stores, have become central cultural and community fixtures in suburbia.[7] More recently, corporate headquarters, long anchored to central city locations, have discovered suburbia. While some cities such as New York, Denver, Houston, and San Francisco are enjoying a continued boom in office construction, much of new growth in headquarters is in suburban areas. Even more dramatic than the growth in office space built in Manhattan is the emergence of Fairfield County, Connecticut, and Westchester County, New York, as the new archetypical suburban sites for corporate headquarter functions. By 1980, New York City was the site of only about half of the corporate headquarters located in the New York region.[8]

As the value of commercial development has been upgraded by suburbia, competition to lure business location has become more intense. Paralleling the concentration of "desirable" residential population in a small set of communities, the concentration of the "best" (that is, the cleanest, most fiscally productive) commercial development is often limited to a small number of suburbs. Usually these are prestige suburbs with high-income populations and attractive residential amenities. The tax rates in these select suburbs are often significantly lower than the rates in other less prestigious communities. In contrast, poor suburbs are less attractive; they have neither the prestige nor the low tax rates of their affluent neighbors. As a consequence, they must either offer heavy tax abatements or other inducements to attract commercial development or they must allow relatively fiscally unproductive development to take place. In either case, they are in a continuing struggle against their affluent neighbors, a struggle they usually cannot win.

Money and Mandates: The Changing Intergovernmental Milieu

The suburban policy environment is also characterized by radical shifts in the system of intergovernmental relations. In the last 10 years, intergovernmental transfer payments from the federal government first expanded radically and then, after 1978, contracted almost equally fast. These swings in federal transfer payments were often paralleled by substantial changes in the transfer payments local governments received from their state governments. In the early 1970s, state governments expanded their own aid programs, enacting new programs using state funds, or passing through funds given to them by federal aid programs. With the growing fiscal problems in the states associated with the lingering recession and with the growing political success of a fiscally conservative ideology, cutbacks in aid are now the order of the day.

The 1970s were also marked by swings in the degree to which higher level governments mandated local service patterns. The New Federalism of the 1970s and 1980s, beginning with the Nixon administration, stresses local options and reduced regulation of local services. The operational mechanisms for this change are block grants and entitlement programs. Yet higher level government decision-makers, Congress in particular, have often been reluctant to surrender control over programs they fund. As a result, local governments have been subject to swings in the degree to which block grants free them from mandated patterns of service provision and the degree to which block grants are "recategorized", i.e., become more restrictive.[9]

Some have argued that the extensive reliance of local governments on federal-state transfer payments has increased the fiscal dependency of local governments, sapping their authority and flexibility. Others have expanded this argument to include "policy dependency"—local governments are said to be under so many rules and regulations that their ability to formulate and evaluate programs responsive to their own local needs is being undermined.[10]

These problems have been discussed mostly with regard to central cities. But suburban governments also participated in the expanding system of fiscal federalism in the 1970s. Thus suburban governments are also vulnerable to the uncertainty of the intergovernmental policy environment and to the wide swings in transfer payments characteristic of today's fiscal federalism.

The Changing Demands on Service Delivery Systems

Suburbs are now faced with tough questions on how to provide services. Given the tight fiscal constraints on local government, solving problems with higher expenditures is no longer a viable option for most suburbs. Instead, the watchwords are efficiency, productivity enhancement, and reductions in service levels.

These changing expectations in turn present substantial demands on suburban service delivery systems. Most notable is the growing stress on "privatization" in the organization and delivery of services.[11]

There are several subthemes in the thrust to privatize that will particularly affect suburban governments. Central to the concept of privatization is the belief that governments should not provide services that can be provided by private sector firms, since the private sector is viewed as more efficient than the public sector. Following this argument, once services are identified as being deliverable by private firms, suburbs would withdraw from the service area and allow their citizens to purchase (or not purchase) a service from private providers. As an archetypical example often cited in the literature, consider garbage collection. In a privatized system, a suburb would set minimum sanitation levels based on health standards and then allow its residents to find their own way to arrange for garbage collection.

Another governmental reform that would increase reliance on private market provision would be for suburbs to subsidize the consumers of a service, rather than the producer. The classic mechanism for this service reform is the use of vouchers issued to residents who would then contract with private suppliers for the designated service. Recent changes in housing programs under the Community Development Act embody this approach. Community Development

Offices certify residents as eligible participants in rent subsidy programs and then supervise the contractual landlord-tenant relationship between their subsidized client and a private landlord.

Many of these ideas have been theoretically combined into the emerging concept of citizen "coproduction"[12] In this approach to service delivery, the analyst distinguishes between regular providers and consumer-providers of services. This distinction flows from the fact that almost all services produced by local governments require the participation and involvement not only of organized local bureaucracies—regular providers—but also of local citizens. Cost savings to suburban governments are possible by changing the relative responsibilities of the different producers.

Again, the archetypical example is garbage collection. The efficiency and cost of municipal garbage collection is in part dependent on the willingness of households to separate their garbage and their willingness to move it to curbs for curbside pickup (as compared to requiring pickup in alleys for example). Suburbs can cut costs by increasing the role of consumer producers, but this of course implies more work by individuals. Similarly, major gains in the efficiency of police patrol work can be gained by increasing the role of consumer producers through such anticrime activities as neighborhood watches. The underlying goal of coproduction is to reduce public costs by shifting part of the burden of service production to individual households.

The emphasis on privatization has also produced changes in the way in which suburbs consider expenditures as possible investments. For example, community development agencies are under pressure from HUD to enter into private-public partnerships for community revitalization. Indeed, Urban Development Action Grants almost always require such a partnership. In this approach to revitalization, suburbs use their own funds to leverage private funds and can take equity positions in community development supported activities. This investment strategy, encouraged by federal guidelines, is buttressed by the self-interest of local community development agencies: given the uncertainty of continued federal grants, profitable investments in private firms can produce a stable source of future income for the local agency.

Another area in which changing expectations have affected the practices of suburban governments is the emphasis on contracts as a means by which to organize services. There has been a great deal of interest in the use of contracts between local governments and private firms, but the actual use of contracts until the present has been relatively limited. Moreover, the use of such contracts has tended to be limited to "hard" services such as street cleaning, garbage collection, and road maintenance. Contracts with specialized professional firms, such as architects, engineers and planning firms, are also relatively common.[13]

In the social services, contracts between local governments and not-for-profit firms are very common. Indeed, such local government relationships with the not-for-profit sector have been called by Kettl the "Fourth Face of Federalism"; but despite their use, they are still relatively underresearched.[14]

Changing Suburban Government Structure

Privatization and the movement away from extensive government intervention also affect the ways in which suburban governments interact with one another and how they interact with other levels of government. In the past, the usual response to claims that suburban government was inefficient and that its small scale and overlapping service responsibilities reduced its effectiveness was to argue for consolidation of suburbs into metropolitanwide government. In its most extreme form, such reforms literally eliminated suburbs, usually through some form of central city-suburban merger. Such major structural changes were evident in Baton Rouge, Nashville-Davidson County, and Jacksonville-Duval County. Other forms of consolidation were found in the calls for federation that led to restructuring of local governments in Indianapolis and Miami-Dade County.

But interest in such major structural reform leading to bigger, more centralized government began to disappear in the early 1970s; at present such structural reforms seem unlikely. Instead, suburban governments are under pressure to reorganize and coordinate services within the present structure of local government. The use of contracts between governments, similar to the use of contracts with private firms, is regarded as a major means of improving service delivery and reducing costs in suburbs. In this intergovernmental use of contracting, local governments enter into contractual arrangements with other governments that can produce services at lower costs than the particular contracting suburb.

The widespread use of intergovernmental contracts originated with the Lakewood or contract-cities plan. Named after the suburban city in Los Angeles County that pioneered the approach in the mid-1950s, the Lakewood plan became an institutional feature of service provision in the county. Under this plan, individual suburbs have several options to choose from when organizing to deliver a service. They can (1) choose to deliver the service directly; (2) contract with another government jurisdiction such as an agency of Los Angeles County; (3) enter into a joint services contract with another local government; or (4) join or create a special service district. Contracting with private firms is a further possibility in the Lakewood plan.

In the contract system, competition is presumed to exist between service providers, creating incentives for producers to reduce costs and providing options for individual suburbs to "shop around". By separating the production of services, which can be handled by large-scale government agencies or private firms, from the consumption of services, supervised by the local government, it is argued that economies of scale and efficiencies in production can be achieved while individual community choice is retained.

Several other mechanisms are available to help local governments produce services more efficiently. They too require change in local government management capacities. Intergovernmental transfers of services are among the most enduring trends of suburban government reform. Conceptually, intergovernmental transfers are based on the belief that a sorting out of responsibilities between different levels of government will improve service performance and increase productivity and efficiency. In this approach to service reorganization, a suburban government usually asks a higher level government to take over policy and financial responsibility for a service the local government previously provided. Transfers between suburbs and county governments are the most frequently found trade, but transfers between suburbs and special districts and state agencies are also evident. The advantage of this form of functional reorganization is that suburban governments still maintain control over many services, but can shift the responsibility for services on a limited basis depending on their evaluation of their ability to manage and fund the activity. For this reason, it has historically been very popular among local officials.[15]

The shift of services between local governments and counties was just noted as the most common form of intergovernmental transfer agreement. This signals one other type of organizational change slowly emerging in suburbia—the growth of urban counties. County governments in suburban regions often have the size, geographic scope, and fiscal capacity to achieve economies of scale in service provision, reduce problems of externalities, and reduce inequities in the financing and level of services across suburban communities. In places where there has been county charter reform, modern and visible government organizations are in place to enact such service reforms. However, many urban counties are still limited to providing "traditional" county services such as jails, courts, and public health. Fewer counties are involved in a wider range of suburban service delivery in areas such as planning, housing, education, or industrial development.

Thus, myriad reforms and directions for improving productivity and efficiency are evident. But central direction and imposed choices from Washington are not dominant in today's policy environment.

Until the Reagan administration took office, a federal presence was evidently supporting the slow centralization of planning in suburban regions and encouraging the coordination of many suburban services. The most notable mechanisms for such coordination were A-95 Review and other policies, such as planning grants, supporting councils of government and/or regional planning agencies. Support for the planning functions of regional bodies is now minimal. A-95 Review is now defunct and what will replace it is unclear. While states may step into this vacuum under the prodding of Reagan's New Federalism or because of the continuing need for service coordination, at present suburban intergovernmental policy relations are certainly less well-defined than they have been for many years.

Capacity Issues

Clearly, the environment in which suburbs must deliver services and plan for the future is rapidly changing. Demographic, economic, fiscal, and governmental forces are all operating to change the expectations and demands placed on suburban governments, often straining their abilities to function. While we have analytically divided these changes into categories, it is clear that most environmental changes are really interactive and often multiplicative; for example, fiscal strain is growing at the same time that a more diverse population in suburbia will require more services than local governments provided in the past. In the following sections, we identify some of the specific capacity issues that seem most pressing in suburbia and identify the prime environmental source(s) of these challenges.

Demographic Changes in Suburbia

A new and more diverse population now lives in the suburbs. The resulting class and racial segregation have clear implications for the fiscal and service problems facing suburbia. Furthermore, at the same time as population growth is demanding the attention of some suburbs, the problems of serving an aging population are beginning to emerge in others.

For many northern suburbs, especially older ones, the pressing issues of growth are no longer central. Instead, supporting municipal investments designed for a larger, younger population are often the central growth issues. The clearest example is the number of excess school buildings found in many suburbs. Yet, newer suburban communities are committing the same errors as their older neighbors, overbuilding capital facilities to serve a young but changing population. Suburbs must plan better for demographic change.

The fiscal management problems of suburbs with disproportionate numbers of blacks and low-income families may be intractable. Their residents need the most services, yet these suburbs usually have the fewest fiscal resources to pay for them. Furthermore, many of the residents of such suburbs may have preferences or tastes for higher levels of services. Reconciling needs and preferences with limited resources is a major task of the least advantaged suburban communities.

The unequal distribution of needs and resources and the fiscal service strains of local governments serving the least advantaged suburban population may not be responsive to the actions of individual suburbs. Higher level government involvement is needed. Fair-share housing plans and interjurisdictional reallocations of resources are necessary, but the structure of suburban government, especially in the north, impedes such actions.

Business and Commercial Development

Suburbs now want commercial development. The single most important issue suburbs competing for economic growth face is their ability to assess the relative tax advantages of different types of commercial-industrial development and to offer inducements not in excess of the fiscal rewards of such development. In the competition for industry, local governments often promise more in tax abatements than they can possibly gain from the business growth they are seeking. The ability to better analyze the costs and benefits of commercial development is crucial in the new probusiness suburban environment, as is the ability to negotiate successfully with business.

Individual suburban governments cannot control the externalities that may be produced by development within another community. In the fragmented structure of suburban government, the existence of such externalities extend beyond the obvious services affected by industrial growth, such as water and air quality. For example, suburbs will use fiscal incentives to attract commercial development. But they often have an equally strong desire not to provide housing for any lower-income workers who may work in the facility. These workers, and the service demands they generate, will be "shuffled off" to a community other than the one in which their firm is located. Fiscal benefits accrue to one community, while service costs are found in another. Responding to this situation is beyond the capabilities of individual suburban communities, and requires the intervention of higher level government such as found under the Fiscal Disparities Act in place in the Twin Cities area of Minneapolis-St. Paul.

Emerging Fiscal Strain

At the same time as the environment in which suburbs operate has been transformed by these radical changes, the fiscal strength of suburbia is being undermined. Changes have resulted from multiple causes—economic recession, growing taxpayer resistance to higher property taxes, and the new fiscal conservatism. But for many suburban governments, the most immediate challenges result from the wide fluctuations in fiscal federalism. The most central issues facing suburbs are related to "cutback management" and the setting of priorities among programs. Empirical evidence is scanty, but wherever fiscal limitations have been imposed several strategies of local budget responses are found: (a) social welfare services are cut first and hardest; (b) capital investments in infrastructure are deferred, as is its maintenance; (c) costs are shifted to alternate revenue sources such as user charges and fees; (d) services and funding are shifted to higher level governments; and (e) debt increases. These choices are politically painful but must be faced.[16]

The need for cutback management will vary significantly between types of suburbs, as will the choices taken by different suburbs. Clearly, suburbs with large black and low-income populations face the worst problems: they have provided as high service levels as they have only by relying heavily on intergovernmental payments. They may be positioned for disaster in the newly evolving intergovernmental system. But it must be noted that the vast majority of middle-income suburbs also participated in the system of expanding intergovernmental aid in the 1970s. Cutback management will also be on their agendas.

Suburbs will face critical management problems in organizing for cutback management. Quite simply, advice and information about successful strategies abound, but their accuracy and applicability are questionable. Policy analysts and managers have not had sufficient prior experience with such reductions.

Managing growing debt in a turbulent financial market will also create problems. Changes in the tax laws reduce the incentives for individuals to purchase tax free municipal bonds. Uncertainty in the bond market has also reduced the desirability of such bonds. High interest rates make debt servicing more onerous. Other changes in tax laws have produced incentives for private firms to enter into "creative" financing arrangements with local governments. All of these changes require new management skills in local government.[17]

Negotiating new relationships with state and county governments will be necessary, straining existing suburban management capacities. In California, the stringent cutbacks associated with Proposition 13 led to a greater interaction between state and local officials. Reagan's New Federalism proposals seek to upgrade further the central role of the states. In the past, many local governments have often regarded state government negatively, as representing an added level of unnecessary bureaucratic red tape. But the ability to negotiate with state officials while still preserving the room to satisfy legitimate local needs will become more crucial as local fiscal resources are strained by reduced aid from Washington.

Expanding and diversifying the local community tax base and tapping other income sources will be the crucial challenge to suburban governments. The residential tax base is simply insufficient to cover the growing expenses of local government during intergovernmental aid reductions. This will increase further the competition for industrial-commercial development. But it also means the imposition of user charges and fees for services, increasing administrative demands. Local governments will now have to price services and try to anticipate the equity implications of imposing new fees on services.

Squeezing More Out of Less: Privatization and Contracting

Faced with the need to satisfy more demands within limited resources, suburban governments will undoubtedly experiment with service reforms that promise greater productivity and efficiency in service delivery. Privatization and contracting services are the most appealing reforms for local governments. Some clear capacity problems result. The new emphasis on contracting seeks to expand a relatively limited past experience into a comprehensive approach to local service delivery. What real impact contracting will have on government costs is debatable, but we do know that the wider use of contracting will change the demands on local government bureaucracies. Successful contracting with private providers requires increased knowledge on the part of local bureaucrats. In order to control the contracting process, program managers will need better ideas about how to monitor the delivery of the service, the cost of various components of the service, the abilities of private firms to fulfill contractual promises, and the extent to which competition between potential private providers can be encouraged and channeled to local government advantage. Possible corruption must be monitored: private interests, kickbacks, bribes, and the like can all be part of a contract process that is not carefully controlled.

The ability to use contracts successfully will differ across communities and across services. For years, the research community has struggled with the development of adequate output measures for "soft" public services. This effort is distinguished mostly by its failures. Given these shortcomings in the policy analytic professions, what can we expect when suburban governments are expected to monitor contracts?

Similarly, if the use of vouchers grows, local governments must develop the staff capabilities to monitor the contractual relationships that their subsidized clients enter into with private providers of services. The extent to which local governments should intervene in these private arrangements is also debated. Such intervention is a normative and political issue related to concepts of taxpayer versus consumer sovereignty, as well as the more narrow concept of fiscal accountability. Many of these decisions will be strongly shaped by the changing ideological climate in Washington and state capitals.

Finally, there are systemwide questions. In a system marked by "load shedding," "coproduction," and "privatization," what happens to different kinds of suburbs? As we rely on market-type mechanisms to allocate services, and as we ask individuals to take up the slack of local government "load shedding," we must remember that there is extensive inequality in the distribution of needs and resources across suburbs. Who pays the bill in the newly expanding market in which suburbs are now expected to operate?

Government Structure

Some of these new issues cannot be solved by local governments operating alone. In the past, the very structure of suburban government has been found deficient. The structure of suburban government will be critically examined even further. However, in the ideologically conservative environment of the late 1970s and early 1980s, the terms and the results of that examination differ from earlier critiques.

Changing expectations create uncertainties in the suburban environment producing greater strains on management capacities. In the present environment, suburban governments have more responsibilities to sort out the assignment of services among different levels of government. This is clearly a positive step in that the upward drift of all services so characteristic of the past was certainly not a guaranteed formula for greater efficiency and productivity. Given the labor intensiveness of most suburban services and the bargaining power of larger bureaucracies and public service unions, it has long been recognized that bigger is not necessarily better.[18] Yet some services clearly need coordination, and some services should be reassigned from individual suburbs to other levels of government. But the proper assignment of functions is a continual item of debate and controversy among service analysts. Despite analytic uncertainty, local governments will have to make concrete decisions.

The diminishing role of regional government and the reduction in planning support and coordination that these agencies provided, even in their minimal way, will produce new demands on suburbs. Service coordination and integration were major goals of A-95 Review, as was the introduction of regional concerns into local community planning processes. These needs have not diminished in the new policy environment, but the mechanisms for airing regional needs have been severely weakened. Public choice theorists would argue that coordination and the introduction of regional needs can be introduced into the negotiations between local governments, but again such negotiations will increase the demands on suburban government officials.

Finally, there are once again the systemwide concerns of equity. One of the driving forces for consolidation and upward transfer of services was to reduce the inequalities of needs and resources across suburbs. Regional governments were supposed to be invested with the capacity to transfer across jurisdictional lines. While the actual extent to which transfers occurred was an unresolved research issue, current trends in suburban government reform mean that even these limited potentials for such transfers have been further limited.

Conclusion

While the problems of managing central cities have dominated much of the research and analysis seeking to improve local government capacity, it is abundantly clear that suburbs are also facing severe management problems. Central cities and suburban governments share many of the same management problems. They are affected by changes in the national and international economy over which they have no control. And they are affected by the changing lifestyles of the American population. All municipal governments are subject to the changing approaches to intergovernmental relations and waves of fiscal conservatism. However, the exact way in which these problems affect cities and suburbs varies. And fundamental differences between the capacity problems of cities and suburbs are evident. Suburbs, as the home of a plurality of the nation's population, deserve further and separate study.

Notes

1. There is a large and growing literature on inequality in suburbia. See, for example, Richard C. Hill, "Separate and Unequal: Governmental Inequality in the Metropolis," *American Political Science Review*, (December 1974): 1557-1568; Michael Danielson, *The Politics of Exclusion* (New York: Columbia University Press, 1976); Mark Schneider and John Logan, "The Fiscal Implications of Class Segregation, " *Urban Affairs Quarterly*, (September 1981): 23-36.

2. Eric Branfman, et al., "Measuring the Invisible Wall," *Yale Law Journal*, (January 1983): 483-508.

3. On black suburbanization see Reynolds Farley, "The Changing Distribution of Negroes within Metropolitan Areas," *American Journal of Sociology*, (January 1970): 512-529; Harold X. Connolly, "Black Movement into the Suburbs," *Urban Affairs Quarterly*, (September 1973): 91-111; Avery M. Guest, "The Changing Racial Composition of Suburbs, 1950-1970," *Urban Affairs Quarterly*, (December 1978): 195-206; John Logan and Mark Schneider, "Suburban Racial Segregation and Black Access to Local Public Resources," *American Journal of Sociology*, (January 1984): 874-888.

4. Mark Schneider and John Logan, "Suburban Racial Segregation and Black Access to Local Public Resources," *Social Science Quarterly*, (December 1982): 762-770.

5. Mark Schneider and John Logan, "Fiscal Implication" and Mark Schneider and John Logan, "Positioned for Disaster." Papers presented at the Annual Meetings of the American Political Science Association, (Denver, Colorado, 1982).

6. Mark Schneider, *Suburban Growth* (Brunswick, Ohio: Kings Court, 1980) reviews much of the relevant literature.

7. See, for example, Peter O. Muller, *Contemporary Suburban America* (Englewood Cliffs, N.J.: Prentice Hall, 1981); Michael Danielson, *The Politics of Exclusion*; and David F. Sly and Jeffrey Tayman, "Changing Metropolitan

Morphology and Municipal Service Expenditures in Cities and Rings," *Social Science Quarterly,* (December 1980): 595-611.

8. Muller, *Suburban America,* chapter 4.

9. See Carl Van Horn, "Evaluating the New Federalism," *Public Administration Review,* (January/February 1979): 17-23. For a general discussion see Deil S. Wright, *Understanding Intergovernmental Relations,* 2d ed. (Belmont, CA: Brooks/Cole, 1982), especially chapters 2-4.

10. Catherine Lovell, "Evolving Government Dependency," *Public Administration Review,* (January 1981): 189-202.

11. The book by E.S. Savas, *Privatizing the Public Sector,* (Chatham, N.J.: Chatham House Publishers, Inc., 1982) is a good polemic of this approach.

12. The literature on coproduction is rapidly growing. See, for example, Gordon P. Whitaker, "Coproduction: Citizen Participation in Service Delivery," *Public Administration Review,* (May/June 1980): 240-246; Richard C. Rich, "Interaction of the Voluntary and Government Sectors," *Administration and Society,* (May 1981): 59-76; Jeffrey L. Brudney and Robert E. England, "Toward a Definition of the Coproduction Concept," *Public Administration Review,* (January/February 1983): 59-65.

13. Committee for Economic Development, *Improving Productivity in State and Local Government,* (New York: CED, 1976); Patricia S. Florestano and Stephen B. Gordon, "Public vs. Private: Small Government Contracting with the Private Sector," *Public Administration Review,* (January/February 1980): 29-34.

14. Donald F. Kettl, "The Fourth Face of Federalism," *Public Administration Review,* (May/June 1981): 366-371. Ruth Hoogland DeHoog, *Contracting Out in State and Local Government* (SUNY Press, 1984).

15. Schneider, *Suburban Growth,* chapter 6. ACIR, *Challenge to Local Government Reorganization* (Washington, D.C., Government Printing Office, 1974).

16. James N. Danziger and Peter Smith Ring, "Fiscal Limitations: A Selective Review of Recent Research," *Public Administration Review,* (January/February 1982): 47-55. Also see Mark Schneider, "The Effects of Changing Intergovernmental Aid on Local Government Expenditure Patterns." Paper delivered at the 44th Annual Conference of the American Society for Public Administration, New York, April 16-19, 1983.

17. See especially Randy Hamilton, "The World Turned Upside Down: The Contemporary Revolution in State and Local Government Capital Financing," *Public Administration Review,* (January/February 1983): 22-31.

18. The work of Werner Hirsch is seminal in this area. See in particular his works: "Expenditure Implications of Metropolitan Growth and Consolidation," *Review of Economics and Statistics,* (March 1959): 232-241 and *About the Supply of Urban Public Services* (Los Angeles: UCLA, Institute of Government and Public Affairs, 1967). Also see, Vincent Ostrom and Elinor Ostrom, "Public Choice: A Different Approach to the Study of Public Administration," *Public Administration Review,* (March/April 1971): 203-216; Elinor Ostrom, "Public Goods and Public

Choices," 7-49 in E.S. Savas, ed., *Alternatives for Delivering Public Services* (Boulder, CO: Westview Press, 1977); and James Buchanan, "Why Does Government Grow?", 3-18 in Thomas E. Borcherding, ed., *Budgets and Bureaucrats* (Durham, NC: Duke University Press, 1977).

6

Capacity Building and Big-City Governance

JOSEPH P. VITERITTI and ROBERT W. BAILEY

Since the mid-1970s, many American cities, particularly in the Northeast and Midwest, have undergone severe governmental crises, with fiscal shortfalls leading to sharp cutbacks in municipal services and the number of public employees. The crises experienced in New York, Philadelphia, Chicago, Cleveland, Boston, and Detroit, to cite only a few, revealed not only the weaknesses of public sector finances but also the inadequacies of management structure and practice. The severe lack of technical and managerial skills in municipal government, casually overlooked during a time of abundance, became conspicuous and troublesome as resources contracted. Many local officials responded to these crises by attempting to upgrade the capacities of large city governments through a battery of organizational and technical instruments.[1] Although these measures have gone a long way toward solving the management problems that plagued big cities, changes instituted to improve municipal government's ability to deal with the demands of the 1980s have generated new problems with important political overtones.

Those who study the concept of capacity building tend primarily to focus their attention on the managerial capabilities of local governments.[2] We share that concern. Large municipalities will not survive unless they learn to make better use of the resources available to them. However, we see capacity in the managerial sense as only one part of

102

the more general issue of urban governance. Urban governance involves much more than the organizational skills needed for the efficient and effective operation of local agencies. The term governance also suggests a more traditional normative concern with the ability of local municipalities to represent the interests of a diverse population, particularly those sectors that are most dependent on public services in order to maintain an acceptable quality of life. Thus, there is a political dimension to governance as well as a managerial dimension.

This essay discusses the capacity-building needs of large cities. It describes the changing demands made upon these municipalities in the last two decades and the progress achieved in addressing those demands. It also examines the managerial and political effects of reform efforts. In doing so, the essay identifies an important dilemma: in improving the managerial capacities of our large cities, we must be wary not to undermine those democratic values that demand that our institutions be representative, responsive, and accessible to the publics they serve.

Defining the Problem: Capacity vs. Governance

Chester Newland has defined "capacity building" as "increasing the ability of people and institutions to do what is required of them."[3] While seemingly general and imprecise as an operational definition, Newland's definition contains an important underlying assumption: assessing the capacity of governmental structures must be done within the context of a basic understanding of our expectations. Over the last two decades we have come to expect very different things from our governmental institutions, particularly in large cities. Recent history reveals a basic tension between our current preoccupation with improved managerial capacities and those values that are fundamental to the proper functioning of government.

By definition, the distinguishing feature of the large municipality is its scale of operation. Thus, by necessity, it is exceedingly bureaucratic. Big-city government is highly specialized, often impersonal, and sometimes dangerously ineffective for many of those who rely on it for service. Managers in big-city government are several layers above the street-level bureaucracy, and it is not unusual for a mid-level executive never to meet a client face to face. Given this complexity, a city administrator must make one of his most important tasks coordination—assuring that the numerous members of a large and diverse service delivery system are cooperating toward a common set of goals.

The job of a big city executive is further complicated by the nature of the external environment which must be accommodated. This environment is characterized by extreme heterogeneity. It ranges from the unemployed teenager, to the local merchant, to the head of a large multinational corporation, to the ward politician. All of these individuals have distinct and sometimes contradictory wants and needs, which they ask local government to satisfy. Large cities derive their political legitimacy from the ability to respond to such varied demands. It is from the requirement that such diverse demands be accommodated that we find one of the most basic dilemmas of urban governance.[4]

As the social diversity of the large city sets the stage for a crisis in legitimacy, its size makes it particularly vulnerable to crises of capacity. Although the scope of the large city provides opportunities for specialization and economies of scale not available to other jurisdictions, there are also problems. It is not just that there is a larger assortment of groups in the political environment of the big city but also that the size of the population allows for interests to be articulated and organized into potent political forces that might in other places remain latent. Groups that are otherwise submerged and peripheral in suburban and rural areas more easily find others in a large city who have similar interests and are willing to press them. The work force of the large municipality, for example, is usually part of a large, well-organized and powerful union which is often capable of circumscribing managerial prerogatives through successful lobbying in the local council or state legislature.

During the 1960s, urban government was deeply affected by grievous social maladies such as racial tension, economic displacement, and political alienation. Spurred by federal policy initiatives and grants as well as local pressures, big-city governments emerged as key actors in dealing with these problems. They greatly expanded the level and range of public services. Between 1950 and 1975 total expenditures on the local level (from all sources) increased nearly ten-fold, and the portion of total government expenditures administered by local governments grew from 24 to 28 percent.[5]

The fundamental challenge to municipalities in the 1960s was political—a questioning of the legitimacy of local institutions and their ability to advance the interests of a changing population.[6] Groups new to the city, or others long present but quiescent, for the first time confronted urban governments with demands for real participation in policy making. Moreover, they demanded equal access to the services and jobs that big cities deliver. The government reforms introduced as a response to this challenge were characterized by community control and decentralization. They were not management oriented.[7] Despite the explosive growth of local government, there was little real change in the pattern of local management that might help municipalities accommodate the inherent difficulties of organization and scale.

There is no real consensus regarding the success of community participation in resolving interest group and value issues. But most scholars would agree that, if these new organizational schemes had any impact on the manageability of urban service delivery systems, it was probably a negative one. Decentralization violated some of the cardinal principles of orthodox management, conceived in a tradition of hierarchy and executive control. But loss of efficiency seemed like a small price to pay in exchange for such cherished democratic ideals as participatory government, equal access, and equitable service. Moreover, it was an exchange that could be accommodated easily in an era of economic abundance.

However, it is not difficult to understand that by the mid-1970s, interest group politics, once viewed as a mechanism for the representation of pluralistic urban populations,[8] was identified as a major factor in the financial decline of cities. Specialization in service delivery had led to comfortable and influential alliances between local bureaucracies and their service clients. The institutions of aggregative politics, those overhead agencies whose priorities were articulated in the mayor's office and budget bureau, simply were not strong enough to withstand the pressures to spend.

The focus of the 1960s on the expansion of service and the dispersion of power has now been shifted by the harsh realities of the 1970s and 1980s. The environment of local government today is shaped by the politics of retrenchment. The current political science literature on local government stresses the theme of limits.[9] Local government, we are told, is simply too constrained by interest groups, by fiscal limitations, by the courts, by intergovernmental regulation, and by a stream of other factors which inhibit the facility with which local policymakers can implement decisions. The breakdown of many large cities into near bankruptcy seems to reinforce the theme. As a result, attention has recently focused on issues of managerial capacity rather than governance.

New Capacities for Large City Governments

Perhaps the most startling fact about local government in the 1960s is that few people understood how large it was becoming. For example, by the time the city of New York was forced to say that it could not meet all its obligations, it was a $15-billion-a-year public corporation. At that point it still had no financial planning process. It actually had two financial accounting systems—one for the mayor and one for the city comptroller—both of which were antiquated, and neither of which reflected the true financial condition of the city. The city's revenue estimating system had been inaccurate for so long that the cash flow position of the city was nearly impossible to fathom. Although the city was attempting to change its management systems, by 1975 there still was little integration of service output measures with allocative decision making in the office of the budget.[10] Fast transfers among accounts and the floating of short-term revenue anticipation notes continued to hide deficits. Under such conditions bankruptcy should not have come as much of a surprise. Indeed, the continued debate as to the causes of the city's financial crisis has focused too much on economic and demographic changes. One can ascribe much of the blame for the financial crisis to inadequate organizational capacity.[11] And while New York was perhaps the most spectacular in a series of near bankruptcies that occurred throughout the nation, its case was certainly not unique.

Throughout the country the traditional systems of fiscal and managerial control, largely introduced by the reform movement to constrain the worst abuses by the machines, were found inadequate for the new responsibilities large city governments took on. In Chicago, the financial management system in the city's public school system failed to provide an accurate measure of the system's fiscal status. Neither lenders nor City Hall could rely on it. In Cleveland, a struggle over the profitability of a public enterprise erupted into both a political and financial confrontation among the city's bankers, its mayor, and the city council. Even in cities that did not face a specific, publicized crisis—such as Chicago, Cleveland, and New York—the dominance of interest groups, clientele groups, and organized professionals in allocative decision making is a major challenge. The new need has been to control costs, to increase productivity, and to provide broader criteria in allocative decision making. The greater interaction between all levels of the public sector and the credit markets requires better systems of control and accountability.

Like periods of reform in the past, the present trend is toward centralization of executive power, the application of rational scientific processes in administration, greater concern for accountability by subordinates, and the movement toward efficiency as the prime criterion of policy judgment. These traditional themes have been proposed in the context of organizational concepts developed in the 1960s and 1970s. Among the most important of the new management concepts for large cities is financial planning. Public sector financial planning is a comparatively new phenomenon. It was made necessary by the proliferation of institutions, functions, revenue sources and cash flow needs associated with an enlarged public sector. Financial planning integrates a series of disparate agendas and budgets. It combines the expense budget, the capital budget, the revenue estimation process, and the debt projections. Since intergovernmental transfers have become so important a part of local revenues, financial planning also involves the legislative agenda of city officials with regard to other levels of government.

Like all planning, financial planning offers a long-term perspective. It forces decision-makers to take into account the cumulative secondary effects of their decisions which, if only annual factors were taken into account, might be omitted. Financial planning also serves to change the focus of politics in allocative decision-making. In ordinary budgetary politics carried out on an annual basis, we see the usual conflict between individuals, groups and institutions which represent the various service interests on the local level (e.g., police versus fire versus education). Because financial planning takes a long-term perspective and focuses on the structure of the assets of local government, conflict in the planning process tends to be across service areas (e.g., personnel costs versus maintenance costs versus material versus debt service). The issues that emerge in the latter case involve more general strategies for improving the productivity and effectiveness of city government.

Another direct effect of financial planning is that it tends to reinforce the power of the chief executive, either the mayor in a mayor/council form of government, or the city manager in a council/manager type of government.[12] In either case, the financial office or office of management and budget is also enhanced. In New York City's budget process, the mayor's Office of Management and Budget now proposes a series of potential cost-cutting devices—some of which would result in service reductions. An agency can then respond if it does not agree with the financial plan, or it may supply alternative budget reductions or revenue enhancements. The political effect of this process is that the agenda of budgetary politics is switched from one in which the budget office must respond to the demands and requests of an agency to one in which the agency is on the defensive. Although the usual haggling and positioning that characterizes budgetary politics has not been removed, the balance of power in that process has changed. While in the past, agencies could submit their budget packages layered with requests for service increases, these demands are now countered by a reduction list that is prepared by central budget authorities. A trade-off process is always present, but now the agenda for negotiations is set by the chief executive.

In addition to providing managers with tools needed to deal with finances at the local level, financial planning also furnishes outside overseers with an essential source of information. A city's reliance on the bond market both for smoothing its cash flow and for its capital borrowing needs has introduced the values of banks and other members of the financial community into the governance of the city.

A second new management concept is that of management information systems (MIS). In some ways, past attempts at introducing program budgeting and management-by-objectives at the local level did include different types of management information systems. However, as some of these more elementary systems were later replaced or discarded, so too were the beneficial aspects that might have been saved. As in the private sector, a good public sector MIS system identifies the critical output factors of service delivery, provides some quantitative indicators of that output, and (when integrated into the budget-making process) establishes criteria for allocative decision making.

In addition to providing a managerial tool, a good MIS system also establishes a channel of political accountability between the chief executive and service agencies. One of the crucial problems that emerged in city politics during the sixties was the constant threat that local bureaucracies would have a greater hand in actual policy making than elected public officials.[13] The professionalization of urban service delivery and the easy alliance between service providers and clientele groups threatened the allocative authority of central budget and political authorities. In the absence of any pricing mechanism to judge the relative values involved in producing public services, the only criterion left was the relative influence of those groups and individuals engaged in the delivery of services. MIS sytems, on the other hand, provide another way of assessing service output. These systems are therefore a potential mechanism for assessing the relative payoffs of investing in various service sectors.

In New York City, the new MIS system is called the mayor's Management Plan and Reporting system,[14] which was originally introduced as a result of a new city charter approved by the voters in 1975. By the time the new system was in place, it emerged as one of the several mechanisms for managerial and financial accountability called for by the federal government, the banking community, and business leaders, all of whom had a direct stake in New York's recovery.

New York complemented its new capacity for operational control with the development of an Integrated Financial Management System (IFMS).[15] Through IFMS, the city, for the first time, could integrate its budget and accounting systems—allowing the mayor and city comptroller to operate with a single set of books. Under IFMS, responsibility centers were set up in each city agency so that managers at all levels of the municipal government could be held accountable for the money they spent.

A third new management approach for large urban governments is increased control over public benefit corporations (PBCs). PBCs, special districts, public authorities, and other such semi-autonomous public enterprises have grown enormously in recent years.[16] Charged with carrying out specific tasks, many of which are in the area of infrastructure construction and economic development, these agencies have enormous influence over public policy in large cities.

The import of these organizations is evident in the degree to which they have contributed to the financial problems of large cities and states during the 1970s. In fact, many of the celebrated public cash flow problems of local governments involved, in some way, problems with PBCs. For example, it was the default of the New York State Urban Development Corporation and the court-imposed delay in the issuance of $500 million in debt by New York City's Stabilization Reserve Corporation that created the immediate environment in which New York City was finally forced to deal with its financial problems.[17] Chicago's financial position was severely hurt by the running deficits of its semi-independent school district. In Cleveland, the publicly owned electric utility corporation—and its lack of profitability—was the focus of a heated political conflict between the mayor and the local banks.

The political accountability of such corporations has been problematic for some time. In the area of economic development, such large corporations tend to be shaped by their ability to raise capital. There is a predisposition toward "large" rather than small projects. The fact that money must be raised in the money markets also means that the values of the market—security, yield, and liquidity—are reflected in the policy making of such corporations. In PBCs that are charged with the delivery of services, there is also a tendency to resist control by outside actors. This tendency minimizes accountability and maximizes professional criteria in policy making. In many places the debts of local PBCs are ultimately paid for through general city funds or by the states. To the degree that these organizations influence policy without being held accountable and impose financial risks on public officials, their independence becomes a problem.

In recent years there has been a series of attempts to control these semi-autonomous agencies. One implication of financial planning is that such corporations must state explicitly their revenue estimates, cash flow needs, debt service and debt issuance projections. They must also indicate those areas where there might be some financial vulnerability imposed on the general fund of local government. As in all plans, the task is to minimize surprises. In the past many such organizations might have created the need for quick cash to resolve some sudden downturn in revenues.

In New York, Mayor Koch has tried another tactic in dealing with public benefit corporations and semi-autonomous public agencies. He has appointed his own key staff members to the boards of such institutions. His deputy mayor has been chairman of the city's multibillion dollar Health and Hospitals Corporation. He has also appointed key officials and close associates to the state's Metropolitan Transportation Authority and has twice attempted (once successfully) to impose his candidate for chancellor of schools on the local board of education. Moreover, new restrictions have been placed on most public benefit corporations in New York State by the state legislature as a result of the UDC default [18] and the financial crises of New York City and the city of Yonkers.

A fourth new approach to management involves changes in personnel policy. At the turn of the century, the introduction of civil service was a key factor in undermining the power of political machines. Civil service was seen as an antidote to corruption and an instrument for the recruitment of qualified personnel. Both of these factors, it was hoped, would lead to better quality service. However, civil service reforms also served to wrest administrative power in personnel matters from local chief executives by placing it in the hands of civil service commissions and legislative committees. Local chief executives, in fact, were greatly restricted in their ability to deal with personnel matters. The emergence of unionized public employees further undermined mayoral or city manager power in these areas. At the bargaining table, unions were able to expand the scope of bargaining beyond the usual items such as compensation and benefits. Now such issues as workload, quality of services, and other areas that would have been left to management might also be considered. These new union prerogatives would not have been so much of a problem if there had been sufficient political power behind the manager or the mayor. But in many cases, employees were able to use other areas of influence, such as the ballot box, campaign organizations and contributions to obtain what they wanted at the bargaining table.

In recent years, public managers have tried to reassert some of their former prerogatives. More forceful bargaining positions, a greater willingness to absorb the costs of public employee strikes, and an attempt to introduce productivity considerations into negotiations are now all evident.The excesses of civil service categorizations also have been modified with the redesign of civil service titles into less specific job descriptions. This practice, "broadbanding," allows public managers to assign a wider range of activities to employees. This more aggressive approach to labor relations on the part of central city officials has been engendered by a political environment that is less tolerant of organized labor and an economic environment that no longer allows for generous personnel policies.

Conclusion: A New Crisis of Legitimacy?

Our large urban governments have come a long way in developing the organizational and managerial capacities called for in a period of economic retrenchment. These new capacities have included improved financial planning, more sophisticated management information systems and more reliable financial controls. They have been bolstered through a reassertion of control over public benefit corporations by elected officials, and more aggressive and enlightened personnel policies.

The self-conscious effort toward capacity building among large urban governments is a much needed response to the fiscal and governability problems of the mid-1970s. It represents the reinvigoration of central political and budget officials against the interest groups, unions, and professional groups that increasingly had come to dominate public policy making in large cities. The overexpansion of local public sectors resulting from local demands and the devolution of national problems on the shoulders of local governments led to profound crises of ideology and finances. Much of this has been reversed in recent years as new tools of public management have been developed. We now understand that large city governments are in fact integrated public sectors with hundreds of millions, if not billions, of dollars flowing through their various instrumentalities each year. Sufficient organizational capacity must be present or else the type of crises that struck New York, Philadelphia, Cleveland, Boston, Detroit, and Chicago will be reproduced.

However, we must be careful not to oversimplify the problems we face, their solutions, or our expectations for the future. The distinction between "capacity" and "governance" is important. Although part of the governability problem of large cities can be resolved by new capacity, improved governance must also reflect a genuine concern for equity and the ability to define and meet citizen needs.

Despite the deep-seated corruption and the excesses of patronage that characterized the political machines of nineteenth century American cities, the truth is that these party organizations provided a significant means of access to a large wave of immigrants who came to the industrial Northeast seeking a better life.[19] Indeed, the early municipality was as much a valued source of employment for unskilled laborers as it was a provider of local service. Thus, it is not difficult to understand why such a low value was placed on efficiency. It was through interest group politics, tempered by ethnic coalitions, that each segment of the population was able to lay claim to a particular share of the resources that local governments had to dispense. It was through public employee unionism, a movement which perhaps reached its peak of power in the late 1970s, that municipal laborers were able to acquire adequate wages, suitable working conditions, and an assortment of legal protections on the job. Finally, it was through the community revolution, inspired and supported by federal intervention, that urban centers began to accommodate the interests of newly arrived populations of racial minorities. Although all of these forces contributed to the financial crises that became evident in the 1970s, each also functioned to enhance the political legitimacy of the American city.

The local party system, one of the significant agents of political socialization in the American city, has become one of the great casualties of the modern era. Political candidates once depended on the well-oiled machines of the ward healer, staffed by an army of worker-soldiers. Now candidates turn to corporate magnates who can provide the financial support needed to finance costly media campaigns. Social services once offered by the clubhouse are now the function of the welfare state. A patronage system, once used as a mechanism to reward good service to the party faithful has been all but eliminated through the civil service. Alas, the final remnant of the patronage system, those political appointments only recently held on to at the upper levels of the urban bureaucracy, is now being eroded by a new form of recruitment that is more likely to turn towards the financial sector than the clubhouse for executive personnel.

We do not deny the importance or necessity of these early and more recent reforms. Each in its own way has enhanced the "capacity" of large municipalities to respond to the organizational and managerial demands of the twentieth century. They have even served as an antidote to lower-level corruption. However, it is important to note that the decline of the old political institutions and practices in the name of efficiency has come at some cost.

True governance is not only an organizational capacity to implement policy or to report accurately on cash flow positions. It is the ability to expand the sense of legitimate authority among those who are governed. Capacity building in large cities has solved some problems, but it has also produced a new source of political division in our cities: between those who represent the new, planning-oriented style of urban governance and those who represent the previous interest-group dominated type of urban government. In the former category are bankers, representatives of the financial community, state officials, central and overhead political authorities at the local level, and urban dwellers who identify themselves primarily as taxpayers. In the latter category are public employees, service providers, clients, bureaucrats tied into the older political agenda, and urban dwellers who identify themselves primarily as service receivers, most notably the poor.

Chester Newland is correct. The capacity of our urban governments must be judged by their ability to do what we require of them. Certainly, the demands of the 1980s far exceed those of previous eras. However, we should be careful not to substitute current organizational and managerial innovations for more traditional and most cherished governmental values.

Notes

1. See Charles H. Levine et al., *The Politics of Retrenchment* (Beverly Hills: Sage, 1981).

2. Beth Walter Honadle, "A Capacity-Building Framework: A Search for Concept and Purpose." *Public Administration Review*, (September/October, 1981).

3. Chester A. Newland, "Local Government Capacity Building," *Urban Affairs Papers*, 3 (Winter 1981): iv.

4. See Joseph P. Viteritti, *Across the River: Politics and Education in the City* (New York: Holmes and Meier, 1983).

5. Statistical Abstract, No. 467, Bureau of the Census (Washington, D.C.: U.S. Government Printing Office, 1981).

6. Peter Bachrach and Morton S. Baratz, *Power and Poverty* (New York: Oxford University Press, 1970); E.E. Schattschneider, *The Semi-Sovereign People* (New York: Holt, Rinehart and Wilson, 1960).

7. See Alan Altshuler, *Community Control* (New York: Pegasus, 1960); Frank Marini, ed., *Toward a New Public Administration* (Scranton: Chandler, 1971); Milton Kotler, *Neighborhood Government* (Indianapolis: Bobbs-Merrill, 1969).

8. Robert Dahl, *Who Governs?* (New Haven: Yale University Press, 1961); Wallace Sayre and Herbert Kaufman, *Governing New York City* (New York: Russell Sage Foundation, 1960).

9. Paul Peterson, *City Limits* (Chicago: University of Chicago Press, 1981); and Douglas Yates, *The Ungovernable City* (Cambridge: MIT Press, 1977).

10. See Charles Morris, *The Cost of Good Intentions* (New York: W.W. Norton, 1980), chapters 6-9; Frederick O'R. Hayes, *Productivity in Local Government* (Lexington: Lexington Books, 1977), chapter 6; Joseph P. Viteritti, *Bureaucracy and Social Justice* (Port Washington, N.Y.: Kennikat Press, 1979), chapter 3.

11. Temporary Commission on City Finances, *The City in Transition* (New York: Arno Press, 1978), section 4.

12. See Robert W. Bailey, *The Crisis Regime* (Albany: State University of New York Press, 1984)

13. Theodore J. Lowi, *The End of Liberalism* (New York: W.W. Norton, 1969).

14. See Joseph P. Viteritti, "New York's Management Plan and Reporting System," *Public Administration Review*, 38 (July/August 1978): 376-381.

15. See Urban Academy of the City University of New York, *An Introduction to IFMS* (New York: The Urban Academy, 1976).

16. Annmarie Hauck Walsh, *The Public's Business: The Politics and Practices of Government Corporations* (Cambridge: MIT Press, 1978); Robert Caro, *The Power Broker* (New York: Knopf, 1976).

17. *Wien vs New York City*, 370 N.Y.S., 2d550, 1975.

18. See New York State Moreland Act Commission on the Urban Development Corporation and Other State Financing Agencies, *Restoring Credit and Confidence: A Reform Program for New York State and its Public Authorities*, Report to the Governor, 31 March 1976, Albany, New York.

19. Lincoln Steffens, *The Shame of Cities*, (New York: Hill and Wang, 1957); Seymour J. Mandelbaum, *Boss Tweed's New York* (New York: John Wiley & Sons, 1965); Alexander B. Callow, Jr., *The Tweed Ring* (New York: Oxford University Press, 1966).

Part III
The Organizational Context of Capacity Building

7

Organizational Incentives in Technical Assistance Relationships

ARNOLD M. HOWITT AND RICHARD M. KOBAYASHI

Efforts to improve management capacity in local government frequently involve *technical assistance* in a variety of forms—aid in designing new accounting methods or improvements in the water supply system; advice on energy conservation or air pollution control techniques; help in planning productivity improvements in a town agency; or workshops to train supervisors to manage personnel better. This advice may come from any of several sources—private consultants, public agencies at other levels of government, academic institutions, or volunteers.

What these situations have in common—irrespective of source or form—is that each constitutes advice from outside the municipal government that is directed toward changing some aspect of that government's operations. Neither the target nor the content of technical assistance efforts necessarily needs to involve state-of-the-art technical ideas or processes. The term "technical assistance" may usefully be applied to any situation in which a government reaches outside of its own ranks for help, even if the change being promoted has been widely adopted elsewhere.

Although some public administrators involved in delivering or using technical assistance have met success, many others have found such aid a source of confusion, frustration, and disappointment. Sometimes officials in the recipient government feel that aid-givers are unresponsive to the real problems, unable to communicate effectively with the appropriate range of people, available for too short a time, or overly concerned with their own agenda. Yet providers of technical assistance, too, frequently have their own frustrations with assistance relationships. Officials in recipient governments sometimes seem more interested in local politics than in needed policy innovations or are unwilling to commit enough time and other resources to make recommended changes work. As a result, assistance relationships are too often sources of conflict instead of opportunities for support and cooperation.

This paper explores one important reason for such disappointment: failure to take account adequately of organizational interests and incentives. Many observers suppose that technical assistance is a valuable commodity and assume that recipient governments are eager to acquire it, whether or not they have to pay. This belief, however, ignores the fact that technical assistance represents external intervention in the recipient government's affairs. The aid giver becomes an actor in the recipient's bureaucratic politics in ways that potentially affect interests inside and outside of government.

Technical assistance should be thought of as an interorganizational relationship in which both the aid giver and the recipient have significant interests at stake and perceive varying incentives for being involved in the assistance activity. From this perspective, effectiveness on both sides depends on understanding—and sometimes influencing—the organization on the other side.

In the absence of such understanding, disappointments with the assistance relationship are bound to arise. Aid recipients form unrealistic expectations about what they will receive from the aid giver, and providers become overly optimistic about what change can take root and flourish in the recipient government. In contrast, a richer appreciation of the organizational stakes involved in technical assistance can help both sides make the relationship more effective and rewarding. The recipient government can make a more informed choice about which source of assistance to tap (where there is more than one potential aid giver) and form practical expectations about the role that the aid giver will play in promoting change. The aid-giving organization, for its part, can develop assistance strategies more likely to result in lasting changes (in the planned direction) in the recipient organization.

This paper does not assert that organizational interests and incentives are the single factor determining the behavior and effectiveness of technical assistance providers and recipients. Other factors such as organizational history, pre-existing relationships between assistance providers and recipients, leadership styles, and the substance of policy clearly make a difference. But organizational interests and incentives deserve careful analysis because they play a major role in structuring technical assistance relationships and substantially influence the outcomes achieved.

In the following pages we shall examine the organizational interests and incentives of technical assistance from both sides. We shall first consider how the stakes of various assistance providers vary and how they affect the way these organizations are likely to behave in an assistance relationship. Then we shall focus on the political context of technical assistance in the recipient government and discuss the implications of this setting for the strategy of the aid-giving agency.

The Interests and Behavior of Technical Assistance Providers

Although a technical assistance relationship can be extremely important to a recipient government, it is also risky. Outsiders are invited to examine management practices critically and to recommend change. The assistance relationship may prove beneficial, but it may also turn out to be impractical, politically embarrassing, and insensitive to important needs and values of the recipient community. Therefore, the aid recipient should have as firm a sense as possible of what perspective the assistance provider brings to the job and how the provider is likely to act during the assistance process.

Types of Assistance Providers and Their Incentives

Several kinds of organizations provide technical assistance. Each has a different configuration of organizational incentives for becoming involved. These differences in incentives, it will be argued, are systematically related to differences in the way technical assistance is delivered to recipient governments.

First, private consulting firms provide aid in specialized areas such as transportation planning or in more general areas such as law, architecture, engineering, planning, or management. As businesses with economic motivations, consulting firms are driven by the market forces that shape demand for their services. Most frequently, they contract directly with a single local government to provide assistance on a fee-for-service basis for a discrete project, but sometimes they are retained by an agency at a higher level of government to deliver assistance to a group of recipients (for example, municipal governments in a particular geographic area) for a specific purpose (for example, to promote energy conservation methods).

Second are "helping" agencies—public entities whose primary purpose is the provision of a wide range of assistance to local governments. These include agencies at higher levels of government, such as a Department of Community Affairs, as well as independent public agencies such as a regional planning agency or a community service institute at a public university. These assistance providers offer services to municipalities free of charge—or for a nominal fee—because they are supported by regular government appropriations or by grants from higher levels of government. Motivated by bureaucratic interests, these agencies strive to sustain or expand their appropriations and grants-in-aid, to respond to policy directives from political overseers, and to engage in activities that are visible to and respected by the professional community to which agency executives belong.

Third are "mission" agencies that are principally concerned with a specific substantive policy area—energy, transportation, health—and offer technical aid to municipalities, often as a means of promoting their own policy objectives. Like the helping agencies, mission agencies are supported by budget or grant funds which permit them to offer free or low-cost assistance services to recipient governments. Mission agencies are also motivated by a set of bureaucratic interests similar to those of the helping agencies.

Fourth, private, nonprofit organizations—such as private universities—also provide technical assistance to local governments. In contrast to the public service institute at a public university, a private university is not primarily established for this purpose and is not dependent on government appropriations; but it will sometimes provide teams of professional school faculty or graduate students, on a courtesy basis or for a nominal fee to defray expenses, to help local governments. The university may be interested in the assistance relationship to enhance its reputation for public service or innovative activity and to contribute to the career development of its personnel.

Fifth, associations of municipalities, such as metropolitan councils of government (COGs) or statewide municipal leagues, provide technical assistance services to their members free of charge or for a nominal fee. This aid is delivered by the organization's professional staff or sometimes by private consultants retained by the organization. It is financed by members' dues or by grants-in-aid from government or foundations. Aside from the potential beneficial effects on recipient communities, the organization provides such aid as a way of increasing members' attachment and loyalty and, where funds are derived from nondues sources, as a means of sustaining the overhead expenses of core staff.

Sixth, volunteers sometimes provide technical assistance. For example, corporations may lend executives to government on a part-time or temporary basis, or local professionals—lawyers, accountants, engineers—may offer their services without fee. These volunteers may be motivated by public-spiritedness, a desire for professional stimulation, or a quest for public visibility that will expand their opportunities for profit-making work with government or other clients. A power company, for example, may offer a program of assistance designed to foster economic development in areas where the company already provides electricity and can increase its profitability by more intensive utilization of its existing capital facilities.

Predicting Behavior

Different types of assistance providers have different behavioral tendencies which are related to their organizational incentives and which can be identified and assessed. While no analysis can offer precise forecasts of how a provider will approach a community's problems, understanding what these tendencies are and why they exist can help an aid-recipient in several ways. First, the recipient can form more realistic expectations about how different kinds of providers are likely to approach their work in the community. Second, when there is some choice about where to seek assistance, better understanding of different providers can help the recipient government match its needs with the capabilities and styles of available aid givers. Finally, when actually working with a specific provider, the recipient government can maximize the value of assistance by improving its ability to direct the provider's work.

Even though such general analysis may imperfectly forecast the actions of specific assistance providers, it can nonetheless be a useful tool for the public administrator. By offering an explanatory model of an aid-giver's behavior, it can help officials zero in on and critically evaluate factors in a particular situation that might result in deviations from general expectations.

One might analyze the behavior of technical assistance providers along many dimensions, but four issues seem particularly important:

(1) How do assistance providers decide which local governments to work with and which projects are appropriate for their attention? (2) How closely attuned and responsive are they to the client's preferences about how assistance will be delivered? (3) Will assistance be "individualized" according to conditions in a specific community or "prepackaged" for application in many municipalities? (4) How long is the assistance relationship likely to last and how intensely involved are providers likely to be with a particular project?

Choosing Projects

Consider the issue of how assistance projects are initiated. What determines which technical assistance relationships a particular provider will enter?

For the private consultant, economic motivation makes market forces the principal consideration. Generally, services are available on a fee-for-service basis at the initiation of the recipient. Under normal circumstances, therefore, a community receives technical services if it has sufficient financial resources to retain the firm. An exception to this pattern arises when the consultant operates under a contract with a third party, usually a public agency at a higher level of government than the recipient. Then the policies of the funding agency generally determine the choice of assistance recipients. Usually, the agency gives very specific direction to the consulting firm, identifying individual communities and projects for it to work on, although sometimes it may offer only broad criteria for choosing assistance sites.

Like the consulting firm with a contract from a public agency, a technical assistance division in a mission agency—for example, a state energy or environmental department—tends to select its projects at the explicit directions of its bureaucratic superiors or funding sources or according to more or less specific criteria they have laid down; technical assistance is one of several tools such agencies use to advance their own policy agenda. Such direction may include particular substantive policy objectives (for example, promoting residential energy conservation) or politically driven distributive requirements (for example, providing assistance to at least one community in each state senate district) laid down by the third party involved in the assistance relationship.

In these cases, a particular community's request to receive assistance would probably figure in the choice but would not be a sufficient reason to provide aid. That would be especially true if there were more requests for technical assistance than the agency's financial resources or production capacity permitted it to satisfy. The "rationing" of demand would be accomplished not by bidding up the price, as one would expect in a fee-for-service arrangement, but rather by external policy direction.

Sometimes, it is true, mission agencies do not receive explicit guidance from either their funding sources or bureaucratic superiors. In these situations, the assistance provider's own professional and political values would be likely to determine the choice of assistance recipients. Either way, the preferences of potential recipients are not likely to be the major factor in the selection process.

Because helping agencies tend to get less explicit direction from their funding sources or bureaucratic superiors than mission agencies do, they are more likely to be guided by bureaucratic interests and their managers' professional judgment about what constitutes worthy projects. In general, they seek a mix of program activity that will preserve their funding base by building a reliable coalition of political support among both funding sources and recipient communities. Because of the low price charged to recipients of their services, these agencies typically face greater demand for assistance than they can satisfy with their existing resources. As a result, they tend to ration demand by looking for "exemplary" projects, which promise to be politically and professionally visible, to have significant opportunity for success, and to encourage other localities to undertake similar efforts.

Nonprofit organizations are likely to choose projects that enhance their reputations for public-serving activity, while also serving more narrow organizational interests. A university, for example, may provide aid because the project is compatible with faculty research interests or can give faculty and students "real world" contacts and field-work experience. A willing aid recipient, therefore, is a necessary but not sufficient condition for initiating an assistance relationship. A project must also have characteristics that make it interesting to the assistance provider.

Volunteers often have similar outlooks, but sometimes they are looking for contacts or experiences they can use to market their professional services, either to the community receiving aid or to another municipality with similar needs. Thus, like the helping agency but for different reasons, volunteers are interested in exemplary projects that can be replicated elsewhere.

Associations of governments usually feel obligated to respond in some way to all legitimate requests for aid from their members. To some degree, this fact limits an association's control of its own agenda; its staff must perform a significant number of routine assistance tasks. But, because demand for services tends to exceed capacity to provide them, associations preserve a degree of autonomy through the methods used to ration demand. Sometimes this may require only referring the municipality to some other source of assistance. Some associations provide a fixed allotment of technical assistance manhours to each community and then charge a fee for services exceeding that amount. Alternatively, some associations accord priority to requests that seem consistent with the association's policy agenda or are professionally interesting to its staff, while devoting fewer resources to others.

Responsiveness to the Assistance Recipient

Different types of assistance providers vary in how attuned and responsive they are to the recipient government's preferences. Therefore, a community should be concerned that the provider's predilections are appropriate for the project at hand.

A critical factor in developing this understanding is determining the assistance provider's principal source of policy cues. Such cues may come from several directions: from the assistance recipient attempting to steer the provider's work, from a third party such as a legislative funding source or a grant-giving agency, or from the provider agency's own professional and political values and objectives.

The recipient's preferences are most likely to dominate the provider's perspective when there is a direct fee-for-service agreement between them. In that situation, the provider is retained to perform a specific task defined in negotiations between the parties. Since payment is contingent on completion of the task according to contractual requirements, the assistance provider will be motivated economically to respond to the client's policy directions.

When the assistance provider's financial support comes from a source other than the aid recipient, however, the outside funding source may prove to be the primary source of policy cues. That is most likely to be the case for "mission" agencies whose technical assistance programs derive their funding from a regular budget and whose policy direction may come from legislative overseers; it may also prove true for helping agencies if their work is being closely guided by legislative sponsors. Outside policy cues are also likely to predominate when private consultants are hired not by the aid recipient on an individual basis but by an agency which contracts to provide technical assistance to a number of communities.

In these cases, the recipient government, lacking economic leverage, may have difficulty in making the aid provider responsive to its concerns and interests. Some responsiveness can be assumed because loud complaints from an aid recipient are politically embarrassing to both the aid provider and the sponsor. Ultimately, though, the aid recipient's most significant source of influence is the power to demand project termination. Some assistance relationships, in fact, are punctuated by such threats; but assuming that the recipient finds the project genuinely valuable, that option would actually be exercised only as a last resort. The recipient, therefore, must contend with an assistance relationship in which its own preferences, even when forcefully asserted, may have relatively little impact on a provider's behavior.

Policy cues may come from neither the aid recipient nor any external source. In many instances, helping agencies like a Department of Community Affairs or a public service institute at a public university are given scant direction by their funding sources or bureaucratic superiors; the same happens less frequently but not unusually for mission agencies. In these situations, the assistance provider is free to determine its policies and priorities on the basis of its own bureaucratic interests and professional norms. The recipient's viewpoint is typically a factor but not dominant in shaping assistance activities. The threat of withdrawal is the recipient's main leverage, although it may not be credible.

Councils of government and state municipal associations may also operate with few external constraints. A particular aid recipient may have little leverage over the assistance relationship, even though it is a member community, because it is not directly paying for the service. To the extent that membership in the organization is voluntary, however, the aid givers will be wary of antagonizing a recipient community. Negative experiences can have an adverse and lasting effect on the organization's relationship with all of its members. Each member has an interest in preventing the organization from making unwanted intrusions into its affairs. (This concern is reduced but not eliminated if membership is required by state law, as it is for some councils of government.) As a result, overall, associations of government tend to be solicitous of, but not wholly controlled by, an individual community's sentiments.

Finally, volunteer assistance providers tend to vary significantly in how responsive they are to the recipient government. If their interest is generating future business or simply basking in the public limelight, they are likely to be attentive to the preferences of their client. On the other hand, if they are motivated by specific policy views, they are likely to behave quite independently. Short of terminating the assistance relationship, a recipient has little leverage in dealing with such a volunteer.

Individualized or Prepackaged Aid

Technical assistance providers vary in the degree to which they offer services that are tailored individually to the needs and circumstances of the recipient government. In some cases, the provider works closely with officials in the recipient government to define precise objectives for the assistance relationship and to determine what methods of assistance will be employed. In others, the assistance provider offers prepackaged aid in which the content and method of assistance is virtually indistinguishable from the treatment offered to other communities.

A recipient government may find it easiest to secure individually tailored assistance through a fee-for-service agreement with a private consulting firm. Then, the assistance provider is most likely to be responsive to the recipient's concerns and to feel fairly compensated for time spent developing a tailored assistance package. That result, however, depends on the recipient exercising careful oversight; otherwise the consulting firm's economic motivation may lead it to cut costs by replicating tasks performed for other recipients. This "boiler-plate" assistance may or may not be responsive to the current recipient's actual needs and preferences.

The probability of receiving prepackaged assistance increases markedly when an aid recipient is dealing with a mission agency or a private consulting firm working on a large-scale contract paid for by a third party. Because the aid provider is dealing with a number of recipient governments, it is likely to have developed a more or less standardized set of services. Moreover, the agency that sponsors and pays for the work is likely to influence significantly the objectives and methods established for the assistance relationship, although the recipient community's preferences are not likely to be ignored altogether. Demonstration programs, in which ideas are tried out in a small number of sites, are sometimes an exception; recipients of assistance in these projects often receive a good deal of individualized attention.

Helping agencies and associations of municipalities that provide assistance to their member communities are likely to provide both prepackaged and individually tailored aid. Because some problems are common to a significant number of communities with which they work, these groups tend to develop standard assistance packages that can be used in a range of sites. For example, a Department of Community Affairs may have a model zoning law or town charter that it recommends to communities that request help in revising theirs. Such "canned" assistance packages are sometimes used for high-priority problems; but, more often, they are used for issues that are not at the top of the provider's priorities. Assistance activities at the cutting edge of the agency's work—generally tasks that are "hot" politically or regarded as professionally exciting—are more likely to result in individually designed services.

Nonprofit organizations, such as private universities and volunteer aid providers, are very likely to offer tailored services. Because providing technical assistance is not their principal business, they tend not to become involved with enough communities to develop a repertoire of prepackaged assistance projects. Moreover, they are often motivated by the novelty of a situation; key staff regard it as professionally stimulating or as an opportunity to train other personnel or students. Consequently, the participating personnel are unlikely to be interested in repetitious tasks.

The Duration and Intensity of the Assistance Relationship

Technical assistance relationships vary in length and intensity— from a single telephone call between a municipal manager and a state official discussing environmental regulations to a major financial management project in which staff of the assistance provider work on site in the municipal government daily for months. To assure that the assistance provider will help a project firmly take root, officials in a recipient government should have a clear sense of how long and how deeply involved the aid-giving organization is likely to be.

A private consulting firm is generally retained for a specific period of time or until specified work is completed according to contractual terms. The firm's commitment and level of effort tends to be directly proportionate to the magnitude of the negotiated fee—except when the firm sees a project as an introduction to a potentially profitable new line of work. For example, a management consultant may help a municipality develop a computerized purchasing system that takes account of new provisions of state law. If the firm has not previously done similar work, it may assign more staff and spend more time than it is being compensated for so that its personnel can develop polished documentation and greater experience with the system. Such projects are seen not as discrete fee-for-service activity, but rather, as marketing and staff training investments. The firm expects that other municipalities will hire it when they learn about work in the prototype site.

Mission agencies and consulting firms working on third-party contracts are less likely to become deeply involved in individual projects. More typically, they sponsor technical assistance programs aimed at spreading a particular innovation to a wide range of communities. They tend to make a relatively low-level commitment in aid to a specific community; such assistance is more likely to involve distribution of printed materials than interpersonal contact and to last for a relatively short period of time.

Demonstration projects, however, frequently secure more resources than the typical assistance effort. Designed as prototypes to be adopted more widely, they are similar to projects that consulting firms use to open new markets. The sponsoring agency has a stronger stake than usual in seeing such projects become fully institutionalized in the recipient government; it hopes to tell success stories to other municipalities.

A mission agency's assistance programs are more vulnerable to shifts in appropriations levels and priorities than other kinds of programs. Because no long-term commitments have been made, a mission agency's assistance efforts may be rapidly altered or phased out. For example, the Reagan Administration cut back and revised federal technical assistance programs in financial management and energy conservation when it took office.

The degree to which helping agencies become deeply involved in particular assistance projects varies widely. They undertake some short-term projects that involve relatively low-level commitments—advising a town on hiring a labor relations specialist or directing municipal officials to materials on interlocal service delivery arrangements. Helping agencies also become deeply immersed in crisis projects. A town's threatened default on its bond obligations, for example, may prompt a Department of Community Affairs to launch an intense effort to improve the community's financial management and budgeting practices. Projects at either of these extremes are an element of the helping agency's *raison d'être*, the sort of activity that its funding sources expect it to carry out as part of its routine workload. But a helping agency may become deeply involved in some projects not because of a crisis or because of its political and bureaucratic overseers' expectations, but because of the agency's own judgment that an issue warrants exploration. To the extent that its financial and personnel resources permit, it will try to develop projects that advance its key officials' professional values or focus on incipient problems and opportunities.

For example, a helping agency might initiate and devote resources to a program encouraging municipal productivity improvements in a state soon to be faced with a tax limitation referendum.

Associations of governments are more likely to make moderate commitments of time and effort to technical assistance projects. Much of their activity requires providing specific information and referral services on request to their smaller and less professionally managed member communities. Other projects typically require distribution of information to a wider spectrum of their members, with the association frequently acting as the agent of a mission agency. Projects that entail more intense involvement tend to occur relatively infrequently; an association rarely has sufficient financial resources to embark on open-ended projects; and its members are simultaneously wary of interference in their internal affairs and expect even-handed treatment in the distribution of organizational benefits.

Nonprofit organizations, such as private universities, and volunteer assistance providers vary widely in how deeply involved they get in particular assistance projects. Because they commit their time and energy with no direct compensation or financial support from either the aid recipient or a third party, they usually shy away from intense involvements. Their participation, moreover, is subject to the ebb and flow of their other commitments, not necessarily to the needs of the project. Businessman-volunteers, for example, respond to the seasonal demands of their firms' work; and university personnel are often governed by the academic calendar, with faculty free time coming in the summer and student participation hewing closely to the structure of semesters or quarters. Sometimes, however, nonprofit organizations and volunteers become deeply involved in a project because its professional stimulation is high or the lure of the pubic stage is particularly strong.

Summary

The preceding sections have explored variations of behavior of different types of assistance providers that result from their organizational interests and incentives. Table 1 summarizes these behavioral relationships.

The Politics of Aid Provision

Discussion so far has concentrated on helping potential aid recipients differentiate the interests and incentives of various technical

Table 1. Behavior of Different Types of Technical Assistance Providers

	Principal basis for choosing projects	Responsiveness to the assistance recipient	Type of aid package	Duration and intensity of the assistance relationship
Private consultants	At initiative of fee-paying clients, except when working on third-party contract	High, except when working on third-party contract	Individualized if supervised or developing new market	Variable as client wishes and can pay for; longer if new market is being developed
Helping agencies	Bureaucratic interests and professional judgment of top staff	Moderate	Both individualized and prepackaged	Quite variable
Mission agencies	Policy set by bureaucratic superiors or funding sources	Moderate-low	Generally pre-packaged unless demonstration project	Generally short
Nonprofit organizations	Projects that are "interesting" to agency personnel	Moderate	Individualized	Variable depending on the "interest" of the project and other pressures on organization
Associations of governments	At initiative of members	Moderate-high	Both individualized and prepackaged	Moderate
Volunteers	Projects that are "interesting" or that serve marketing purposes	Variable, depending on whether they are seeking business or professional stimulation	Individualized	Variable, depending on interest of the project and other pressures on organization

assistance providers to make better predictions about their behavior. In this section, we consider the interests of the aid recipient with the aim of improving the provider's assistance strategies.

Establishing the Assistance Relationship

As argued earlier, technical assistance providers often assume that recipient governments are eager for their help. Too often, however, they ignore the fact that technical assistance is external intervention in the recipient government's affairs and that they therefore become actors in the recipient's internal politics. Some local officials may genuinely welcome the assistance provider, but other key individuals and constituencies in the recipient government may regard assistance as bothersome because it disrupts traditional ways of conducting government business. Some may feel that their jobs, influence, or status are threatened. In fact, some actors may oppose both the aid giver and the assistance project.

Effective provision of technical assistance requires an acute sensitivity to the political stakes of different parts of the recipient government and of outside constituencies. In important ways, one should think of the aid giver's task as helping a client in the recipient government build a political and bureaucratic coalition influential enough to secure the adoption, implementation, and institutionalization of the policy change about which assistance is being offered.

The provider's first step should be to clearly identify a client within the recipient government. Broadly speaking, the provider might think of the entire government or community as his client, but practically that designation leaves ambiguous his internal source of policy direction and strategic advice. More narrowly, he should identify a specific client, preferably an actor who invites him to intervene, on behalf of whom he can work, whose objectives are compatible with his own, and whose cooperation can be won for the organizational changes needed.

When a key actor in the recipient government seeks out technical assistance and expects to pay for the service, the aid giver usually has little difficulty in defining who an appropriate client is. At other times, however, identifying the client may prove problematic. Sometimes the assistance relationship is initiated by a subordinate actor whose principal may be weakly motivated or uncommitted to seek outside help. A mayor's assistant, for example, may seek help with a project about which his boss is ambivalent or which ranks low in his priorities. Or, there may even be *no* person or organization in the recipient government who cares strongly about the success of the assistance effort, a situation that may arise when aid is being provided through an intergovernmental program that seeks to upgrade capacity in a large number of governments. Sometimes, in fact, the nominal local sponsor of an assistance project may be responding to unwanted pressure or merely trying to capture available grant money; he actually may hope that the assistance effort fails.

To be effective in such situations, the assistance provider must usually find or create an ally influential enough to help him pursue the objectives of the assistance project. However, he must also exercise care, both to avoid political pitfalls and to deal with potential ethical dilemmas that arise in trying to press an unwilling community to accept outside advice.

Diagnosis

A second step for the aid giver is to consider carefully the needs for assistance. A starting point ought to be the client's objectives. The client may publicly articulate reasons for requesting assistance or cooperating with the provider, for example, making financial management more effective or taking advantage of new service delivery technology. The client, however, may also have unspoken political and bureaucratic reasons for seeking assistance. A project may be symbolically significant to a key constituency outside government, or it may work to the client's advantage in competition for influence within the affected agency or the government as a whole. Such objectives may be confided to the aid provider or may have to be inferred from the client's cues. Even when not overtly stated, though, the assistance provider should be highly sensitive to such motives. These political and bureaucratic objectives may be more important than his client's public reasons for seeking aid.

Beyond the objectives that the client identifies, an aid giver may have reasons of his own for believing that organizational change would be appropriate; technical assistance is frequently a tool for agencies at higher levels of government to promote their own policy agendas. Staying strictly within the bounds set by the client may not, in fact, best serve the client's interests. Because the client is seeking an expert's best judgment, it is quite appropriate for the provider to point out additional issues and try to educate and persuade the client that they justify adopting new government practices.

However, pressing a recipient government to accept the assistance provider's definition of objectives potentially raises ethical dilemmas for the provider because it can verge on coercively imposing change from the outside. When a client has independently retained the assistance provider and is paying for his services, this problem is less acute. The client has enough influence in the relationship to guide the aid giver's orientation and control his behavior. The problem can be more troublesome when the assistance provider is a volunteer or is being supported financially by sources outside of the client's government. In that case, the client may have too little influence over the assistance provider's actions to prevent him from acting mainly in his own interests or serving those of an outside funding source.

It is difficult to lay out precise guidelines to govern relationships of this sort, if only because accepting free outside assistance often involves overt or tacit acceptance of a larger agenda of objectives and interests than the client would otherwise define. That is clearly the case when acceptance of an intergovernmental grant also entails acceptance of administrative regulations promulgated by a higher level of government. In technical assistance arrangements, the key to these relationships lies in the clarity of expectations on both sides and the degree to which obligations are freely incurred. Except when the regulatory requirements of a higher level of government are involved, the recipient government ought to retain the latitude to back out of a relationship which threatens its interests or values.

Technical assistance providers must be sensitive not only to the benefits but also to the costs of organizational change. There is a tendency for proponents of change—the client inside the government and others (including the aid giver) who are promoting innovation from outside—to become enthused by the potential positive impacts of change and to ignore its disadvantages even to themselves. In effect, they overvalue the benefits and discount the costs. Yet costs are inevitable: proposed change may alter the content of some individuals' jobs in ways they find unpleasant, consume scarce financial resources, absorb large amounts of staff time and energy, alter power relationships inside the organization, and annoy important external constituencies. If in their eagerness to see organizational change the proponents of innovation tend to understate the costs even from their own viewpoint, it is understandable that they fail to notice costs that others find quite substantial. It is others' perceptions of costs, however, that prompt resistance to proposed change and lead to foot-dragging or sabotage if change actually is implemented.

An effective assistance provider, therefore, will carefully assess the quantity and distribution of both costs and benefits of organizational change, as perceived by key actors in the recipient government's political environment. These include the client, his bureaucratic superiors, the government's elected chief executive, the city council, and various constituencies likely to be concerned.

Assessing in advance the effects of organizational change is a tough but important task. The costs and benefits that actors perceive vary according to the number of officials and citizens likely to be affected by change and its visibility. Quite significantly, particular impacts of change will not be evaluated in the same way by every actor. What one regards as a benefit may well appear to be a severe cost to another.

A Strategy of Assistance

Diagnosis of organizational interests is critical information for the aid provider's development of a strategy of assistance. The aid provider ought to be particularly interested in identifying any significant variations in the distribution of benefits and costs. Which actors are likely to be net winners or losers if the proposed change is actually implemented? This analysis can be extremely helpful in picking out potential supporters and opponents of change.

The aid provider should be concerned with finding and keeping allies. That initially requires sustaining the support of the client by appreciating his risks and taking actions to minimize tensions and threats that arise from the process of organizational change. Keeping the client's active support sometimes proves difficult, though, especially if his benefits and costs are distributed asymmetrically through time. Some clients of a technical assistance project may reap all—or nearly all—of the benefits when a project is announced, even if it is never fully implemented and institutionalized by the recipient government. A mayor running for reelection, for example, may wish to radiate with the positive aura of reform without actually paying the price of promoting bureaucratic change. He may therefore take advantage of the "an-nouncement effect" of a proposed reform having no intention of following through. That will pose difficult problems for an assistance provider that assumed the mayor's support for his efforts.

Whether or not the client remains a committed supporter, the assistance provider can use the access gained to the recipient govern-ment as a base for seeking broader backing for the proposed assistance project. The key question in determining who might prove to be an ally is whether the project can serve other actors' interests. Assistance providers sometimes limit their search unnecessarily by thinking exclusively in terms of their own or the client's interests rather than seeking ways to make the project appeal to other actors in terms of values and objectives that matter to them. Assistance providers can be far more persuasive and advance their cause by taking care to understand fully what others care about and how the project might legitimately be represented to serve their interests.

Similar analysis of the benefits and costs of organizational change can help the assistance provider anticipate who his opponents will be and possibly suggest ways of reducing or even neutralizing their opposition. One step that may prove helpful is to alter *perceptions* of benefits and costs. If the reasons for opposition are successfully forecast, that can sometimes be accomplished by careful consultation with potential opponents before a project is formally announced. Another possibility once benefits and costs are identified is to alter the original plan for change—perhaps only marginally, perhaps more substantially—to take account of potential opponents' interests. Yet another possibility is to arrange for some form of compensating change—perhaps in a wholly different policy arena—that will attract new support or at least minimize opposition. Even if the only course available is to meet opposition head on, the assistance provider and the client will be better off as a result of anticipating objections and resistance than they would have been concentrating exclusively on the reasons that change would be beneficial to themselves.

Institutionalization

A final consideration for the assistance provider, but one that should be taken into account from the outset, is institutionalizing the organizational changes that technical assistance aims at fostering. Ultimately, the assistance relationship will terminate with the provider leaving the recipient government to carry on by itself. Can the project survive? Frequently, changes wrought on a temporary basis while the assistance provider is present to sustain them are swept away when the provider leaves the scene. That is always a risk in assistance relationships, but it can be reduced if the provider explicitly considers how to make the assistance project self-sustaining.

As with all aspects of an assistance relationship, there are technical dimensions to this problem, for example, assuring that requisite skills are present in the recipient government's permanent management team. The assistance provider, however, should also recognize a political dimension. Change will persist only if there are actors in the recipient government who have both incentives to maintain the project and sufficient influence to accomplish that. These actors may or may not be the original proponents of change in the recipient government; quite possibly, they may be actors who discover benefits that they did not initially appreciate. To increase the chances of an innovative practice surviving, therefore, the assistance provider should work to stimulate such support.

Conclusion

This paper has explored the importance of organizational interests and incentives in providing technical assistance. The potential recipient of assistance needs to recognize that different types of aid providers have varying interests which make them behave differently in an assistance relationship. Assistance providers, in turn, need to understand the political context in which they will work in the recipient government. Improved understanding of organizational interests on both sides can reduce the frustrations, disappointments, and wasted resources that technical assistance efforts frequently produce.

8

Inducing Capacity Building: The Role of the External Change Agent

Bruce Jacobs and David Leo Weimer

Improvements in the managerial and analytical capabilities of local government agencies may be desirable because they lower costs, increase quantity or quality, or contribute to better distribution of the services provided to the public. In some instances, the stimulus for improvement may come from within the agency, as officials become aware of the possibility of desirable changes and initiate capacity building[1] efforts without external support or direction. In others, however, we would not expect to see new and potentially productive technologies, procedures, personnel and the like without the participation of external agents or institutions, e.g., state or federal government agencies, foundations, research institutes, or consulting firms. In this paper, the authors consider several strategies that might be used by those outside local government to help build its capacity to make decisions, implement decisions, or monitor their impact.

Capacity building can be thought of as a special case in the study of organizational change and innovation. Local public agencies are likely to innovate at slower-than-socially-optimal rates in the absence of external support because of deficiencies in knowledge, funds for start-up, or technical expertise. A general framework for the analysis of external efforts to induce innovation in local public agencies should consider how information, funding, and technical assistance can be combined to overcome these deficiencies and take into account the implications of the proposed changes for the perceived well-being of key organizational actors.

Local decision-makers have multiple goals that are unlikely to be fully consistent with the goals of program sponsors. This may result in the diversion of resources from the uses envisioned by those who initiate change. Additionally, some program designs create incentives that may lead program sponsors to support innovation where it is unlikely to provide net social benefits.

In what follows, we analyze several generic strategy types. For each we consider the process of capacity building and the organizational factors that may either promote or inhibit its implementation. We begin with a brief discussion of the decision-making environment in which capacity building must occur.

The Organizational Context of Capacity Building

To understand the opportunities and constraints faced by the external change agent and to assess the potential effectiveness of each of the strategies he or she might use, we must place capacity building in the context of organizational decision making.[2] Capacity building involves organizational change. It may consist of adding new personnel, administrative units, equipment, and staff responsibilities, or it may require partial reallocation of existing organizational resources. In either event, at least some of the agency's staff will be affected if the required changes are successfully implemented. Their response may aid the process of implementation or hinder it. For the external change agent to ignore the important role of agency officials and staff is to invite program failure.

During the 1930s and 1940s, students of organizational behavior challenged the notion that all members of an organization pursued the same set of objectives, i.e., the organization's goals. Instead of viewing a firm or bureau as an anthropomorphic entity with a single order of priorities, Chester Barnard, Herbert Simon, and others argued that an organization comprised individuals cooperatively engaged in a mutual enterprise.[3] Each participant belonged to the organization because it was in his or her interest to do so. In exchange for the contributions made to the agency's operation (e.g., carrying out its tasks), the member received a series of inducements or incentives. These inducements might include salary and benefits, as well as nonmaterial rewards, such as the prestige of office, the camaraderie of coworkers, or the satisfaction that one's work is effective and helps achieve a desirable objective.

The important point here is that agency staff need not (and in fact do not) share an identical set of individual, rather than agency, goals. Different participants may not seek the same inducements and may not value a particular inducement equally (e.g., the satisfaction derived from an innovation). For any staff member, the net satisfaction from participation is the difference between the benefits derived from the inducements offered by the organization and the costs of carrying out the tasks assigned. As long as the net satisfaction is positive (and sufficiently large) it is rational for the staff member to continue making the contributions necessary for the operation of the agency. In addition, this "surplus" of incentives leads the employee to accept the authority of superiors.

Any capacity-building effort will require some members to experience a change in costs (e.g., tasks) or a change in benefits (e.g., job security or prestige). The individual (or, in most cases, the individuals) responsible for the maintenance of the inducements-contributions system is the organizational executive.[4] Executives alone have the task of seeing to it that the requisite contributions are made by their staffs and that sufficient quantities of inducements flow to them. If the changes necessary for the capacity-building effort decrease the net satisfactions of a sufficient number of staff members, an executive may face a situation in which the operation of the agency in other areas might suffer, or his or her capacity to govern (i.e., authority) might decrease. In his analysis of the process of innovation, James Q. Wilson has characterized these difficulties:

> The greater the cost in scarce inducements, the more radical the innovation, regardless of the prospective benefits. . . . Loosely speaking, the executive of the organization assesses the cost of any innovation in terms of how much must be done to keep affected parties happy or (if the innovation calls for adding new members to the organization) what must be done (or 'spent') to induce new members to contribute. Money costs are often very important, of course, but other costs may be of equal or greater importance: soothing ruffled fur, reducing uncertainty-induced anxiety, bolstering members' self conceptions, appealing to their sense of duty, eliminating interpersonal tensions and hostilities, changing the norms of informal work groups, familiarizing workers with new technologies, finding ways to compensate demoted members for their loss of prestige and power, reformulating statements of organizational purpose.[5]

The executive, therefore, would like to have a store of surplus inducements so that he can distribute them where appropriate in the process of capacity-building change. However, there are other uses to which the executive might put these resources. William Niskanen provides an important insight into the logic of executive choice.[6] He argues that, for the executive, the benefits derived from participation are partly a function of the difference between the maximum budget of resources flowing into the agency and the minimum costs of carrying out the agency's tasks.

This difference, the discretionary budget of the executive, is part of what has been called organizational slack.[7] An executive may spend part of his budget to increase the slack enjoyed by some of the staff. He may also, however, channel some of these resources to "pet projects" or to alleviate deficits in other parts of the agency's work. *Ceteris paribus*, the executive has an incentive to expand his or her discretionary budget. This can be achieved either by increasing the resources coming into the agency or by decreasing the costs of some of its operations.

The inducements-contributions formula and the logic of executive choice have important implications for external change agents who seek to induce capacity-building innovations in public agencies. If agency members feel that a particular change will decrease their slack or place their benefits from participation in some future jeopardy, they have an incentive to resist the capacity-building program. Their resistance need not be in the form of disobedient behavior. More frequently, staff members may exhibit unexpected limitations in learning rates or may respond to new tasks by "going through the motions" without achieving the objective.

These symbolic responses are, of course, well known among those who have studied patterns of resistance to organizational change. Their importance in this context is that, whatever the putative organizational benefits of a capacity-building change, there may well be organizational members who believe that the change is not in their interests and will act accordingly. These behaviors, in turn, increase the costs of change as seen by the executive. Moreover, if the executive is not committed to the capacity-building effort, he or she may calculate that it would be more "profitable" to allow (or avoid noticing) the staff's behavior than to go through the difficult process of implementing the change.

More generally, we should expect agency executives to view each capacity-building proposal in terms of the costs and benefits as they appear to them in their positions. The overall effectiveness and efficiency of the organization will, in most cases, be important in their calculations. But so will the perceived impact on their discretionary budgets, their authority, and the willingness of agency staff to perform other functions. Where the priorities of the agency staff and the executive are not in conflict with the capacity-building agenda of the external change agent, there should be more rapid adoption with less conflict. Where either has conflicting priorities, the change agent's strategy must recognize the different calculations being made by those in the local agency.

One approach to the external inducement of capacity building is the provision of financial resources to help fund desired changes. These resources may come in the form of grants or they may consist of income in-kind (e.g., lending personnel to a local agency for the purpose of introducing new skills or procedures). With the tremendous expansion of the intergovernmental grant system and other federal initiatives started during the Great Society period, much has been learned about local governmental response to externally supplied financial resources.[8] Many of these lessons are important to external change agents who participate in the process of capacity building.

The resources that flow to a grant recipient may be spent by the local agency in three ways. Expenditures on the aided function (i.e., on capacity-building changes) may increase beyond what they otherwise would have been. However, grant monies may also be spent on other activities of local government or they may be used to provide some tax relief to local constituents. The expenditure pattern that a grant produces will be a function of the structure of the grant and the priorities of local agency executives and staffs.

Grants may be characterized along several dimensions.[9] Perhaps most important for our discussion is the degree to which a grant is targeted for a categorical purpose, such as capacity building. Categorical project grants tend to be allocated at the discretion of the sponsor according to criteria that are meant to ensure substantial compliance with the objectives of the grant. Typically of limited duration, they may be expanded or not renewed on the basis of the sponsor's satisfaction with local agency performance. At the other end of the spectrum are revenue-sharing grants intended to improve the fiscal situation of local governments, but not targeted for particular purposes. With much less uncertainty regarding the amount and duration of these grant monies, local officials have little incentive to devote new resources to activities not high on their priority list.

Political scientists and economists have studied the impact of grants on recipient institutions.[10] Most have concluded that both the structure of the grant and the priorities of the recipients affect the degree to which the donor's objectives are met. In general, more tightly categorical grants have a higher probability of achieving the desired outcomes.[11] However, even narrowly defined project grants may be spent in ways other than those intended by the external change agent. To see why this is so, we must look at these grants as executives of local organizations see them.

For the local official, a grant represents both costs and benefits. While the grant increases the size of the agency's budget, it also requires the expenditure of resources for particular purposes. If these purposes are at odds with the official's preferences or those of the staff, then slack resources may have to be spent in order to meet the minimum requirements of the grant. In this case, the discretionary budget of the executive may actually be reduced, thus providing an incentive for noncompliance with the program's objectives. To ensure success, the external change agent may have to monitor the grant closely or donate the financial resources through the direct provision of the desired services.

Generic Strategies for Inducing Capacity Building

Because our concern is with the role of the external change agent in capacity building, the theory of induced innovation provides a starting point.[12]

It can be argued that local public agencies are likely to innovate at slower-than-socially-optimal rates because of the resource constraints and incentives their managers face. Competition for scarce, local resources makes it difficult for public managers to secure start-up funds for new projects, especially if the projects are not intended to produce reductions in future operating costs. Unlike their counterparts in the private sector, public managers are usually not allowed to accumulate funds within their agencies or to enter capital markets independently. Unlike their private counterparts, the public managers cannot look to the profitability of competitors as an indication of successful innovation, and they are not punished in the marketplace for failing to adopt the most efficient technologies. When public managers do decide to innovate, they are often disadvantaged by deficiencies in technical expertise (a lack of capacity) that may limit the extent to which they can effectively use outside consultants. These factors—limitations in funding, knowledge and expertise—combine to make rates of innovation in local public agencies slower than in competitive, private sector firms. If the latter are assumed to innovate at rates less than or equal to the social optimum,[13] absent external assistance, it follows that innovation in local public agencies will be too slow from the viewpoint of social efficiency.

One way to classify change agent strategies for inducing innovation in general, and capacity-building in specific, is in terms of the way they are intended to mitigate the factors inhibiting innovation by local public managers. Some strategies provide local managers with *funds* to cover start-up costs of capacity-building changes. Some provide local public managers with *information* about desirable capacity-building activities. Others attempt to enhance levels of local expertise—itself an element of capacity—through the provision of *technical assistance*, which can be thought of as providing information relevant to the circumstances of the local agencies. The strategies are summarized in Table 1.

Funding Strategies

Each of these four general funding strategies implicitly assumes that short-term funding can contribute to longer-term increases in capacity. That is, once the funding is withdrawn, gains in capacity building will not completely disappear.

Skills Seeding

Local agencies often do not have the personnel needed to perform newly required tasks or to introduce technological changes in the performance of traditional functions. Facing constraints of resources and knowledge, these agencies can benefit from the provision of funds by another organization for the purpose of hiring specialists to help carry out the new tasks and to provide the agencies with the capacity to do so in the future. Such skills seeding can be initiated by local officials who are aware of the need for specialists they do not currently have (e.g., a systems analyst in a budget bureau or an epidemiologist in a local health agency). Change can also be initiated, however, with an offer of funding from another institution that desires, or requires, the introduction of new technical capabilities.

Skills seeding will typically involve funding for a fixed period of time. The specialist hired with the funds given to the local agency may be a consultant or may join the agency's staff for the funding period. The impact of his or her efforts, however, should last beyond the initial grant. This can occur in at least three ways. First, the specialist can teach agency staff members how to perform the new tasks and depend on them to continue these efforts in the future. Second, the local agency

Table 1. Strategies for Inducing Capacity Building

Strategy	Assumed Contribution to Capacity Building	Major Implementation Problem
A. Targeted Financial Subsidies		
1. Skills seeding	Sponsored persons are retained or transfer skill to permanent employees; builds staff expertise.	Status as temporary employee limits opportunities to demonstrate skills.
2. Functional unit building	Helps establish units with management, analysis and planning responsibilities; units become part of organizational structure.	Line bureaus resist reallocations of resources.
3. Tool introduction	Information systems facilitate better decision making or lower operating costs.	Design and organizational cooperation problems can hinder data quality and use.
4. Evaluation requirements	Encourages jurisdictions that participate in general grant programs to develop evaluation skills.	Lack of monitoring and enforcement encourage testimonials as substitutes for evaluation.
B. Information		
1. Exemplary projects	Indicate how some jurisdictions have dealt with problem to encourage replication or adaptation.	Diversity among jurisdictions may lead to inappropriate adoptions.

2. Strengthening information networks.	Encourage the transfer of information among jurisdictions through professional and government associations.	Bias toward transmission of apparently positive results.
3. Personnel and performance standards	Offers guidance and external validity to efforts of internal change agents.	Establishment of realistic standards in the face of diversity.
C. *Technical Assistance*		
1. Direct training	Local personnel participate in training program sponsored by external change agent.	Local agencies may not be able to spare staff who would gain most from training.
2. Personnel exchanges	External change agent and local jurisdictions swap personnel to broaden their experience.	Limited by size of the change agent organization and willingness of personnel to deviate from standard career paths.
3. Joint projects	Consultants are provided to work with local jurisdictions to provide critical expertise for specific projects.	Gap may exist between technical expertise of consultants and contextual knowledge of local personnel.

may offer permanent employment to the change-agent-sponsored specialist. Third, the agency may hire other staff to do the work after the specialist has departed.

There are several factors that may limit the impact of skills seeding. Since the period of funding is fixed, local managers may not want to commit future intergovernmental resources that might not be forthcoming. The temporary status of the specialist in the agency may also limit his or her ability to influence and teach other staff members. Moreover, absent a clear message from the local manager, agency staff may discount the desirability of new technologies or functions.

In many cases, local political and institutional factors not known by the change agents can limit the impact of their efforts. Sometimes these constraints stymie the implementation of capacity building. The less contact the change agent has with local officials before the project begins and the less time spent learning about (and dealing with) important contextual problems, the greater the potential impediments to successful change.

A related point is that both the manager and his or her staff should perceive the usefulness of the innovation. (Solutions to unimportant problems or failed attempts to solve important ones will limit the impact of the specialist's work.) It is important for the change agent and the local agency officials and staff to see that new skills are targeted at relevant, but tractable, problems that are soluble in the near term.

Functional Unit Building

To introduce new decision-making capacity in a local government, it is sometimes desirable for a sponsor to commit funds for the development of a new office. Typically given responsibility for policy analysis, program planning and evaluation, or management control, these new functional units will most likely be in the office of the chief executive or operate as a support agency in the legislative branch.[14] In some cases, however, they may be devoted to a single area of public policy, e.g., a criminal justice planning agency. Most often, the division will have some new staff but also will have to borrow or recruit staff members from the agencies.

While the development of offices of evaluation, planning, and the like might seem inherently desirable to the donor, there are several forces within the local jurisdiction that may limit successful implementation of the change.[15] The process of planning and evaluation implicitly involves judgments about the distribution of local government resources. Line agency personnel may see the external division as a threat to their budgets and therefore may calculate that it is not in their interest to cooperate fully with the new office. At the initiation of the effort, they may also be reluctant to "lend" their better staff members to the division, especially if the loan may be perceived as becoming permanent.

The information needed to assess the effectiveness and efficiency of local programs is rarely available in analyzable form. Constrained by this limitation, analysts in the new office may require substantial allocations of other local government resources or, absent these resources, may be restricted to program descriptions rather than program analyses. This problem may be compounded when a staff member on loan from a line agency expects to return to that agency and appropriately is concerned with the interests of his or her former office.

As was the case in skills seeding, the success of new functional units is quite often a function of the local executive's support. If the relevant officials make clear their desire to use the new division as an administrative resource, the likelihood of line agency cooperation will increase. Additionally, it is important that the analysis division select tractable problems, the solutions to which are perceived as of value to the executive and at least not in great conflict with the priorities of the affected bureau. If a recommendation or evaluation is felt to be quite threatening to a line agency, the executive may well face a reduction in organizational slack that is more costly than the benefits of the analysis. Poor selection of issues may effectively doom the office to the status of window dressing, for it may no longer be a net benefit to the executive.

Tool Introduction

The effectiveness of existing staffs might be increased through the introduction of tools, such as information systems, that contribute to management control, problem analysis, program evaluation, or strategic planning. Where functioning tools can be directly bought from private sector vendors, contributions of funds toward purchase prices may be sufficient to induce adoption and facilitate successful implementation. If the tools are more complex, requiring modification to fit the circumstances of the agencies or requiring changes in organizational routines, funding for consulting services may also be needed. The tools might contribute to capacity directly by increasing the information available to decision-makers or indirectly by reducing the staff time that must be devoted to routine activities.[16]

Perhaps the tool with the greatest potential for capacity building is the computerized management information system (MIS). However, several interrelated problems combine to make MIS implementation difficult in local public agencies.[17] The common disjunction between those who bear the costs of data collection and those who realize information benefits, the strain on clerical personnel during the start-up period when both the MIS and the manual system it is replacing must be supported, and the need for continuous training in data collection procedures in the face of personnel changes all contribute to the problem of collecting and monitoring quality data in the MIS. Reliance on shared computer systems whose operators face weak incentives to cooperate fully in implementation and use, lack of in-house resources for special studies, and lack of technical expertise to alter the MIS in response to the changing environment, combine to hinder effective use of the MIS capabilities. Without regular use of the MIS, errors in data are not detected and corrected. The resulting deterioration in data quality further discourages use.

Because information is a political resource, the introduction of an MIS can alter the distribution of influence within a jurisdiction.[18] To the extent that these shifts are anticipated by the losers, their cooperation during implementation may be less than full. For example, line personnel who expect an MIS to be used to monitor their performance more closely may subtly undermine its implementation by providing incomplete or inaccurate data.

Evaluation Requirement

If the change agent is a source of general funding for local public agencies, it can attempt to induce capacity building by requiring the recipients to evaluate their use of grants as a condition for further funding. In preparing the evaluations, the local agencies might develop expertise that they could use to assess the effectiveness of the distribution of locally generated funds. The more importance the change agent places on the evaluations, the more likely that evaluation expertise will actually be developed at the local level.

Local executives who believe that the quality of the evaluation products will have little effect on future funding are unlikely to place high priority on evaluation efforts. Personnel whose time is least valuable to the executive may be given responsibility for completing the evaluations; it is unlikely that their product will include sound measures of impact or skillful diagnosis of managerial problems. Consequently, the value of evaluation will remain undemonstrated to local executives.

Resource and political constraints may make it difficult for the change agent to increase the stringency of the evaluation requirements for the local executives. Monitoring the evaluations and providing feedback to local executives on their quality should place heavy demands on staff time. Simply identifying inadequate evaluations would have little impact unless the change agent could make credible threats of reductions in levels of future funding. If the donor is a federal agency, however, it must be concerned with the political support for its programs; "moving" money and geographically distributing it may be viewed as politically necessary, particularly for funding programs intended to provide general support of service delivery.[19] Threats may be credible for discretionary grant programs, but the change agent runs the risk of excluding from participation not only those recipients who choose not to devote resources to building evaluation capacity, but also who do not have an adequate skills base to develop evaluation capacity on their own.

Information Strategies

Information strategies require the change agent to invest resources in the generation and diffusion of information among local public agencies.[20] The information is intended to increase the local executives' knowledge of the capacity-building innovations that might or should be adopted.

Exemplary Projects

The change agent can designate "exemplary projects" that he believes are worthy of replication in particular circumstances. The change agent would evaluate capacity-building efforts that have been or might be attempted. Documentation describing the potential benefits and costs of the most promising projects and indicating how they could be implemented would then be disseminated to target jurisdictions. The change agent might also help adopters secure funding and technical assistance from various sources to aid implementation.

The great diversity in organization, procedures, and resources of even like-functioned local public agencies suggests that no exemplary project will be appropriate for all jurisdictions. Unless the change agent is careful in determining and communicating the local conditions prerequisite to successful implementation, advocating exemplary projects is likely to lead to inappropriate adoptions. But evaluation is difficult, requiring sophisticated analysis on the part of the change agent as well as cooperation from local experimenters. It may only be possible to determine the prerequisites of successful implementation with confidence after experience is developed in a variety of jurisdictions. Because it may take a considerable length of time to implement exemplary projects and then to generate data useful for evaluation, the exemplary project may be widely diffused before reliable information about its appropriateness is available.

There is a danger that the change agent will become "locked-in" to specific exemplary projects.[21] The change agent, particularly if it must show activity to satisfy budgetary sponsors, may seek to encourage rapid diffusion of the projects it sponsors by disseminating information that provides an optimistic view of the likely benefits of their adoption. Both the change agent and certain of its personnel identify, and become identified, with particular projects. Because systematic evaluations of the optimistic claims may show them to be unjustified, the change agent has little incentive to conduct evaluations of projects that are being widely diffused; negative findings would harm their credibility with the local executives who have adopted on their advice.

The tendency toward lock-in may be reduced if the change agent follows a two-stage diffusion strategy.[22] In the first stage exemplary projects would be repeated in a limited number of local agencies on an experimental basis. Data generated in the first stage would then be used in the second stage to diffuse exemplary projects selectively to jurisdictions where they would be most appropriate. Unfortunately, this strategy is costly to the change agent and may conflict with the desires of budgetary sponsors for widespread geographic impact.

Strengthening of Information Networks

An important constraint faced by officials in thousands of local agencies in our decentralized federalism is lack of knowledge about innovations that might improve their agencies' performances. In some cases, lack of knowledge is more important than financial constraints. To disseminate such information to local jurisdictions, both public and private organizations have used a variety of information-transfer mechanisms.

The federal government uses several strategies to promote local use of successful new techniques and programs. Many federal agencies publish periodicals that contain descriptions of effective local programs.[23] Others issue reports or information about studies on an occasional basis.[24] Individual studies are made available from the U.S. Government Printing Office and from federal departments directly.

Conferences are held by federal agencies to acquaint local officials with new developments of relevance to their offices.[25] Finally, the federal government funds information centers that are intended to serve as clearinghouses and promoters of new programs.[26]

Though many federal information transfer efforts are aimed at officials in urban and metropolitan areas, rural officials may also benefit. In the Department of Agriculture, for example, the Economic Research Service and the Extension Service influence rural capacity building.

Associations of government officials and professional associations are also important sources of information. By financing journal publications[27] and holding conferences, these associations disseminate great quantities of news, program analyses, and conceptual studies.

A third source of potentially important information is the national advocacy organization. Though primarily interested in furthering the interests of its membership, the advocacy organization can also play a useful role in disseminating information through its publications and its conferences.[28]

The transfer of information, however, is not always helpful for capacity building. Often descriptions of successful projects overestimate the benefits derived or under-report the costs involved. There is an almost uniform bias toward news about successful local programs and against the description of local failures. This tendency distorts local officials' bases for decision making.

Conferences can help alleviate the bias, though there is no guarantee of this. In a proper setting, agency staff might openly discuss problems it has been unwilling to put on paper. Also, other officials may have the opportunity to cross-examine those who describe their successful program. However, puffery remains a potent force in both written and verbal presentations.

Finally, there are some circumstances in which it is not in a local official's interest to report the details of successful programs. If government or private institution grants are won on a competitive basis, the successful grantees may have little incentive to provide others with information on what made their proposals or programs successful.

Personnel and Performance Standards

The change agent may invest in the development of personnel and performance standards for local public agencies. These standards may help local executives determine which aspects of their capacity are relatively underdeveloped. They may also be valuable to local executives as a source of external validity in their efforts to mobilize local resources for capacity building. In some circumstances, such as when the change agent is a state legislature, the standards may be mandatory, in which case the local executive is more likely to view them as constraints rather than resources.

The setting of reasonable voluntary standards is made difficult by the diversity of local public agencies. Standards appropriate in some jurisdictions may be inappropriate in others.[29] For example, a recommended number of building inspectors per capita may be appropriate for the Midwest but too low for the older cities of the Northeast and too high for the newer cities of the Southeast. Additionally, clear rationales for any particular standard often do not exist. In such cases the change agent may disseminate information about average levels so that local executives can more easily determine if their personnel or performance levels are substandard. However, there is also the possibility that the change agent will not wish to be seen as advocating mediocrity and therefore set overly high standards that are irrelevant to local circumstances.

The effectiveness of mandatory standards depends on the willingness of change agents to impose sanctions for noncompliance. Cutting off funds or shutting down facilities is likely to involve substantial political costs for the change agent. Unless credible threats to do so can be made, however, compliance is unlikely.[30]

Technical Assistance

Change agents may directly share their expertise with local agencies through technical assistance.

DIRECT TRAINING. One way to introduce new skills into a local agency is to provide training for its staff. This strategy for capacity building can be implemented in several ways.

A team of specialists may be imported into the local community to act as consultants for a fixed period of time.[31] Having detailed knowledge and experience, these advisors can provide valuable instruction on how to carry out new tasks. A disadvantage of this approach may be that the consultants will not be available for needed follow-up advice and instruction.

Another approach involves funding for training in a centralized location not in the local community. This procedure lowers the cost of delivering instructional services to larger numbers of local staff. However, the local agency may face the higher costs of travel and transportation, as well as the loss of staff members for days or weeks. A critical element in the success of this approach is whether the local manager feels that the skills taught will be of substantial value to the operations of his or her agency. If not, the manager may be tempted to send some of the less capable staff members, therefore avoiding the loss of more important staff during the training period.

A third mechanism by which local governments can provide training is to fund coursework done by members at local universities or other educational institutions. Thus, for example, local budget staff may take courses in accounting or systems analysis. Again, however, it is important to know how much of the value of the training accrues to the staff member and how much is enjoyed by the executive as an increase in the agency's capacity.

When training takes place away from the agency, its impact may be limited by the fact that other personnel whose contributions are important to the implementation of the change have not received the training. This may also occur in an on-site training exercise if key workers cannot be spared during the time allotted to the change agent.

The success of direct training will be contingent on how new skills can be best put to use in the context of the local agency. Some capacity building requirements may be common to local governments in general. Changes in federal grant program administration, new federal (or state) regulations, and the economic impact of rising energy costs are examples of common problems. In these circumstances, generalized training programs may fulfill the capacity building purposes of many local agencies. In other instances, problems may be particular to a community, or the governmental infrastructure may be based on specific systems not common to all local agencies. Differences in budgeting and accounting procedures, in the distribution of local government functions, or in personnel systems may limit the applicability of a generalized training program.

More generally, the total costs and benefits to the manager must be taken into account. External funding or "free" training may limit the impact of the program on the manager's discretionary budget. However, in some cases, the attractiveness of a training program may be concentrated on the staff member (who might pick up marketable skills or enjoy a week in an attractive setting) and be of little use to the agency.

PERSONNEL EXCHANGE. Local agencies may benefit by lending personnel to other agencies, jurisdictions, or private institutions. Funding for this purpose may be provided by the government, the host institution, or private institutions.[32] The organizational purpose of this loan is the benefit that would accompany the acquisition of new skills, experience, and information from the host institution.

Another approach that can be of benefit to the local agency is for it to host personnel from other agencies, governments, and private institutions.[33] In this instance, the host institution should be able to gain useful capabilities and advice that are based on the experience of the temporary staff member in his or her regular position.

Though apparently an attractive strategy for capacity building, personnel exchanges can sometimes be of limited value. A local manager may be unwilling to release a valuable staff member for periods up to a year (and sometimes more). In some instances personnel exchanges have been used to "farm out" staff members who are viewed as incompetent or who are advocates of policies not favored by current officials. In other cases, neither the temporary staff member nor the host (or lending) institution is quite sure of the purpose of the exchange. Finally, capable temporary staff may have the opportunity to switch positions, thus losing the benefit to the lending agency. On the other hand, a local agency may benefit by hiring its temporary employee.

JOINT PROJECTS. The change agent may make available consultants to work with local personnel on specific projects.[34] The projects themselves may be demonstrations of some capacity-enhancing organizational change. Additionally, the consultants are intended to provide on-the-job training to local personnel. A successful joint project might leave the local personnel better able to implement similar projects in the future.

There may be a conflict between the goals of completing successful projects and transferring skills. Taking time to teach local personnel technical skills diverts limited consultant support from timely and successful completion of the project. Because it is probably easier to measure project success than training success, one might expect the consultants to emphasize the former. In fact, it has been argued that the ready availability of consultant support may actually decrease local capacity.[35]

Finally, the consultants may face technological lock-in, which may be encountered in exemplary projects. The consultants develop specialized expertise needed for the joint project; their services will likely be in demand for similar projects in the future. Hence, they have an incentive to provide the sponsoring change agent with favorable evaluations that will encourage replication. Because the consultants may be the change agent's primary source of information about the joint project, bias in the information they provide is likely to be important.

Conclusion

Change agents have several strategies available for inducing capacity building in local agencies. In addition to the direct investment of financial resources, the dissemination of information and the provision of technical assistance may contribute to the process of change. The diversity of circumstances in local agencies requires careful choice of appropriate capacity-building strategies. An understanding of the incentives faced by local executives and staff members is critically important if the capacity-building effort is to succeed.

We have outlined ten general strategies that can be used by external change agents to induce capacity building. For each we indicated how the strategy is intended to contribute to capacity building and the organizational factors that tend to hinder its implementation. We hope that it will provide a starting point for prospective change agents.

Notes

1. See the definition of capacity building provided by Beth Walter Honadle elsewhere in this volume.

2. Much of this discussion is derived from Bruce Jacobs, *The Political Economy of Organizational Change* (New York: Academic Press, 1981), chapter 2.

3. The seminal works were Chester I. Barnard, *The Functions of the Executive* (Cambridge, Mass: Harvard University Press, 1938) and Herbert A. Simon, *Administrative Behavior* (New York: Macmillan, 1947). See also Peter B. Clark and James Q. Wilson, "Incentive Systems: A Theory of Organizations," *Administrative Science Quarterly*, 6, 2 (September 1961), 129-166.

4. In practice, any agency is likely to have several executives. The logic of executive choice, which we describe in what follows, would apply to each official individually, as well as affect the overall pattern of resource allocation in the agency. As a matter of convenience, we will discuss the executive as a single person.

5. James Q. Wilson, "Innovations in Organizations: Notes Toward a Theory," in *Approaches to Organizational Designs*, ed. James D. Thompson (Pittsburgh: University of Pittsburgh Press, 1966), 197.

6. William A. Niskanen, "Bureaucrats and Politicians," *Journal of Law and Economics*, 18, 3 (December 1975) 617-643.

7. Richard M. Cyert and James G. March, *A Behavioral Theory of the Firm* (Englewood Cliffs, N.J.: Prentice Hall, 1973), 36.

8. See Jacobs, *The Political Economy* 44-52.

9. See Advisory Commission on Intergovernmental Relations, *Categorical Grants: Their Role and Design* (Washington, D.C.: U.S. Government Printing Office, 1978).

10. See, for example, Martha Derthick, *Uncontrollable Spending for Social Services* (Washington, D.C.: The Brookings Institution, 1975); Martha Derthick, *The Influence of Federal Grants* (Cambridge, Mass.: Harvard University Press, 1970); Edward M. Gramlich, "Intergovernmental Grants: A Review of the Empirical Literature" in *The Political Economy of Fiscal Federalism*, ed. Wallace E. Oates (Lexington, Mass.: Lexington Books, 1977) 219-239; and David R. Beam, "Economic Theory as Policy Prescription: Pessimistic Findings on 'Optimizing' Grants" Paper presented to the 1978 American Political Science Association convention.

11. Grantors whose objectives are too narrowly defined, however, may limit their own effectiveness by not taking into account the organizational context of the local recipient.

12. David L. Weimer, "Federal Intervention in the Process of Innovation in Local Public Agencies: A Focus on Organizational Incentives," *Public Policy*, 28, 1 (Winter 1980) 93-116.

13. Richard Nelson, "The Allocation of Research and Development Resources: Some Problems of Public Policy," in *Ohio State University Conference on the Economic of Research and Development*, (Columbus: Ohio State University Press, 1965).

14. For a description of one such office (the San Diego County Office of Program Evaluation) see Gale G. Whiteneck, *Assessment of State and Local Government Evaluation Practices: An Evaluation Unit Profile*, (Denver: Denver Research Institute/University of Denver, March 1977).

15. An excellent discussion of these forces is presented in Aaron Wildavsky, *Speaking Truth to Power: The Art and Craft of Policy Analysis* (Boston: Little, Brown, 1979), chapter 9.

16. For a detailed discussion of the various ways computerization can contribute to capacity in local government, see Kenneth L Kraemer, William H. Dutton and Alava Northrop, *The Management of Information Systems* (New York: Columbia University Press, 1981).

17. David Leo Weimer, "CMIS Implementation: A Demonstration of Predictive Analysis," *Public Administration Review,* 40, 3 (May/June 1980) 231-240.

18. For a discussion of potential power shifts see Kenneth L. Kraemer and William H. Dutton, "The Automation of Bias" in James N. Danziger, et al. eds., *Computers and Politics: High Technology in American Local Government,* (New York: Columbia University Press, 1982), 170-193.

19. For a discussion of "moving money" see Jeffrey Pressman, *Federal Programs and City Politics* (Berkeley: University of California Press, 1975).

20. For example, the office of Policy Development and Research in the U.S. Department of Housing and Urban Development endorses the use of policy analysis and program evaluation teams by local government, Public Technology, Inc., *Program Evaluation and Analysis* (Washington, D.C.: Government Printing Office, 1978).

21. For a discussion of the Law Enforcement Assistance Administration's "lock-in" to PROMIS, one of its first exemplary projects, see David Leo Weimer, *Improving Prosecution? The Inducement and Implementation of Innovations for Prosecution Management* (Westport, Connecticut: Greenwood Press, 1980).

22. See Lee S. Friedman, "An Interim Evaluation of the Supported Work Experiment," *Policy Analysis,* 3, 2 (Spring 1977) 147-170.

23. An example is the Administration on Aging's publicaton, *Aging.*

24. The Department of Housing and Urban Development's publication, *HUD User,* falls into this category.

25. The Bureau of the Census, for example, has offered a series of conferences intended to instruct local personnel on how most effectively to use the data from the 1980 census.

26. One example is the National Center for Home Equity Conversion, funded by the Administration on Aging to help develop local programs that allow elderly homeowners to spend some of their home equity without having to sell and move.

27. One of the larger efforts in this regard is the *Journal of the American Planning Association.*

28. Often there is a fine line between an "advocacy organization" and a "professional association." Sometimes they are impossible to distinguish (e.g., the National Education Association).

29. For a discussion of this problem in the context of federal and state regulation see Eugene Bardach and Robert A. Kagan, *Going By the Book: The*

Problem of Regulatory Unreasonableness (Philadelphia: Temple University Press,1982).

30. For example, state-set standards appear to have been largely ineffective in improving local jail conditions. Karen A. Reixach and David L. Weimer, "American Jails: Still Cloacal after Ten Years," in Jameson W. Doig, ed., *Criminal Corrections: Ideals and Realities* (Lexington, Mass.: Lexington Books, 1982), 95-108.

31. For an example of the successful use of consultants in this regard see James D. Marver, *Consultants Can Help*, (Lexington, Mass.: Lexington Books, 1979).

32. The major federal program for this purpose is the Intergovernmental Personnel Act.

33. In some instances, corporations have lent executives or staff members to local agencies for limited periods of time.

34. For a discussion of demonstration projects see Walter S. Baer, Leland J. Johnson, and Edward N. Merrow, *Analysis of Federally Funded Demonstration Projects* (Santa Monica: Rand Corporation R-1926-DOC, April 1976).

35. Elliot H. Kline and C. Gregory Buntz, "On the Effective Use of Public Sector Expertise or Why the Use of Outside Consultants Often Leads to the Waste of In-House Skills," *Public Administration Review*, 39, 3, (May/June 1979), 226-229.

IV
Improving Management Control Systems

9

Harnessing the Computer

PETER F. ROUSMANIERE AND SHELDON S. COHEN

Computer technology is the invisible sleeping giant of local government. It can't be seen, felt or heard: computers do not appear in uniform to direct traffic or in vans to deliver hot meals. But computer technology touches the lives of those who live and work in urban America in many ways. Police emergency dispatching, vehicle ticketing, tax billing, and hospital lab testing are among thousands of tasks accomplished daily by local government employees with the help of computers.

In this chapter the authors trace the emergence of computer technology in local government from the early 1960s to the mid-1980s. They adduce from a case study of the city of Boston key problems associated with managing computer resources in the 1980s. Then they analyze how to make local officials more accountable for computer-related decisions, how to ensure an effective review of options, costs and benefits of computer alternatives, and how to add discipline to the computer-system-acquisition process. This review is pertinent to large and small governments.

Twenty-Five Years Of Computer Technology

In the early 1960s, most local government employees performed paperwork operations, such as tax and utility billing and accounting, by hand or with the aid of mechanically driven bookkeeping machines. Now computers perform much of this workload. They produce a thousand times faster than the most sophisticated bookkeeping machines, while performing multiple tasks simultaneously.

The IBM 360 was the most popular large computer of the late 1960s and early 1970s. Only large, local governments could afford them, and trained staffs were required to operate them. As a consequence, many localities contracted with computer service bureaus which, using their own 360s or competing models, processed government work off-premises. A few arranged through cooperative agreements with other localities to share computer resources. Computer systems introduced in the late 1970s and early 1980s delivered further extraordinary advances in speed, convenience, and price.[1]

With the commercial introduction of minicomputers in the mid-1970s, the acquisition of computer technology by local governments began to spread. Because of their comparatively low price and ease of use minicomputers opened the door to automation for medium to small-size local government units. Even large local governments began to buy minicomputers when it become evident that minicomputers were well suited to support specialized tasks, such as library circulation control, police dispatching and high school courses in computer programming. For many local government officials, the computer age began with the on-site installation of an IBM System 34, a Digital Equipment PDP/11, a Data General Micronova, a Wang 2200, or a similar minicomputer system.

In the late 1970s word processing systems and microcomputers began to appear in municipal offices, thanks technologically to the development and subsequent mass production of microprocessors, or tiny solid state chips within which the operation of the computer is integrated. Technological advances occurred at virtually every stage in computer design and manufacture. Vendors proliferated. As a result, computers for every budget became more powerful, easier to install and cheaper to maintain. By the mid-1980s, a large city would have acquired microcomputers, word processors, and minicomputers dedicated to help individual departments, with one mainframe with sufficient power to serve simultaneously a hundred or more workstations throughout city hall and district offices.

The advancing sophistication and affordability of computer hardware only partly explains the expansion of computer use by local governments. Federal agencies in charge of grant programs flourishing in the 1970s encouraged innovation in the use of computer technology.[2] Federal dollars helped to fund municipal computer budgets in the mid-

1970s, through grant programs in areas such as public housing, community development, and public safety. Examples include systems for police dispatching, public housing management, and CETA employee tracking. In addition, computer technology became an increasingly better buy compared with traditional, labor-intensive methods. Labor costs rose steadily with general inflation. The cost of performing a typical task on a computer—for example, the entering and storage of data and the generation of reports—dropped sharply. And computers performed with quiet efficiency tasks which were difficult to do well manually, such as preparing hospital bills or checking large files of data for errors.

As the local government market for computer systems grew in size and its needs became better defined, a revolution occurred in the marketing of computer resources. "Turnkey" system vendors arrived on the scene. A turnkey system is a package of hardware and software put together by vendors who in the computer industry are usually referred to as OEMs (original equipment manufacturers) or dealers. These vendors assume total responsibility for hardware, software, installation, training and support. They can offer postinstallation support, often through "remote diagnostics"—phone links permitting a vendor, in San Francisco for example, to monitor a customer's system in New York. Small systems no longer require the attendance of the full-time technician. Some vendors offer to operate the large system on the customer's site under a facility management contract, thereby eliminating the customer's need to hire and supervise computer specialists.

Prior to the 1980s smaller communities had simpler problems in computer system planning and management because the options available to them were few and relatively unattractive. During the 1980s computers became significantly more powerful and easier to use, and the supply and quality of software designed for municipal use improved. Thus thousands of communities have been able to acquire computer systems at attractive prices, purchase predeveloped software, and operate these systems with little or no in-house programming talent.

The small community, like its big-city neighbor, invests today in several computers, which may be partially linked in a network but are more likely to operate independently. In the small community, a multi-user minicomputer usually performs high-volume work, such as payroll, accounting, and tax billing. This minicomputer is managed by a one- to three-person computer department, or by a major agency, such as finance, schools, or utilities. In addition, microcomputers are often owned by individual departments and dedicated to word processing, record keeping and computational tasks. In the big city, too, computer resources are spread between centralized and distributed nodes. At the center is a large (or mainframe) computer, while major departments may have their own minicomputers and microcomputers.

A Case Study Of Boston

As of 1984, the city of Boston owned about fifteen large and medium-sized computers and up to fifty smaller systems, without counting personal computers. It was party to several computer service contracts, each in excess of $1 million in annual fees. In fiscal year 1984 about 200 employees were engaged full-time as computer technicians; they were complemented by consultants operating under several dozen separate contracts.

In 1967, a year before the White administration took office, the city established a data processing unit within the Division of Administrative Services. Throughout the White administration (1968-1983), this unit was the focal point for efforts to coordinate the use of computers. In the late 1960s the Data Processing Division acquired two IBM 360 computers. However, other departments including police, schools, and hospitals continued to operate their own computers autonomously. In fact, the Department of Health and Hospitals had already acquired computers and spent more on computers than the Division of Data Processing.

The Data Processing Division stagnated during the 1970s. The division failed to gain control of the data processing budgets of the major line agencies. It did upgrade its IBM computers from 360s to the more advanced 370 series. It failed, however, to develop and maintain application software at anywhere near the pace it aspired to or line agencies demanded. In 1980 the city's financial accounting was, for example, still being done on a 1960s vintage bookkeeping machine.

The mayor responded to mounting line agency complaints in 1981 by reorganizing the Data Processing Division. It was given a new name and a new director, who was directed to develop a comprehensive plan to upgrade and integrate the use of computer technology in the city. In nine months the newly named Management Information Systems (MIS) Department released a five-year plan. This document was, at the time, a heroic effort to articulate computer priorities for the city. For the first time in the White administration, it inventoried computer systems, services and expenses. It evaluated the options for purchase of and control over hardware. And it outlined an ambitious program for cost-saving and system development.

As a rational planning exercise, however, the five-year plan was a failure. It was written chiefly by consultants with at best tepid support by key line agencies. The MIS Department and line agencies subsequently ignored virtually all specific recommendations contained in the plan. For example, the MIS Department later quadrupled its computer capacity despite the plan's finding that the city was using a fraction of its current computer capacity. The MIS Department and the semi-autonomous School Department continued to use incompatible operating systems on their respective IBM computers. On balance, however, the highly visible planning project had a profound impact upon the scale of computer spending. The planning process goaded line agencies to promote their most valued and often long-delayed computer project and to apply their cunning to secure mayoral support. The chief reward for mayoral support for initiatives was money, which the mayor's budget aides disbursed in large amounts and without regard to the plan's guidelines. Four examples of funded initiatives were:

Parking Ticket Collection

Computers assisted in a complete overhaul of the procedures for collecting parking tickets. As a result, annual gross revenues from parking ticket collection shot from about $8 million to $25 million. Parking ticket collection, a massive billing and dunning operation, requires rapid, accurate and impersonal processing of notices, a task at which computers excel. In 1982 the city contracted with a computer service firm specializing in municipal parking ticket administration. Under the contract, the vendor logged in tickets (about 7,000 per day) within forty-eight hours, matched tickets with registration data for Massachusetts and other states, and was responsible for depositing of receipts. The service cost the city $4 million annually, but more than paid for itself by the growth in gross receipts.

Computers in Assessing

Until the early 1980s the city's assessing procedures were almost entirely manual. Property values had not been systematically revised since the 1930s. Data on over 100,000 parcels were recorded by hand or by typewriter. The procedures were vulnerable to error, delay and abuse, judicial decisions on taxpayer suits and numerous studies concluded. The city was under a long-standing court order to equalize the assessments of taxable property.

Computer-assisted mass appraisal (CAMA) systems have become increasingly more powerful, reliable and affordable. CAMA systems can make numerous checks on the quality of the data collected in the field; they can flag a record showing a five-floor house with one bathroom or highlight for a field worker recent sales of properties he or she has reviewed. They can also compute proposed assessments using a program that logically compares each assessment to all other assessments, thus ensuring a modicum of consistency. In addition, a computer can prepare reports for a variety of purposes, including taxpayer reviews, court defenses, and assessment projections.

For three years the city, through the specially created Office of Property Equalization (OPE), tried to acquire such a system. In December 1980, OPE requested bids from vendors for a CAMA system for the city's upcoming 100 percent revaluation program. After reviewing eight bids, it selected a vendor and, in June 1981, signed a contract. The contract stipulated that the vendor was to deliver a working CAMA system by the summer of 1982 at a cost not to exceed $145,000. The city bought a system that had not been installed elsewhere and required additional programming to meet the city's specifications. The vendor never delivered a functioning product; still, the city subsequently awarded the vendor over $1 million for work through January 1983. The computer system contracted for, however, was scrapped.

In 1983 the city and the State Department of Revenue, which oversees municipal assessments, signed a formal memorandum in which the signatories agreed that the "city's CAMA system had to date been unable to generate values which meet the minimum standards, statistical and otherwise, set forth in guidelines published by the Department of Revenue." They also agreed that the city would acquire and use a satisfactory CAMA system to help generate entirely new assessments. By the time the Flynn administration took office in January 1984, the Assessing Department had not contracted for a new system.

Payroll/Personnel

The city's first comprehensive professional audit (for fiscal year 1977) triggered a recommendation to create a new centralized data base for all city workers. In 1981 the same auditors dusted off their recommendation and submitted it again. At the time the auditors submitted this reminder, the city was processing over 600 payroll runs per month. The names on the runs were not being compared. The total number of individuals paid by a specific department was not known. Nor were key personnel data—such as vacation and sick time accrued and taken—recorded centrally.

In 1981 the administration sought to contract out for a turnkey personnel/payroll system. A request for proposals for a system went out in 1981. The review of proposals for package systems ended with a request by the MIS Department that it be allowed to design the system from the beginning, using MIS Department staff and consultants. The leadership of the department was anxious to prove that its staff could deliver on a high visibility project.

Departmental staff and consultants prepared an initial version of a permanent system and had parts of it operating by July 1982. Since then, every person receiving a paycheck has had his or her record on a single data base, and all payrolls have been checked against employee records prior to their release.

The city's independent auditors made a detailed inspection in 1982 and concluded that improvements were needed. The system worked well in certain respects, for example, responding to on-line inquiries about individual employees and producing employee rosters on short notice. However, the system did not log attendance data, and the accrued sick and vacation information was unreliable. Nor did it carry Health and Hospital personnel data; these data were handled by a service bureau at an annual cost in excess of $200,000. These shortcomings illustrate the two steps forward, one step back nature of innovation in computer systems: a system is introduced to solve some pressing problems, but is not fully exploited because the data entered at the outset are flawed, data errors and omissions remain uncorrected, and user agencies are reluctant, or not adequately trained, to use the system correctly.

Word Processing

In the early 1980s, the city's MIS Department was receiving an increasing number of requests for office automation capability. Word processing was becoming a widespread technology, and much interest was expressed by city departments at the time.

The MIS Department's primary concern was to undertake a coordinated approach, leading to a consistent solution for city departments. Thus, a request for proposals was issued in 1982 for a single vendor to provide office automation resources for all departments. Wang Laboratories was awarded a contract. Within two years, twenty-five departments installed Wang systems, which cost about $1.5 million.

The MIS Department's five-year plan, prepared while the selection process for office automation systems was underway, included the following statement of objectives: "integrate word processing with the city's data processing plans; standardize the utilization, training, and support for the use of word processing equipment; plan for the natural interface of the MIS Data Processing Center." The department achieved some of these objectives. The city acquired compatible systems, which were sold and maintained by a single vendor. Also a small unit in the MIS Department was set up to coordinate technical assistance. But other objectives were not met. The Wang installations did not communicate with the city's IBM and Digital Equipment Corporation (DEC) computers. Some offices had one set of terminals connected to a locally installed Wang system and another set of terminals connected to an IBM or DEC computer.

The Implications of Boston's Experience

On balance, Boston's experience with computers resembles the struggles of thousands of other local governments over the past twenty-five years to master this technology. Acquisition of computer technology seems to happen not at all, or at high pitch of activity. Boston's experience with computers is not unusual for American cities. Boston's budget for computers during the sixteen years of Mayor Kevin White's administration (1968-1983) grew on average over 50 percent per year. In 1968 the city spent about $900,000 on computer-related activities; in 1979 the budget was about $8 million. In FY 1984 the city spent about $15 million for computer systems and services, including hardware, software, programming, staff and contracted services. This growth in spending took place without a coherent plan or visible central leadership.

When asked, most municipal officials indicate general satisfaction with their computer systems. But when pressed further, many admit they have found it exceedingly difficult simultaneously to encourage innovation in the use of computers and to control the plans and uses for these computers. To create within a municipal bureacracy a positive regard for computers is an important and difficult undertaking. Once innovation sets in, the more aggressive agencies run roughshod over attempts to coordinate and conserve the expenditure of funds. Although reliable comparative data do not exist, the authors believe that computer-related spending by municipalities rose in the first half of the 1980s at an annual rate of 25 percent or more per year.

As is the case in many for-profit organizations, this growth of computer spending has outstripped policy and control. Most municipalities do not account for computer-related spending on a consolidated basis; rather, spending is distributed throughout dozens of personnel, supplies and contractual accounts. The evaluation of options, costs and benefits is more often than not haphazard and biased. Most municipalities are not skillful at selecting appropriate computer products and services, at negotiating and enforcing contracts, and at implementing systems. Many municipal attorneys are simply incompetent to negotiate computer contracts. Few municipalities know how to allocate authority and responsibility between a central MIS shop, line agencies and finance departments. These deficiencies in management may gradually be resolved as local governments gain experience with computers, especially as more elected and appointed officials bring into government knowledge of computers gained at school or in business.

Senior members of Boston Mayor Raymond Flynn's administration, which took office in January 1984, had almost no experience with acquiring or managing computer resources at a scale higher than a microcomputer. The one exception was the pollster for the Flynn campaign. His own experience with large computers was limited but he knew that the leading problems of computers in the city in 1984 were not lack of computer capacity or lack of initiatives. Rather, the new administration had quickly to consolidate control over computer resources and set priorities for future system development, as adverse trends in the city's financial prospects forced the administration to question whether it could afford to fund computers at increasingly higher amounts.

Local governments, both small and large, are confronting the same questions:

1. How to make local officials managerially accountable for decisions relating to computers;
2. How to ensure effective review of options, costs and benefits of computer systems; and
3. How to add discipline to the computer-system acquisition process.

The balance of this chapter addresses each of these issues in terms applicable to large as well as small communities in the United States.

Establishing Control Over Computer Resources

Advice at the top

Computer technology has become essential to the implementation of local government policy; it is no longer merely an option. In order to maintain property assessments at full and fair value as required by state constitutions and statutes, localities are forced to use computers. And certain mayoral directives, such as personnel hiring guidelines and spending freezes, are extremely difficult to administer and enforce without well-designed, well-managed, automated financial management systems.

Local administrations need to create and protect sources of advice on computer technology. City budget offices have typically developed no noteworthy expertise in computer technology. MIS departments are themselves contenders for computer resources because of their substantial staffs and operational responsibilities. As a result, they are unable to provide independent internal review of proposals regarding computer technology that can be presented in annual budget requests. Furthermore, many cities have no formal mechanism for monitoring the development of multiagency and multiyear system development projects, or capital projects, as they are difficult to track through the annual budget process.

Some cities, however, have found ways to secure objective and expert advice on computers. They engage consultants to help prepare long-range plans, evaluate the performance of current systems, and assess the day-to-day management of MIS resources. Another approach has been to create a high-level MIS advisory position, reporting directly to the mayor's office, and filled by an individual known to enjoy the mayor's trust. A third approach has been to create a standing committee of public officials and private citizens to monitor computer activities and advise the mayor from time to time.

Small communities experience essentially the same challenges in computer system planning and management as large communities. Small communities, however, find it more difficult to pay for computer expertise, either in the form of regular staff or consultants. They must therefore rely more on voluntary assistance from state agencies, university extension services, or private citizens. Community residents who have a special understanding of computer systems are particularly valuable advisors in computer system planning because their endorsement of a system acquisition plan or an internal computer management plan often ensures a positive response by the local legislative body. These residents are usually business proprietors who have purchased computers for their own enterprises or administrators who use computers daily in their jobs.

Asserting Budgetary Control

Every new local administration has an opportunity to revise budget office policies for allocating dollars for computers. Every budget for spending on computer technology reflects trade-offs among competing items—staff, development of new applications, modification and enhancement of old applications, specialized systems software, hardware, communications, and contracted maintenance. Many budget offices need to strengthen their abilities to understand these trade-offs. In order to do so, budget offices should find out what hardware, software, personnel, and contracted resources are being assigned today. They should inventory the current backlog of major projects in progress to upgrade old systems or acquire new systems. They should carefully account for the real costs of these projects.

Another step toward budget control is to require departments to submit project plans, thus ensuring a minimum level of independent review of those plans. This step would permit at least certain questions to be asked about the merits of the project. Are the project expectations realistic? Has the best case been made for undertaking the project at the proposed time? Who will be accountable for project management? Are the project budget and project timetable realistic? These are the questions for which the central administration in a large locality (or the few senior executives in a small locality) will want answers for all projects that are pending or in progress.

These questions treat computer technology as a capital investment. A capital budget process is appropriate for reviewing computer system budgets, as major hardware and software investments have lifetimes of five or more years.

The budget office could also require departments to submit annual computer budget requests that break out their computer expenses into industry-accepted categories. The departments would thus have to show how much they expect to spend on new system projects as compared to projects to maintain old systems, contracted services provided by computer vendors, contracted programming, and contracted planning cosultation. Most budget forms today lump costs into meaningless aggregates.

Evaluating Options, Costs and Benefits

Prior to the cost/performance advances of recent years, the benefits attributed to computer systems were frequently conjectural, often nonexistent. Many early projects to install large, complex systems, such as library data bases and comprehensive land use data bases, were flawed by excessively high expectations of computers, technicians, and users. But by the end of the 1970s, with labor costs rising steadily and the relative costs of computers dropping dramatically, computers became easier to justify. Computer technology was still relatively new and poorly understood by municipal officials. By the middle of the 1980s, even the more recalcitrant local government entities began to acquire computer systems.

These decisions produced mixed results. Boston's investment in an automated parking ticket collection system was paid for many times by increased receipts. The city's CAMA system investment was almost a total financial loss. The economic benefits of the city's personnel/payroll system and word processing installations were arguably positive, but never independently evaluated. Though economic considerations have been a key factor in local government purchases of computer resources, there is little documentation to confirm that computers have been a good buy, and many local officials feel reluctant even to venture an informed guess because of the technical nature of the subject. Those who do attempt to analyze computer system proposals struggle with the problems of quantifying all cash flows associated with computer investment, giving appropriate weight to noneconomic factors, and counterbalancing the natural tendency of the system advocates to defend investment decisions vigorously. Thus, many computer system projects proceed without any serious effort to look at options, costs, and benefits objectively. This can be done, however, as the following brief example illustrates.

Assume that a local government wishes to purchase a turnkey system to assist accounting, payroll, tax collection, and utility billing. This system is budgeted to have sufficient terminals, storage capacity and processing speed to serve up to thirty users simultaneously. The total cost of a turnkey system would include vendor charges at the time of system acquisition, installation costs, and annual operating costs. These costs, drawn from the authors' consultative experience with local governments, can be classified as follows:

(1) Vendor charges for equipment and software acquistion;

(2) Pre-installation preparation cost, including the computer site and other facilities and a possible substantial investment in data communications facilities, which may approximate 20 percent of vendor charges;

(3) Cost of data base preparation, conversion, salaries of staff involved in system acquisition, and consultant fees;

(4) Staff development and training—assume 5 percent of one-time costs;

(5) Post-installation hardware and software maintenance contracts, typically 10-15 percent per year of one-time costs;

(6) Post-installation costs of new system staff—10 percent per year of vendor costs; and

(7) Post-installation, annual, semidiscretionary system maintenance cost, including special programming by the vendor and equipment upgrades—5-10 percent of vendor costs.

Table 1 shows a generous budget for acquisition of the system for a jurisdiction of 30,000 population for the first three years of operation. One way to analyze the investment is to estimate the marginal financial return per terminal. There may be 30 terminals hooked up, but many are used daily for only a few hours. Assume that town employees daily use about 120 hours of terminal time. The town's computer investment can be distributed among 15 full-time equivalent (FTE) terminals (i.e., 120 hours divided by 8 hours). Amortizing the system rapidly in three years, the locality incurs a cost per FTE terminal month of $1,111 (i.e., $600,000 divided by 540 terminal months). The next step is to estimate if the marginal economic benefits equal or exceed $1,111 per month, per FTE terminal.

It rarely is the case that a system can be evaluated exclusively on the basis of measurable savings or additional revenues. More difficult to estimate, but potentially of great weight, are other factors such as the investment's potential impact on staff recruitment and training, responsiveness to citizens and other private parties, and statutory compliance. A good CAMA system, for example, should improve the credibility of property assessment and reduce the amount of litigation arising from assessment disputes.

Table 1. Estimate of Three-Year Costs of a Computer-based CAMA System

Vendor charges		$250,000
Pre-installation costs (facilities and communications),		
20% of vendor charges		50,000
Other preparation costs		25,000
Staff development costs,		
5% of vendor charges		12,500
Subtotal (cost through installation)		337,500
Annual costs:		
Contracted maintenance,		
15% of vendor charges (item 1)	37,500	
Annual systems staff cost,		
10% of vendor charges	25,000	
Semidiscretionary costs,		
10% of vendor charges	25,000	
	87,500	
Subtotal for three years (87,500 × 3)		262,500
Total three-year system cost:		$600,000

System Acquisition Process

Acquisition of computer resources in a locality usually can be handled in at least two of the following ways: custom programming; purchase of a turnkey system, including both hardware and software; a service contract for a remote site to provide data processing services via phone link; or a service bureau to provide services by picking up data in hard copy form for keypunching at a remote site.

Frequently the system development process boils down, sooner or later, to a decision to buy packaged software or to acquire a turnkey system. The acquisition of computer resources may take up to one year, but should be viewed as a unitary, interrelated process. Key milestones in this process are the definition of system requirements, the drafting of a request for proposal, evaluation of the submitted proposals, and negotiation of a contract. These milestones apply to small as well as to large local governments.

Defining System Requirements

A sensible cost-effective acquisition process depends on the jurisdiction being reasonably explicit about its functional requirements. For example, a municipal library system that wishes to automate should have a clear idea of what specific applications are to be automated, e.g., circulation, public access on-line catalog, cataloging, acquisitions. For each application, local officials should have thought through the total number of records to be held by the system, the data to be kept on each record, and the expected volume of transactions. Likewise, the physical organization of the system should be reasonably well defined—the number and location of terminals and printers, for example. Moreover, there needs to be at least a tentative concept of the performance requirements of the system—maximum response time, expansion capability, and performance in the event of down time, for example.

The process of converting data from the existing system or systems to a prospective new system should be thought out well in advance. The entire system development process could be sabotaged, for example, by use of corrupted data.

Defining system requirements can rarely be done by the line department or a central MIS department alone. A mixture of points of view and expertise is important, and well-written descriptions of system requirements are almost always the result of many drafts and meetings.

The Request for Proposal

Assume that a decision is made to acquire a turnkey system from one vendor. The next milestone is preparing the request for proposal (RFP). The RFP establishes a scope of goods and services—hardware, software, training, support and ancillary items—which the locality expects to receive and which the vendor relies on in formulating the proposal. This is the blueprint of the system, subject to future refinement and mutual approval of detailed system specifications. The process is not aided by having surprises appear at later stages.

It is essential to clarify expectations of both the vendor and the city at the outset to prevent disagreements and to strengthen the city's position should disagreement later arise regarding the party's intent. System acquisition projects often falter due to flawed communications between the buyer and the seller, and this can be avoided in part by early attention to the terms under which the system would be accepted by the city. The RFP is just one step in a documentation trail that ends at acceptance testing and includes the vendor's proposal, all correspondence between the vendor and the city, and all materials submitted anytime by the vendor to the city.

Evaluation of Proposals

The evaluation of proposals received in response to the RFP has its basis in several earlier steps. The assessment of requirements occurs at the very beginning of the system acquisition process. It identifies the specific functional requirements of each department. This statement of functional requirements forms the core of the RFP. The evaluation of proposals examines in depth the proposers' ability to meet these functional specifications.

The first task of the local government is, through initial screening, to make sure that the vendors have, in fact, submitted proposals that are equivalent. Has each vendor responded to the full scope of functional requirements, or are there holes—functions to which the proposers do not respond? If holes exist, the proposals need to be adjusted to make the proposals functionally and financially comparable. Is the proposed hardware too much or too little? Is the vendor practicing a popular industry ploy of underestimating hardware requirements in order to get its foot in the door?

One of the most cost-effective steps in evaluation is making reference calls—to the right people. The locality should call persons who use the vendors' systems daily, especially clerical and mid-level personnel. Elected officials, city managers and even MIS department managers are generally unreliable references for two reasons: they probably do not know how the system performs daily, and they often were involved in the selection of the system and therefore are inclined not to confess any problems.

An adequate demonstration of the vendors' products is essential. It usually takes one or two days, depending upon the scope of the applications and the size of the jurisdiction. These demonstrations are more effective if they are held at the local government's offices, with the vendor accessing its home office computer through a telephone dial-up.

After careful reading of the proposals, the demonstrations and reference calls, the prospective vendors should be narrowed down to a few finalists. Each firm should be invited back separately to spend as much time as necessary to understand the locality's requirements and

make last-minute modifications of the proposals. The amended proposal of the finalist deemed the best becomes the basis of contract
negotiation.

Contract Negotiation

Computer contracts are poorly understood, even by computer
technicians and attorneys. Early actions and decisions bear directly
upon the strength of the local government's position in negotiating a
contract that protects its short- and long-term interests and the
performance of the acquired system.

Local officials should not try to beat the vendor in negotiations or,
at the other extreme, assume that good faith will make up for
incomplete documentation. A locality should make sure that it and the
vendor see eye to eye on all issues, and that system-acceptance-testing
procedures are fully understood.

The elements of a complex computer system cannot be separated.
Near the very beginning of the contract, "system" should be defined to
include hardware, operating systems, software, applications software
and supportive programming aids. From the city's point of view , there
is no substitute for acceptance testing of the system in its entirety: this
principal should be nonnegotiable. Exemplary terms for acceptance
testing include the following: a thirty- to sixty-day period for acceptance
testing, keyed to specified response times with a specified number of
terminals being used on specified applications; and correction of any
hardware failures.

The local government can expect that response time problems,
should they occur, can result from a combination of software and
hardware limitations. On one hand, the primary cause of down-time
problems is software. Regardless of the source of a particular problem, a
system that does not perform to standard in certain respects is a system
that does not perform at all. The vendor is naturally inclined to gloss
over the problems, and some city officials may also be tempted to
ignore them. On the other hand, the problem could have been caused
by the city deciding at the last minute to change the specifications of the
system it wants (for example, doubling its terminals) without carefully
thinking through how the system should operate under acceptance-
testing conditions. The city should modify the acceptance-testing
procedures to accommodate any changes it makes to the system
specifications after contract signing.

Concluding Comments

Computer systems have become significantly more capable, easy to use and affordable during the 1980s. These trends can be expected to continue throughout the remainder of the decade, to the benefit of local governments of every size, charter and structure. The city of Boston's experience with computers foreshadows the experience of thousands of communities in the 1980s, as computer technology comes within the economic reach of virtually every local government. Computers have come to America's city halls and its rural villages. Technical knowledge of systems, managerial know-how, and informed confidence are permeating local bureaucracies, though more slowly than some would wish. Technical assistance is available for many localities from their municipal associations, state oversight agencies, university-based municipal programs, public accounting firms, and consultants. The best guidance, however, is found internally, among local appointed and elected officers. As the country's population becomes generally more adept at using computers, elected and appointed officials should expect to be held more accountable for management of computer resources.

Notes

1. Montgomery Phister, Jr., *Data Processing Technology and Economics*, 2d. ed. (Bedford, Mass: Digital Press, 1979), and Edward L. Price, "The Coastal Plain Computer Cooperative, Valdosta, Georgia," *Public Management* 59 (November 1977): 15-16.

2. Kenneth L. Kraemer and James L. Perry, "The Federal Push to Bring Computer Applications to Local Governments," *Public Administration Review* 39, 5 (September/October 1979): 260-270.

Selected Annotated Bibliography

American Society for Public Administration, "Mini-Symposium on Micro-Computers in Local Government," *Public Administration Review* (January-February 1984): 57-78. Five essays on local government applications.

Auerbach Publishers, Inc., *Computers in Local Government: Finance and Administration* and *Computers in Local Government: Urban and Regional Planning* (Pennsauken, N.J.: Auerbach Publishers 1980). Two large compendia of articles on computer technology planning and management.

Boston Computer Society, *Update Magazine*. Largest microcomputer user association in the United States (20,000 members), with extensive technical assistance programs for microcomputer users.

James N. Danziger, "The Use of Automated Information In Local Government", *American Behavioral Scientist*, Vol. 22, Nbr. 3, pp. 363-392. Jan/Feb 1979. One of numerous studies prepared in the 1970s on computer technology policy for local governments by the Public Policy Research Organization, University of California at Irvine.

International City Management Association, *MIS Special Report: Joint Powers Agreements, Regional Resource Sharing and other Cooperative Approaches to Local Government Data Processing*, 1978. One of several special reports published by ICMA on computers.

Southern Rural Development Center, Mississippi State University, *Computers and Local Government: Synthesis and Annotated Bibliography*, n.d. 543 items cited. None published after 1981.

10

Developing Financial Management Capacity: Integration at the Local Government Level

RICHARD G. HIGGINS, JR.

The consensus of professional and academic literature on local government financial management is that while progress has been made, much more in the management capacity area remains to be done. In this chapter I will expand upon the financial management techniques discussed in most treatments of the subject (budgeting and accounting) and add capital facilities planning, debt administration, and cash management. Only through a comprehensive or integrated approach to financial management will officials achieve the most efficient and effective use of increasingly scarce local government revenue. In fact, the financial management techniques by themselves have the potential to generate additional revenue to support services where tax dollars would be either difficult or impossible to come by.

This chapter treats the "what" of local financial management (descriptions of these techniques and their purposes) and the "how" (the steps involved in their partial or complete implementation). There are several basic ingredients for successful utilization of a financial management system, or changes in an existing system.

(1) Strong top-level management support is essential, not only in the introduction of the technique and process, but throughout the use of the financial management system.

(2) A core of competent analysts and support staff is very important. Sophisticated quantitative training in accounting and economics is helpful, but the most useful skill is that of judgment, i.e., the ability to ask the right questions.

(3) While there are general guiding principles involved in each financial management technique, there is no single right way to design and implement financial management systems for local governments. There are a wide range of approaches and techniques which can be adapted and tailored to the particular needs of the jurisdiction. For example, in areas where local governments are not large enough to have trained staff for financial management improvements, quite often interlocal arrangements can be made by the state to facilitate technical assistance and training.

(4) Specific financial management techniques, such as budgeting and accounting, should be viewed as related to each other and interdependent with other management procedures, such as personnel administration and program operations.

For a financial management system to be useful it need not be large and sophisticated, but it must be responsive to local needs and flexible enough to be used and understood by many parties. Local officials can best meet their current fiscal pressures and prepare themselves for future challenges if they develop an integrated approach to financial management. Before developing the integrated approach to financial management, it is necessary to briefly describe the fiscal austerity environment that affects nearly all local governments.

Fiscal Austerity

Evidence of the factors of fiscal austerity—weakened economic bases, tax and expenditure limits, and reduced levels of federal assistance—are present for nearly all local governments as we move into the last half of the 1980s. While the literature on financial problems appears to be skewed toward accounts concerning large urban areas in the Northeast and Midwest, small- and medium-size local governments nationwide are also struggling to make ends meet. The challenge before elected and appointed officials to deal with fiscal austerity has already proven to be a difficult one. Most predictions point toward a long and difficult adjustment period to the forces of New Federalism and a slower growing public economy (particularly in the area of domestic expenditure).

The two most common responses to this situation at the local level are:

> *Diversification*—the search for new tax and nontax revenue sources; and

> *Managerial improvement*—changes in either existing central or program administration designed to maximize the utility of existing resources.

Local government officials generally turn to these two options before they consider either private sector cooperative relationships or selective cuts in service levels. Experience in most local governments to date suggests that even where state law and local political and economic circumstances permit, revenue diversification alone is unlikely to yield sufficient revenue to avoid service-level reductions. The potential of managerial improvement, particularly in the financial management area (budgeting, accounting, capital facilities planning and financing, and cash management), shows promise for all local governments. Local government financial managers have learned a lot since the New York City fiscal crisis. Officials who thought financial management was just line-item budgeting for expenditure control purposes are, in the words of one author, "coming of age".[1] The evidence is that:

> Municipalities whose accounting practices were so out of step with generally accepted accounting practices (which are themselves undergoing scrutiny and revision) as to make audits impossible are being forced to uproot their obsolete systems. Municipal borrowers who had been accustomed to furnishing only sketchy financial reports to prospective lenders are now finding a market that demands information in great detail.... In conclusion there are plenty of hopeful signs that sound financial management is beginning to be treated as an essential aspect of operating local governments....[2]

The current fiscal challenges will provide a stern test for the "coming of age" thesis. As mentioned before, financial managers have been preoccupied with budgeting to the point that other useful financial management techniques, such as municipal accounting and capital facilities financing, have been viewed as foreign and intimidating. In order to have a comprehensive approach to financial management, these barriers must be removed. A number of recent efforts have been devoted to this purpose; for example, one of the basic goals of the U.S. Department of Housing and Urban Development's Financial Management Capacity Sharing (FMCS) program was to "tie together budgeting, accounting, and auditing".[3] The work of Hayes, et al. in developing the concept of "integrated financial management" (budgeting, accounting, performance management, and auditing) is also related to the U.S. Department of Housing and Urban Development conference theme.[4]

Financial Management Capacity

In recent years, there has been a reexamination of the structures and processes of public management, both across and within the levels of American government. One of the most common ways to divide the tasks of administration is into policy management, resource management, and program management. The activities that correspond to each of these divisions are as follows:

> *Policy Management* involves the strategic functions of setting goals and priorities, mobilizing and allocating resources, and providing guidance for the development of policies, processes, and programs.

> *Resource Management*—functions such as personnel administration, property management, information processing, and financial management. In essence the across-the-board support functions fall in this category.

> *Program Management* —administrative functions directly related to implementing and overseeing programs, activities, and services.

This approach to public management not only provides a functional breakdown of activities, but also fits the traditional, hierarchical structure model of top-level or macro activites (policy) as distinct from operational-level or micro activities (program) with an organizational level linking the two (resource).

This schema suggests that financial management falls entirely within the middle category of resource management. Financial matters have always been of great importance to top-level policy-makers as well as program managers, rather than confined to the domain of the "green eyeshade types." Related to this theme is the suggestion that emphasis on expenditure control, rather than on management and planning, has characterized the narrow approach to municipal financial management.

> The account structures and basic accounting reports (i.e., balance sheets, change of surplus statements) are exclusively concerned with fiscal accountability and are largely irrelevant to the functional concerns of management. *Even budget status reports provide very limited information of operational significance to city governments because their structures of accounts are geared toward accounting for things purchased rather than activities undertaken and results achieved.* In addition, few municipal financial reporting systems are integrated with the operational reporting systems of the line departments. In short, *the entire municipal finance process tends to be self-contained, geared to legal requirements with little operational relevance, and maintained for the convenience of accountants and auditors rather than the enlightenment of policy makers and management.*[5] (emphasis added)

Since 1975, there has been considerable progress in breaking down the barriers within local government financial management, between budgeteers and accountants, between elected and departmental officials and most notably between central office staff and program managers. Much more needs to be done in this area. Financial management capacity building has been and must continue to be more than just technique oriented; it must also be directed toward human resource development, making the most of local government personnel of all kinds to build a flexible team orientation to financial management activities. This approach to resource management is essential in order for the concept of integrated financial management to be successful.

Traditional Practices

Budgeting

Most depictions of budgeting emphasize the political (interest-group struggles) or the economic (resource redistribution) aspects. The focus here is on the managerial perspective, which relates to other depictions but is in itself distinct. The essence of budgeting as an administrative tool is captured by the following statement:

> The budget is a central element in decision making—if, indeed, it is not the central element. The budget is the locality's plan for how it will allocate its resources to meet the most pressing requirements for personnel, equipment, and facilities. While there are other important decisions that face the executive and legislative leadership of a locality, there is little question that virtually all governmental decisions are at least conditioned and constrained by the harsh realities of the budget. This fact of public life is true at all times, but it has come to the fore with unusual force at the present time because of the continued pressures of inflation and tax revolt that create today's reality in most local governments.[6]

The practice of budgeting has been the core function of local government financial management over the years. Some experts have criticized local officials for focusing solely on budgeting (technique, format, processes, etc.) rather than supplementing it with other financial management tools. Despite the development of other components in financial management at the local level, the budget continues to occupy the primary position. There are several very important reasons for this:

(1) The universe of local governments in the U.S. is both large and diverse; there are many different sizes, titles, and structural forms. One of the few (perhaps the only) common threads that they all share is that every locality goes through a process of preparing and adopting a budget as a principle step in its annual decision-making cycle.

(2) Even where more sophisticated documents and processes are utilized, the budget is likely to be the personification of local government operations to the citizenry. To the extent that the external community (i.e. that beyond the city or town hall) is aware of the operations within the hall, that awareness most likely emanated from a public hearing on the budget or from a review of some form of the budget.

(3) In regard to the internal operations of local government, the budget also plays the central role. All of the officials of the jurisdiction are involved in one or more stage of budget preparation, enactment, and execution. This is a process that involves not only the chief executive and the local legislature but

also the central budget agency staff and the operating departments.

In response to the growing demands placed on local government
over the years, the scope and purpose of budgeting has also grown. The
essence of the evolution of the budget function through the three
phases of control, management, and planning was first described by
Allen Schick.[7]

(1) Control—The emphasis during this period was on the budget as a
tool to enforce financial accountability. The line-item approach
represented a detailed breakdown of expenditure items. The
purpose was to avoid incurring deficits. In addition, very little
flexibility in transferring funds once appropriated was allowed.

(2) Management—The approach to budgeting at this time shifted
somewhat from expenditure control to the performance of local
government, namely efficient provision of public services. At this
time budgets were re-cast in functional terms. Workload measures
and productivity analysis became inputs in the budgeting framework.

(3) Planning—Influenced by systems analysis, budgeting from the
planning perspective is seen as much more closely related to the
overall goals and objectives of the local jurisdiction. The planning
approach to budgeting has several important elements that serve
to distinguish it from the control or management approaches.
They are:

— emphasis placed on budgeting as community decision making
rather than as an internal administrative procedure;

— program choices made by evaluating the cost-effectiveness of
alternative means; and

— multiyear planning, programming, and budgeting introduced.

Accounting, Performance Management, and Auditing

True to evolutionary form, modern budgeting currently serves all
three purposes, i.e. the maintenance of financial control, the improvement of service delivery, and as a guide to community goals and
objectives. The difficulties of effectively achieving each of the objectives

is obvious. In most instances these orientations require different types of information, methods, and staff training. As the unit of government grows, the demands on all three intensify. Despite the scale of the task, many units of local government have developed budget systems that effectively serve all three functions. This is where the value of integrating the budget function with other financial management operations becomes more apparent. Figure 1 and the brief descriptions of public management activities and financial management functions show how processes such as accounting, performance management, and auditing both complement and supplement budgeting in meeting the basic requirements of public management (expenditure and revenue control, service delivery, and evaluation).

Why Integration?

Over the years the following problems have been identified by local government officials in regards to their financial management operations:

(1) The system is too fragmented; budget staff are concerned with preparation, the accountants focus on expenditure control, department heads focus on their activities, and no one looks at the overall operation.

(2) Decision making in the budget process is hampered by the lack of information on program performance and on overall financial data.

(3) Monitoring of program operations and revenue conditions is not always done in a way that allows for necessary adjustments within the current budget year.

(4) Assessments (audits) are usually confined to financial/legal compliance rather than evaluating program operations.

Financial management system integration is not quick or simple, but it can improve the problem situations mentioned, for when financial information and performance information are integrated, the result is an overall management (planning and control) system. To illustrate this point, consider the value of a municipal accounting and reporting system. A municipal accounting and reporting system is the cornerstone of the whole financial management process. A good accounting system can result in budgetary control, sound investment decisions, and prudent management. Good accounting procedures also help prevent theft and misuse of funds. Most importantly, timely and accurate financial reports enable officials to evaluate governmental performance and set a course of future action. An effective, integrated financial management system can best be built in a gradual manner, dealing first with the most obvious linkage needs, and in the process building support and understanding among affected staff.

The concept of integration may seem overly simple to large jurisdictions with large financial problems and amazingly complex to small jurisdictions with limited staff and reorganization resources. To each group the process of examining the nature of its existing financial operation with an eye toward the potential benefits of integration (large and small, short-term and long-haul) would likely provide useful information to aid in more efficient service delivery and administrative processes. The proof of this point lies in the observation that most of the fully developed financial management systems are found in small and

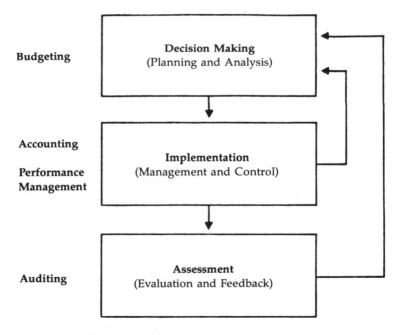

Figure 1. Model of integrated Management
Source: Frederick O'R. Hayes, et al. Linkages: Improving Financial Management in Local Government (Washington, D.C.: The Urban Institute Press, 1982): 2–3.

Figure 1 continued

$$\overline{}$$

Public Management Activities

Decision Making. Planning and analysis are the starting points, where decisions are made about what services local government will provide, how much these services will cost, what agencies will do the work, and where the money will come from. Budgeting is the key activity in this process.

Implementation. Management and control refer to the actual operations of government, where control systems are needed so that the budget is not overspent and so that managers know what is happening to public services. There are two basic fiscal control systems:

> *Accounting* reports on actual spending so that management knows if it is sticking to its budget plan.
> *Performance Management* reports on operations so that local officials know if they are meeting their service delivery targets.

Assessment. Evaluation comes after the fact, to tell local management whether results conformed to its plan. These functions are best met by two types of audit: financial and performance. Both are necessary for full-scale evaluation.

Financial Management Functions

Budgeting—the process of preparing and carrying out a locality's financial plan.

Accounting—the basic financial record-keeping and expenditure control tool of local government and potentially the most valuable information system available to local managers and legislators.

Performance Management—the improvement of public service delivery by establishing and monitoring targets for agency performance. It often includes a focus on increasing productivity.

Auditing—the process of evaluating the locality's fiscal and service operations. Auditing provides vital feedback insights for better budgeting, management, and control.

Source: Frederick O'R. Hayes, et al. *Linkages: Improving Financial Management in Local Government* (Washington, D.C.: The Urban Institute Press, 1982): 2–3.

medium-size jurisdictions. In the quest for integration it should not be overlooked that the best route to that goal is through the high-quality performance of the individual financial management functions. Even if total integration is a long way off for the local government, life can be improved for both officials and citizens through budgetary or performance measurement innovations discovered through interdepartmental teamwork or information exchanges with other jurisdictions.

New Financial Management Practices

In the aftermath of the major developments of the 1970s—fiscal crises, Proposition 13, grant reform/reductions, and recessionary pressures—there has been a dramatic increase in the attention paid to local government financial management.[8] While attention has always been focused on budgetary reform and updating accounting systems and information for decision-making purposes, considerable attention has also been placed on the new and, in some cases, more sophisticated functions of financial management. Capital facilities planning, debt administration, and cash management are three examples of the new entries into the world of local government financial management. The following organization chart illustrates the number and scope of the functions and activities that typically occur in a local government finance department.

The variety and sophistication of the activities listed on the organization chart (Figure 2) should put to rest the myth that local government finance departments are little more than budget and treasury operations. Over the past two decades the growth of financial operations at the local level has resulted in many new positions being created for budget analysts, capital planners, economic development specialists, and grants managers. In many jurisdictions financial management has been adding employees while other departments were losing positions.

Before embarking upon brief descriptions of the new entries in local government financial management and how they fit into the integrated system model, several points need to be made:

(1) The label "new" as it is used here is not meant to suggest that capital facilities planning, debt- and cash- management activities have not been part of many local government operations for some time. Rather, the phrase "new" refers to the greater emphasis

Figure 2. Finance Department Organization Chart

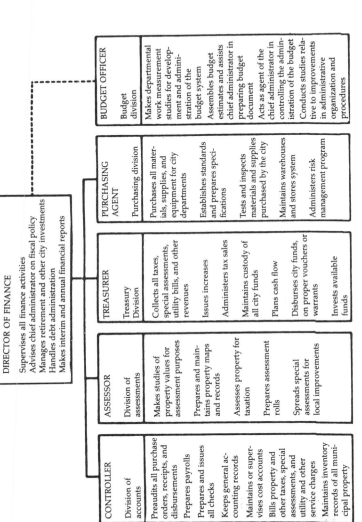

DIRECTOR OF FINANCE

Supervises all finance activities
Advises chief administrator on fiscal policy
Manages retirement and other city investments
Handles debt administration
Makes interim and annual financial reports

CONTROLLER

Division of accounts

Preaudits all purchase orders, receipts, and disbursements

Prepares payrolls

Prepares and issues all checks

Keeps general accounting records

Maintains or supervises cost accounts

Bills property and other taxes, special assessments, and utility and other service charges

Maintains inventory records of all municipal property

ASSESSOR

Division of assessments

Makes studies of property values for assessment purposes

Prepares and maintains property maps and records

Assesses property for taxation

Prepares assessment rolls

Spreads special assessments for local improvements

TREASURER

Treasury Division

Collects all taxes, special assessments, utility bills, and other revenues

Issues increases

Administers tax sales

Maintains custody of all city funds

Plans cash flow

Disburses city funds, on proper vouchers or warrants

Invests available funds

PURCHASING AGENT

Purchasing division

Purchases all materials, supplies, and equipment for city departments

Establishes standards and prepares specifications

Tests and inspects materials and supplies purchased by the city

Maintains warehouses and stores system

Administers risk management program

BUDGET OFFICER

Budget division

Makes departmental work measurement studies for development and administration of the budget system

Assembles budget estimates and assists chief administrator in preparing budget document

Acts as agent of the chief administrator in controlling the administration of the budget

Conducts studies relative to improvements in administrative organization and procedures

*The dotted line between the director of finance and the budget officer indicates that the latter is often primarily responsible to the chief administrator, being physically located in the finance department to prevent the duplication of records. In many cities the finance director handles the budget.

Source: Leonard I. Ruchelman, "The Finance Function in Local Government" in Aronson and Schwartz, *Management Policies in Local Government Finance* (Washington, D.C.: International City Management Association, 1981), 18.

placed upon these functions in recent years as well as an explosion in public attention and concern about the nature of these activities and their consequences. This is not surprising given the fact that nearly everything that local officials have done recently has gone under the microscope for close scrutiny.

(2) The typical organization chart shown here may be a source of frustration to smaller units of government which cannot command the resources to organize their finance operations on such a grand scale. Chances are very good that this large an operation is not necessary. The chart can serve as a model for division of responsibility for financial operations that could easily be adapted and adjusted for local circumstances.

(3) As has already been mentioned many of the activities that larger jurisdictions engage in frequently (municipal borrowing, idle fund investment) are beyond the reach of small- and medium-size jurisdictions for either technical or scale of operation considerations. In many states, intergovernmental arrangements have been established to deal with this issue.

Capital Facilities Planning

For most jurisdictions, this activity is called "capital budgeting," the other half of the "double budget system" commonly referred to in public budgeting textbooks. With the notable exception of the federal level, separate operating and capital budgets have long been the rule in American public management. Typically, capital expenditures result in the purchase of items that have useful lives well beyond a single budget year—land, buildings, bridges, motor vehicles, computers, and office equipment. Given the expectation of long-term use of these assets, local governments generally finance their acquisition by selling long-term bonds, rather than by committing current operating revenue. Several other characteristics of capital facilities create special concerns for the local official:

Most capital projects not only have large price tags, but also take several years to complete.

Most local governments have the capacity to finance only a limited number of projects during a given year. This forces choices to be made among various projects that on the surface are all likely to be justifiable expenditures and very difficult to compare.

The capital facilities plan and the resulting capital budget are very important elements in the local government's long-range planning and economic development program. The current concern over the nation's infrastructure, i.e. the importance of maintaining the country's physical plant and the resultant cost figures certainly brings this point home forcefully.

Each of these characteristics of capital projects forces officials to engage in more long-range planning than is traditionally associated with operating-budget deliberations. The technical aspects of many (if not most) capital projects also require a merger of physical and financial planning activities. Engineers from the Public Works Department and planners from the Community Development Department need to combine their knowledge of the specific functional needs with the economic, demographic, and financial information and considerations that others contribute. The function of the capital planning and budgeting process is to provide the mechanism for this integration. A typical process in the development of a Capital Improvement Program (CIP) includes the following steps:

(1) An annual review of the jurisdictions's capital needs.

(2) Hearings to get public input concerning potential capital projects.

(3) Identification of revenue sources for potential projects.

(4) Establishment of criteria in order for policy makers to choose among competing projects.

(5) Scheduling selected projects when they are needed and funds are available.

Most jurisdictions attempt to develop five year CIPs, and the capital budget component for the current year represents the annual installment of the overall CIP. Given the nature of the activity, capital facilities planning should be viewed as part of the "Decision Making" process in the model of integrated financial management described earlier. The mechanics of financing capital projects and the monitoring of the capital budget during the year, however, fit into the "Implementation" component of the model.

Debt Administration

As mentioned, capital expenditures at the local level are financed by the issuance of local bonds. Because of its high visibility and long-term consequences, debt administration is a particularly important function in local government financial management. While there has been an explosion in the variety and complexity of municipal borrowing in recent years, there are basically two types of long-term borrowing available to local governments. Bonds may be either general obligations, supported by the full taxing and credit power of the local government, or revenue bonds, supported by that revenue either earned by the asset created or dedicated to its financing. Usually, general obligation bonds pay lower interest rates, but many local governments utilize revenue bonds where possible because they are not subject to either voter approval or state limitation as to the total volume involved.

While the policies and circumstances surrounding the borrowing practices of local governments vary considerably, the policy and debt-issuing procedures should meet four basic requirements:

(1) Guidelines as to the appropriate and prudent uses of borrowing;

(2) Statutory and constitutional requirements placed upon the use of debt;

(3) Acceptable disclosure practices as enforced in the private financial markets; and

(4) Consideration of questions of timing and design to maximize the efficiency of borrowing under various market conditions.

The primary purpose of municipal borrowing is to permit governments to achieve timely financing of needed expenditures without unsettling fluctuations in tax rates. Debt sold today must be repaid in the future with interest, so current borrowing decisions create fixed obligations on future budgets. Another very important way in which current borrowing practices have a major impact on the future financial condition of the government jurisdiction is through the operation of bond-rating firms. A bond rating for a local government debt issue represents a subjective judgment concerning two factors—the appropriateness of the use and size of the debt issue in question and the current fiscal condition of the jurisdiction as it affects the ability of the debt (principal and interest) to be repaid in a timely manner. The judgment of the rating agency has a direct bearing on the interest charges that the municipal market places on the borrower. On many occasions in recent years, local governments have been forced to either scale down debt issues or withdraw them entirely due to high interest costs. The activities of the rating agencies, particularly the depth of their examinations of the fiscal conditions of issuing jurisdictions, has itself been subjected to intense scrutiny. This has resulted in a number of incidents of "downgrading", i.e. lowering the bond ratings of local governments with a resulting increase in interest costs.

As with capital facilities planning, debt administration falls into two positions on the model of integrated financial management. Given the managerial and legal significance of total outstanding debt, debt policy obviously must be a factor considered in the planning and analysis that occurs in "Decision Making." Also, much of debt administration is concerned with monitoring current market conditions and assessing the performance of current long-term borrowing on a monthly or quarterly basis. This activity relies on the performance management activities that occur in the "Implementation" component.

Cash Management

In contrast to debt administration, which is long-term borrowing, many local governments have recently discovered the value of short-term investment of previously idle cash balances. As recently as 1965, state and local governments in aggregrate held 25 percent of their financial assets in either demand deposit (checking account) or currency (cash) form. Given the current pressures on local governments to raise as much revenue as possible, it is almost inexcusable not to investigate the earning potential of investing idle cash balances.

The primary goals of a cash management program are to maximize the availability of cash to meet daily needs and for investment purposes and to earn the highest possible return on cash consistent with acceptable levels of risk.[9] The central responsibility for setting up a cash budget generally lies with the treasurer, under the supervision of the finance director or the chief executive. The cash budget is the first step in the overall cash management program whereby the flow of revenue into the treasury is monitored and the specific timing and amount of each anticipated expenditure charted. Successful cash management programs make extensive use of municipal accounting systems. Given the important role of time for cash management purposes—that is, the time between the earning of revenue and the point at which expense payment clears the bank of the jurisdiction—many other government officials are involved in the execution of the cash management program. The treasurer must have the cooperation of all officials involved in the collection, handling, and disbursement of cash, including elected officials, the comptroller, tax collector, capital improvements coordinator, and department personnel.

Of all the steps involved in cash management, the most crucial is that of collecting and processing incoming revenue. Many jurisdictions have resorted to the "lock box" technique for this purpose. Both regularly scheduled payments, such as property taxes and license fees, and unscheduled fees, such as traffic fines, are mailed directly to a lock box at a local bank. Receipts not sent directly to the lock box are deposited daily, and up-to-date records kept of all fund balances. Of course, it is equally necessary to monitor and anticipate other revenues, including federal and state grants-in-aid, income on investments, utility revenues, bonds, trust funds and return on sale of property.

An example of an innovation designed to minimize processing time comes from Texas. Rather than await delivery of state-collected city sales tax through the mail, cash managers of large Texas cities fly to the state capital to pick up these checks, which they deposit immediately. The interest earned on this money during the extra time it is in the bank easily exceeds the travel costs involved in this procedure.

It would be a mistake for the reader to assume that cash management is a simple and straightforward process; it is generally a complex and a time-consuming process. Most governments attain a degree of proficiency only after several years of experimentation and adjustment. An indication of the difficulty of developing a cash management program is the fact that such a system is very dependent on the local government officials' ability to forecast revenue and expenditure flows. Local government forecasting is itself a very recent innovation that few local governments are proficient in. Forecasting and cash management program development are areas in which local governments make extensive use of private sector consultants. While independent progress is slow in the cash management area, the potential of idle fund investment to provide revenue without additional burden on taxpayers is clearly worth the effort. Due to the day-to-day financial monitoring essential for a successful program, cash management fits into the "Performance Management" component of the integrated financial management model.

Implementation Issues

As previously mentioned, there are several factors that serve as prerequisites for successful implementation of an integrated financial management system. For that matter, these factors are essential to ensure success in any of the various financial management functions. They are:

(1) Support of top-level policy-makers;

(2) A core of competent analysts and support staff;

(3) A recognition that there is no single best way to financial solvency and service-level stability; and

(4) A recognition that the separate functions can and should be interdependent without serious interference with their basic structure and purpose.

Hayes, et al. have expanded upon these basic issues:

Financial management should be developed as the centerpiece of the government's overall management system. It is not an esoteric matter that should be left entirely to technicians.

Getting everyone together on an improvement program is important and, in some local governments, critical.

Some significant incremental expenditures—especially for information systems—will be required in most local governments. The exceptions are those local governments with financial management functions already well advanced and those small enough to function without large investments in information systems.

Potential cash benefits—in savings or increased revenue—are also likely to be significant. A strategy for the early realization of these benefits may be feasible in some local governments.[10]

Advocates of integrated financial management are suggesting little more than the exchange of expertise and information between financial staff and departmental (program) officials. A flexible set of accounts and procedures should be mutually beneficial. This, of course, flies in the face of general bureaucratic resistance to change and the traditional distrust and distance that exists between "financial types" and "program types". This distance often makes decision making difficult, as Jan Lodal comments:

> It makes no sense to have separate budget and accounting systems. The available balance of funds is determined simultaneously by the approved budget and the amount spent to date. Any new system worth its salt should provide timely reports to all managers on available funds. Many governmental financial systems are oriented almost exclusively toward financial control. . . . But for adequate planning, both executives and legislators must know the full cost of programs they wish to undertake. . . . Thus spending should be classified according to the programs they are part of, in addition to the traditional accounting classification.[11]

Nearly every article or study on local government management addresses the ever-present issues of structure (political versus professional administration) and size (large versus small jurisdictions). Without demeaning the importance of these two issues, in general they should be viewed as less important in the financial management area than they currently are.

The basic thesis on the structural question is the notion that political systems (mayor-council) find it more difficult to respond to fiscal pressures that force either tax increases or service reductions than do professional systems (council-manager). The argument is based on the notion that mayors rely on interest groups for electoral support, whereas city managers are more insulated from that form of pressure and therefore better able to make the necessary decisions on financial matters. Related to this is the notion that the professional form of local government would likely be more receptive to innovations and new techniques, such as integrated financial management.

To date there has been no research (empirical or case study) that provides strong support for the notion that the local government structure concept has a direct relationship to a jurisdiction's ability to respond to fiscal austerity. What does appear to be important is the degree of centralization of decision making, particularly in the areas of financial management and personnel administration. This suggests that the issue of whether the chief administrator has the capacity to recognize the problems that exist and muster support for their ultimate resolution is much more important than whether the individual is appointed or elected. The concept of integrated financial management developed here is appropriate for either form of government structure. The literature on financial management improvements, such as budgetary reform and innovations in capital facilities planning and financing, also does not suggest serious problems due to structural issues. In the financial management area, factors such as state restrictions and local economic conditions are usually much more influential than local political traditions.

The issue of jurisdiction size, while more serious than structure for financial management capacity, is still not an insurmountable obstacle. It is obvious that smaller jurisdictions will have fewer staff and support resources to devote to developing a financial management system. The image of a finance director with five separate divisions under his direction is likely to be both foreign and frustrating to the jack-of-all-trades three-person operations found in some of the small local communities across the country. It is quite likely that most of the financial problems in smaller jurisdictions can be handled well with existing budgeting practices and that innovations in accounting, debt administration, and cash management are less necessary. On the other hand, few local governments, regardless of size, have not experienced the following:

Problems of inadequate information on expenditures.

Shortcomings in the performance of public programs.

Lack of coordination between departments and central administration.

The value of the general guidelines for greater attention to information exchange and coordination suggested here transcend the sophistication of the model or the associated financial management techniques. As always, local officials would have to tailor the model of financial management, based on local economic conditions and administrative procedures. The concepts addressed here suggest techniques and issues that should be considered, but even those that have near-universal value will result in vastly different programs and results once implemented at the local level.

An additional comment on the variable of jurisdiction size is that where local governments are indeed too small to engage in certain practices, such as debt insurance or cash management, state agencies have often stepped in to assist them. That is the topic of the next section.

The State Role

States have always played varied roles in regard to the financial management practices of their local governments, both large and small. Among these roles have been those of regulator, supervisor, and provider of technical assistance. The basic pattern appears to be an emphasis on regulation and control of the traditional financial management practices (budgeting and accounting) and a mix of control and technical assistance with reference to the "new" financial management practices (debt administration and cash management). The following is a brief summary of these developments with reference to specific states in some instances.

> *Budgeting.* Budget procedures for local government—hearings, timing and format—are now established in more than half of the states. There has been renewed pressure in recent years for states to require local budgets to be submitted on prescribed forms to state officials prior to local enactment. State efforts in this area are not totally control-oriented inasmuch as many states sponsor or conduct workshops to assist local officials in developing sound budget techniques and processes.
>
> *Accounting and Financial Reporting.* In the wake of New York City and other close calls, state regulation and supervision of local accounting and financial disclosure practices are definitely on the increase. There is pressure on states to have local government financial statements prepared on a uniform and more timely basis for both state oversight and comparison purposes.
>
> *Debt Administration.* Since the 1930s, states have placed special restraints on local borrowing behavior. These generally include limitations on total outstanding debt and requirements of local referenda prior to the issuance of bonds. Other limitations may be placed on the purposes for which debt can be incurred and the specific design features of the debt issue. States also assist smaller local govern-

ments in preparing to enter the bond market, particularly for those communities that have had little or no experience in that regard. The Oregon Municipal Debt Advisory Commission is a leading example of this activity. Many states have also created loan guarantee programs to assist local borrowers and some have centralized borrowing through state bond banks.

Cash Management. There are various state laws regulating local government investment practices. Among them are requirements that local governments maintain certain levels of cash balances and restrictions on the types of securities (purpose, time period, and degree of risk) that local cash managers can invest in. Most states adjust the limitations on local governments based on the size of the jurisdiction and the track record of its cash management program. In addition, small units of government, frequently without large cash balances or available expertise to determine sound investment practices, are aided by state-wide investment pools in a number of states.

While every state engages in regulation, supervision and technical assistance for local financial management, few states have comprehensive programs that provide across-the-board services for local communities regardless of size. The states of New Jersey, North Carolina, and Oregon are considered national leaders in this area. It should be noted that qualitative analysis of these programs often reflects on the solid performance of local financial managers as much as it involves the nature of state efforts.

Where To Go For Help

One of the best sources of information and assistance regarding improving local government financial management are workshops conducted by state municipal finance officers associations and municipal leagues, which operate in many states. In addition, the following national professional associations (all located in Washington, D.C.) have long been active in these activities:

(1) The Financial Management Resource Center of the Government Finance Officers Association (GFOA) is the

national contact point for technical support under the Department of Housing and Urban Development F.M.C.S. Program.

(2) The International City Management Association (ICMA) catalogs exemplary financial management practices, particularly in small- and medium-size localities. ICMA also publishes handbooks and provides technical assistance through national and regional workshops.

(3) Both the U.S. Conference of Mayors (USCM) and the National League of Cities (NLC) have recently published handbooks and newsletters related to financial management improvement in both large and small cities.

(4) The National Association of Counties (NACO) also provides technical assistance to local governments, particularly in rural areas. In recent years the National Association of Towns and Townships (NATaT) has also stepped in to assist the smaller communities that have needs unmet by the larger associations.

(5) The Council of the State Community Affairs Agencies (COSCAA) is the national organization that coordinates the activities of the state agencies involved in state-local relations. Originally, COSCAA concentrated on functional areas, such as community and economic development, but lately it has been engaged in specific financial management training and assistance activities.

Conclusion

It is generally thought that in order to reform existing procedures or structures, additional financial resources are required. Additional resources, sometimes referred to as organizational slack, are required to either reward employees for their cooperation or to fund training sessions on the new operating procedures being implemented. Following that line of thought, advocating organizational or procedural reform in a declining resource environment may be viewed as an exercise in wishful thinking. However, many of the suggestions assumed under the heading of financial management capacity building, such as the integration concept, do not require additional resources as much as they require reconfiguration of existing resources and decision-making processes. Where new resource commitments are required, they may well result in financial returns in excess of costs as various local cash management programs have illustrated. The essence of the challenge for local government officials is well stated in a recent International City Management Association (ICMA) publication:

> An important consideration is whether the tax revolt can be put to use in improving municipal finance administration. A seeming contradiction is that citizens' endorsements of lower taxes have not necessarily meant support for fewer services. The challenge ahead, then, is to achieve cost reductions through improved productivity. This means delivering more and better public services with fewer resources. Management strategies should include devising new patterns of organizations ... [12]

As the quote from ICMA suggests, in recent years the public has made its feelings very clear at the local level; they definitely want lower taxes, but at the same time they want to retain the current level of services. Improvements in both program administration at the departmental level and financial management centrally seem to be the areas that local officials must concentrate on. As mentioned previously, very few local governments have been successful in identifying alternative revenues in sufficient amounts to meet their growing expenses. The potential for cost savings through financial management improvement as well as revenue generation (in the case of cash management innovations) does show considerable promise. The message of this chapter is that the concept of integrated financial management deserves consideration as an approach to meeting all of the pressing needs that local officials currently face.

Notes

1. Bernard Jump, Jr., "The Coming of Age of Public Financial Management", *Urban Affairs Papers*, 2, 2 (Spring 1980).

2. Ibid, 3-4.

3. U.S. Department of Housing and Urban Development, *Local Financial Management Techniques in the 80s: Techniques for Responding to the New Fiscal Realities* (Washington, D.C.: U.S. Government Printing Office, January 1980).

4. Frederick O'R. Hayes et al., *Linkages: Improving Financial Management in Local Government* (Washington, D.C.: The Urban Institute Press, 1982).

5. J. Ward Wright, "Building the Capacities of Municipal Governments", *Public Administration Review*, Special Issue (December 1975):750.

6. Frederick O'R. Hayes, et al., *Linkages: Improving Financial Management in Local Government*, 3.

7. Allen Schick, "The Road to PPB: The Stages of Budget Reform", *Public Administration Review* (December 1966):243-258.

8. An excellent handbook on both the new and the old practices of financial management is J. Richard Aronson and Eli Schwartz, ed., *Management Policies in Local Government Finance* (Washington, D.C.: International City Management Association, 1981).

9. For a more complete treatment of the steps involved in setting up a cash management program, see Frank M. Patittucci and Michael H. Lichtenstein, *Improving Cash Management in Local Government: A Comprehensive Approach* (Chicago, Illinois: Municipal Finance Officers Association, 1977).

10. Hayes et al., *Linkages: Improving Financial Management in Local Government*, 161.

11. Jan M. Lodal, "Financial Information System Should Serve Managers", *Public Management* (June 1979).

12. Leonard I. Ruchelman, "The Finance Function in Local Government" in Aronson and Schwartz, *Management Policies in Local Government Finance*, 22-23.

Part V
Human Resources and Management

11

Capacity Building in Municipal Labor-Management Relations

JONATHAN BROCK

Most books on management put labor-management relations into a separate chapter, as does this one. Many top managers and elected officials assign it to specialists in the law or personnel departments. However, labor-management relations affects so many aspects of municipal service delivery and costs that it requires constant attention from top program managers and policy officials.

Such constant attention is required simply because most public services are provided primarily through the efforts of people. While computers, trucks, or other forms of capital are used, most public services are labor-intensive. In order to improve a public agency's performance, some alterations must usually be made in the way people feel about or do their jobs. Therefore, most attempts to change or improve public services will have some effect on the terms and conditions of employment. Such matters are ordinarily part of collective bargaining and thus will concern employees and their representatives.[1]

This chapter examines the need for a conscious connection between day-to-day municipal management and the policy and practice of labor relations. The chapter suggests several ways of building capacity for more constructive and effective labor-management relations.

209

Labor Relations and Public Employment

The idea of capacity building seems especially appropriate to municipal labor-management relations. In many jurisdictions, collective bargaining is barely twenty years old; in some states or localities, there is no bargaining at all. Therefore, in many public jurisdictions, the capacity of either side to bargain effectively is not well established. In contrast, where bargaining exists in private employment, it has been in place for a much longer period of time, and as a result, the players and institutions know their roles well. But in the public sector, where roles and practices have generally had less time to become defined, establishing stable labor-management relations is more difficult.

Apart from this relative experience, there are some additional factors which differentiate public from private sector labor-management relations:

(1) Periodic changes in political leadership and appointed managers.

(2) Electoral and political considerations of top executives in making program or labor-management decisions.

(3) Union activity in the elective and appointive politics of its own managers and related legislative activities and relationships.

(4) Legislative ratification of contract funding and other legislative activities.[2]

These factors complicate public sector labor-management relations and explain, in part, the difficulty in establishing stable practices, even where unionization and bargaining have existed for a long period.

Despite these complications, labor relations is important to virtually every public manager and political leader. While unionization in the private sector covers just under 20 percent of the private nonfarm work force, growth in private sector unionism appears to have leveled off in the last decade or so. In contrast, about 50 percent of public employees are already unionized and both public and private sector unions have been working to increase that proportion.[3] Over the last two decades, bargaining and other labor rights have been extended steadily to state and local government employees through state-by-state legislation.

With growing unionization and expansion of bargaining rights, it is a rare manager or leader who does not encounter contract negotiations or other daily manifestations of established labor-management interactions. Since job security and gains in wages and benefits have been eroded by recent economic and budgetary difficulties, the frequency of stress and confrontations between labor and management is likely to increase. More attention to labor management relations will therefore be a necessity in most jurisdictions.

Affecting the Outcome of Collective Bargaining

Many public managers behave as if collective bargaining and the contract are the only important factors in labor relations, and therefore become interested and involved for only a few months every year or two. But the contract itself is a product of far more than annual bargaining. It results from decisions and interactions that take place throughout the year and that may or may not directly be part of the contract itself. For management to influence a contract, it must give equal attention to these other factors in the employment environment. For example, management must recognize that policy and program decisions affect the work force; new initiatives increase or alter workloads and create new tasks; the performance appraisal system, promotions and work assignments affect groups and individuals' feelings about the workplace, as do reorganizations and other change activities that take place. The way in which management handles grievances and the daily actions of supervisors will affect the attitude of the work force and how it perceives management.

It is not uncommon for difficulties with management policies or with a particular manager to result in a high grievance rate or, later, in demands at the bargaining table for compensation or altered work practices. Activities in these areas and their effects can have an important effect on the atmosphere at the bargaining table and the resultant ability to resolve important issues. Many times, economic demands at the bargaining table are a result of unresolved or unattended problems related to working conditions or methods of supervision.[4]

Thus, noncontract actions can affect the relationship and the outcome of bargaining. Effective labor-management relations depend upon how management handles the totality of decisions and actions that affect the ways people do their work, their attitudes about the workplace, and their feelings about management. Therefore, carefully

formed labor and personnel policy—related to policy and to programmatic objectives and decisions—and effective channels for problem
solving can help to effect constructive contract changes.

A Structure for Labor-Management Relations

Even if a manager wishes to improve labor relations in a
municipality or department, it may take considerable time and effort to
influence established policies, practices, and attitudes that affect
employees on their jobs and at the bargaining table. Primarily, it
requires that the department or municipality be organized to anticipate
and integrate the handling of issues that affect personnel and labor
relations into day-to-day management decisions. That requires what I
shall call here a labor relations "structure."[5] If management is reasonably well organized in this respect and able, therefore, to take the
actions necessary for effective employee relations, both its contract
bargaining and day-to-day management will benefit. This structure, in
essence, provides the capacity to carry out a labor relations policy, to
improve labor relations practices, and to engage in mutual problem
solving to the benefit of managers, employees, and the public.

Defining a Structure

The structure of labor-management relations is not necessarily
large, formal, or complex. Rather, it is that basic set of relationships,
responsibilities, and mechanisms—recognizable by both parties—that
permits labor and management to interact. From a management
standpoint, it consists of two parts: internal processes by which
management can make and implement decisions affecting workers and
bargaining; and channels through which to relate to the bargaining
unit.

An adversary relationship between labor and management can be
productive; but if it is unstable and there are not clear and useful
channels for resolving differences, the instability will pervade day-to-
day management and the organization becomes vulnerable to the
influence of external critics or pressures. Without undue labor-
management confrontation or external pressures to contend with, the
organization can better expend its energy on providing good service.

Developing a structure of the sort that this chapter will describe
helps labor-management relations in several ways. It can avoid poorly
thought-out solutions and positions on labor relations and other issues

that affect the work force; reduce the possibility that communication difficulties, either within management or between management and labor, can occur; and provide a much better way to prepare for bargaining and to develop a more positive bargaining atmosphere. A structure that contributes stability to labor-management relations will contribute to improved day-to-day management and quality of services.

What are some of the elements of such a structure?

Needed: A Point Person with Broad Perspective

First, an effective structure requires a central focus of responsibility for labor policy. In this respect, a central labor relations person on the management side is necessary so that both union leadership and others in management know whom they are supposed to call on in labor relations matters. More than one strike or difficult grievance has been precipitated by the lack of an open communication channel or knowledge of whom to call at the critical moment.[6] A grievance can often be settled when the union leadership can get a direct informal line to an authoritative or knowledgeable management representative. Moreover, a clear focus of labor relations responsibility is necessary to discourage an opportunistic union from "forum shopping" or "whipsawing" management by getting different answers from different management representatives. Many managers blame the union when it "shops" for an answer. As often as not, the shopping is made possible, or necessary, by lack of organization on the management side.[7] Who can blame the union if management does not know who has responsibility?

Essentially, the function of a central labor relations person is to seek consistency in personnel policy and management actions that may affect the work force or the bargaining climate. Workers may perceive various management actions as signals or symbols of their attitude toward the work force, even when innocently undertaken. Therefore, a single individual with responsibility for labor-management relations should have thorough access to discussions on all major organizational decisions. That person should be prepared to speak out in management councils on the impact of such decisions on labor-management relations.

Ideally, the individual selected for this labor-management job should have the full confidence of and easy and informal access to the head of the organization. The labor-relations person should also have the trust and confidence of the union. Otherwise, the labor-relations person may be less than effective. The union may then find someone else in the organization to talk to or find another channel through which to make known its concerns, such as the legislative branch, the media, or the courts. This does not mean the union has to be enamored of the choice, but it must be able to use the channel. Finally, top management and others must utilize and support that person (and staff, if any) and prevent "end runs" by referring problems to and soliciting advice from this central source.

Who is this person? Many small municipalities hire an outside attorney or consultant on a contract basis to do their labor negotiations. In others, the mayor or town manager performs the task. In larger cities, it may be the personnel officer, an assistant city manager, or a specialist in the personnel department or budget office. Elsewhere, it is simply someone who has a knack for negotiating or who has a good relationship with the union. Where departments within the municipality are large, individual departments have their own labor relations person whose primary responsibility is to advise managers and deal with officers of employee organizations on collective bargaining matters. Appropriate coordination with the central person for the municipality is ordinarily sought by departmental representatives.

Too often personnel and labor policy is made mainly by isolated staff specialists or by labor attorneys. Personnel and labor policies instead should be made from a broad perspective, with the involvement of key operating people from across the municipality or department, not just by personnel and labor relations specialists. Because personnel and labor relations policies should support major operational goals, municipal policy-makers and operating managers must be involved in shaping labor policy and providing guidance to the labor relations person. Those involved in these decisions might include the head of the municipality—the mayor or city manager—representative department heads, and key budget officials. Reflecting this, in some municipalities there is a "labor policy committee" which meets periodically, especially at bargaining time. Sometimes members of the legislative branch are involved. Policy and line officials do not have to be involved every day—that is what they pay a specialist for—but they must, throughout the year, assess the impact of most major decisions on labor-management relations. By the same token, personnel and labor relations specialists should be involved with or consulted on other policy and management matters so that the effect on employees is properly considered.

This sort of labor policy coordination might be encouraged by placing employee relations issues on the regular agenda of some existing group of top decision-makers. In such a forum, upcoming problems can be addressed before they adversely affect the labor-management relationship. For example, if a new municipal service or reorganization is being proposed, its effect on workers and management's obligations under the labor contract should be considered to avoid unnecessary bad feelings or a contract violation. The latter can lead to unrest or difficulty at the bargaining table.

While program and service delivery consistent with a good employment environment are management's overriding responsibilities, legal advice should be sought in forming or carrying out labor policy, since there are many legal/technical aspects to labor relations. Nonetheless, while lawyers or personnel specialists have an important role to play, successful labor relations requires a broader array of views, reflecting both the most important goals and constraints of the organization and the day-to-day labor-management climate. Managers should not allow labor policy to be formed primarily by legal experts, but legal requirements and rights are important to forming a proper strategy and in selecting tactics.

The central labor relations person should keep abreast of any external forces that might impinge upon internal labor-management relations and personnel policies. For example, political and legal developments affecting the jurisdiction should be monitored. Prospective changes in the bargaining laws, union organizing activities, internal union politics, and recent court decisions can all have a pronounced effect on relations in the agency and on the strategy and behavior of both management and the union.

Building Middle Management and Supervisory Capacity

Labor relations are strengthened most by making even-handed and consistent labor policy a part of day-to-day operating level management. Otherwise, many good intentions from policy-makers or by a negotiator will not have much effect. All too often, line supervisors unwittingly antagonize employees and their representatives by violating the spirit or letter of the bargaining agreement. Therefore, there should be regular communication—through training, staff meetings, or other mechanisms—to ensure that middle managers and line supervisors learn about and influence, where appropriate, developments in labor policy.

Training middle managers and supervisors in good personnel

management, in general labor relations concepts as well as in specific local rules and policies, is necessary for building capacity. It will make them better managers and will improve the organization as a place to work. Errors and violations of contract provisions are frequent causes of labor-management difficulties. Therefore, it is important for supervisors to know what is permissible and what is not—in disciplining, making assignments, and so forth. In one case, a seemingly straightforward reorganization was held up for months because management failed to notify properly the union of the impending change as the contract required.[8]

In order to ease their task, these middle- and lower-level managers will need training, briefing, and access to the central labor relations staff so that advice and assistance will be accurate, consistent, and readily available.

Handling Grievances

A municipality should have a grievance procedure that is satisfactory to both management and the union. An unresolved grievance without a ready means of resolution can strain relationships between managers and workers and between workers and union leaders. People may become consumed by the need to win rather than the need to solve the problem. Pride and bitter feelings then interfere with identifying legitimate needs and acceptable solutions. Unresolved grievances and leftover bitterness can interfere with other, perhaps more important, interactions, including contract negotiations.

Pressures from poorly resolved or constant grievances frequently lead to harder union positions at the bargaining table and can substantially affect the atmosphere in which bargaining takes place. In a poor atmosphere, with little trust between labor and management, progress on substantive problems involving improvements in working conditions, service delivery, or in other significant aspects of cost and quality of service can be hampered.

Besides causing problems, patterns of grievances may point to solutions. Do they occur at certain locations? Do they most commonly arise under certain supervisors? Do they relate to a particular promotion or compensation policy? Often, grievance patterns have roots, and by watching these patterns, fundamental problems can be identified. With an effective labor relations structure, those underlying problems can more easily be addressed. If there are informal channels of communications between the union and management, the underlying causes are more likely to emerge, permitting management or joint action to correct the situation.

By resolving the problem at the point at which it occurs, interpersonal problems that may have caused the grievance are more likely to be resolved. The higher in the organization a grievance goes, the more likely it is that the outcome will further harm the relationship between employee and manager and adversely affect labor and management cooperation. Thus, improving the capacity of supervisors to avoid and resolve grievances is an important ingredient of a labor relations structure.[9]

Joint Problem Solving

Joint labor-management committees often have been successful in improving productivity and developing and maintaining good bargaining relationships. They have been used in a variety of productivity experiments and in various forms of problem solving throughout the public sector and in private industry. For example, they have tackled job safety problems, developed quality circles, improved the quality of work life, and identified areas for costs saving and productivity improvement.[10]

A joint committee is composed, usually, of an equal number of labor and management representatives, selected by each side, who either work on a specific problem or are available as a standing committee. Joint committees often achieve dramatic results.[11] Getting labor and management officials together on a regular basis (sometimes with neutral assistance) pays many dividends, not only for solving the specific problem but for recognizing their ability to work together effectively. This beneficial impact on the overall relationship can spill over into more productive bargaining.

Joint committees can explore issues too complex to resolve in a single bargaining round. Complex pension and benefit issues may be suited to such committees. By working together, away from the bargaining table, it is often possible to make progress or resolve difficult issues that plagued the last bargaining round. Where any restructuring of work or jobs is contemplated, a joint committee is almost a prerequisite in a unionized workplace. These items are often too complex and emotionally charged to be resolved during contract bargaining.[12] Ordinarily, the union's knowledge of the work flow will be crucial to any substantial revisions. It would not be unusual for the union representatives to know more than management about where costs can be cut, quality improved, and productivity increased.

In organizations where there is an overall (rather than an issue-specific) labor-management committee, subcommittees can be formed to address specific issues. Specific expertise can then be assigned to solve specific problems. In this way, members of the organization other than those on the main committee, can thereby work together constructively. Where there has been bitterness and mistrust, such joint work can improve trust among even greater numbers of people in the organizational hierarchy. It can divert union and management from prejudices that they may hold about each other on certain issues.

Cooperation can also lend strength to follow-through measures. A joint committee, while it may come up with a less perfect process design, is more likely to implement that which it has designed itself and has endorsed. Consultants' recommendations may not be implemented nearly so well. Besides, given the informal power and formal rights of unions, there are few important management or service delivery decisions that do not depend, to some extent, on union input and agreement. Joint committees, formed in good faith, with time to work on the problem and the latitude to come up with their own solutions, can be extremely important tools for managing a public agency.

Several factors are important if joint committees are to work well.[13] A successful joint committee has the consent of both sides, appoints members who are likely to make a contribution to the effort, and secures commitment by labor and management to carry through the process and to be attentive to the work and recommendations of such a committee.[14] Where the relationships or issues are difficult, the help of a neutral should be sought.

The use of joint committees outside of negotiation periods has several spin-off benefits to both parties. It can assist labor and management, respectively, to "get their act together" prior to bargaining. The interaction helps each side avoid surprises at the bargaining table. (Surprises, while they may have a certain dramatic effect and may gain some results in the short-run are likely to provoke undesired reactions as well as desirable ones.) By building relationships and channels of communication through interaction on a joint committee, trust can be built between management's chief labor-management officer and the union leadership. Problems can be resolved in a timely way and handled away from the table if labor, management, and key subordinates are in touch. Similarly, greater trust results in more effective problem solving at the table. Finally, informal channels formed during the year can be used during difficult moments in bargaining and can be invaluable in avoiding impasses, strikes, and other disruptive actions.

Bargaining

Preparation for Bargaining

Bargaining can be both a game and an art. It is best carried out by people who understand its many aspects, but must be directed by the organization's best interests. Contract bargaining, as we have described, has substantial importance in determining the cost and quality of services. While each side will be seeking to come out well, problems can be worked on and resolved when the parties maintain a constructive relationship between bargaining rounds. Successful bargaining takes place when both sides have their most important priorities attended to and when no one feels the need to "get even" during the course of the contract or the next bargaining round.

A Bargaining Strategy

For management, a bargaining team should be working in the months before bargaining so that the municipality or department's priorities can be established and plans made to follow those through the bargaining. For example, a city may wish to hold down wage rate increases, get major changes in work rules, and reduce the costs of health and welfare benefits. It is unlikely that all of those things can be accomplished in any one bargaining round. It is important to assess which are the most important in the next bargaining round. Initially, management may ask for concessions in all areas. The skilled negotiator will need to know which are most important and which things can be traded at the bargaining table. It is rare that a contract settlement does not represent some ranking of issues and trading between the parties. It is better to do this explicitly.

Organizing for Bargaining

Bargaining positions and strategy should match the organization's overall purposes, priorities, and resources. Therefore, it is crucial to formulate bargaining positions in conjunction with top management, key operating people, and key staff. Often, these are represented on a labor policy committee.

Effective bargaining for management requires that a person or team be designated well ahead of actual bargaining. Close attention should be given to the composition of this management team. It should relate closely to, if not be, the labor policy committee. In most instances, the person who has primary responsibility for labor-management relations should be the team's head. Generally, this person should be from within the organization, someone who will have to live with the consequences of the settlement. Persons who know the operating needs of programs affected by the contract should also be included. A labor-management relations expert can be expected to be good at bargaining but may not be easily able to anticipate how certain work rule changes might affect operating units. It will also be important for someone on the team, or in close touch with the team, to know how local civil service and personnel rules and state regulations and statutes affect the contract.

In smaller jurisdictions, one person may suffice. Even so, this person should be guided by an informal policy committee so that settlements reflect the reality of operating in the city or bargaining unit. Whatever policy mechanism is used, the chief negotiator must be able to check his or her perceptions and bargaining positions with those who will have to operate under the terms of the contract.

The bargaining team should also analyze the impact of different proposals on costs, operations, and day-to-day management. Grievance patterns, joint committees, and the activities of line supervisors can provide important data for evaluating bargaining issues before the sessions begin. By anticipating issues and possible positions, their impacts can be evaluated and the less desirable ones avoided. Proposals hastily agreed to frequently have undesired operational or financial consequences. Therefore, the bargaining team should solicit a wide range of input prior to bargaining.

Legislative Relations

The local legislature will normally have to ratify the financial provisions of any contract agreement in a jurisdiction. Therefore, capacity building must include development of a systematic and mutually acceptable executive-legislative protocol. Municipalities differ in how they do this. Techniques range from no consultation at all to an elaborate system of joint priority setting and review of possible negotiating positions.

One fundamental principle is to keep the legislative branch from being surprised. Involvement as part of a labor policy group or briefings by the central labor relations person throughout the year and especially just prior to bargaining can be of substantial benefit. The need for confidentiality in bargaining is likely to complicate communication with the legislative branch as bargaining draws near. In jurisdictions where union leaders have close ties to members of the legislature, this may be especially tricky.

If the legislature fails to ratify a contract agreed to by management and the union, it may be very difficult to renegotiate. Moreover, a management-negotiator who cannot make a deal that will "stick" may get less than full attention from the union in the next round. The political relationships between the union and legislature, and legislature and executive, will help to determine the sort of legislative-executive relationship that is appropriate regarding contract bargaining.

Hired or In-House Negotiators?

Small- and medium-sized municipalities often wonder whether or not to hire an outside negotiator. A small town, especially after a bad experience or two in bargaining, may seek an outside attorney or professional negotiator to handle its contracts. An in-house person is better simply because he or she has to live with the settlement and the day-to-day response of the union. On the other hand, sufficient talent may not be available within the city, or it may be difficult to obtain resources necessary to recruit and support such a position. If engaging outside counsel or a professional negotiator is the only alternative, it is important to check his or her credentials and professional reputation with both management and unions.

When engaging such outside services, it is crucial for the town to remember that it is not buying a labor relations policy; it is only hiring a negotiator. The function of developing a labor policy and carrying on day-to-day relationships with the union must still be undertaken. The goals in bargaining should be related to service delivery and the type of working environment that the municipality or department wishes to maintain or create. It is difficult for an outside person to support such goals without substantial input and almost daily working relationships with the municipality's key policy-makers and managers.

Where the alternative is no leadership or professionalism in dealing with the union, it may be better to go outside for help rather than to muddle through. Muddling does not usually create stable or consistent labor-management relations or effective contract bargaining. Outside help may be a necessity in the short-term while the city "gets its act together" and develops capacity for handling its total labor relations function.

Labor Laws

Better and more stable labor laws usually result when both sides' interests are well reflected. The most practical, acceptable and therefore, most stable laws seem to result as the product of agreement by the key labor and management interests in the local public sector. Such laws must recognize their effects on the incentives to bargain and, unlike many existing statutes, they pay careful attention to providing adequate systems for solving disputes and other problems. The lack of a closure mechanism for impasse resolution increases the chances of bargaining conflicts escalating and continuing. Then one must face the possibility of illegal strikes, which disrupt services, bargaining, and constructive relations.

The development of good labor laws and dispute resolution systems can avoid or minimize illegal strikes. Such laws will more likely be produced if they result from state-level leadership of both sides working together. Often, labor and management leadership support very different sorts of labor laws, resulting in sloppy compromises, or laws and mechanisms that raise the opposition of one or both sides. The unhappy side fights the law by challenges in court or by lobbying for its demise. Thus, a law developed with the consent of both sides can do a great deal to stabilize labor-management relations.[15]

Ordinarily, state-level labor and management leadership has the ability to influence state laws and politics. Therefore, the structure of public employee labor laws must be recognized and made part of the capacity-building strategy of responsible management organizations. Where labor and management leadership can agree, state legislators and key executive branch officers no longer have to decide or determine policy in the face of competing interests. Thus, the possibilities for legislative approval are high, and the prospects for more stable local labor relations enhanced.

Summary

As local managers think about capacity building in labor-management relations, the following observations may be helpful.

First, management should think and act systematically. Labor relations is not a separate or separable aspect of management. Most program activities of a public manager will affect the work force in an "industry" that relies heavily on people to deliver its services. Therefore, most policy decisions and management actions that affect employee relations should be considered with the input of the person with major responsibility for labor-management relations, operating managers, top policy officials and others. In this way, the various interests and resource centers affected by policy decisions can make their views known, and reasonable and practical trade-offs can be made.

Second, localities should establish a proper structure for handling labor relations. The structure should govern how management handles its internal policy and issues affecting employees and how it builds and carries out relationships with union leaders and employees.

Third, responsibility for overseeing labor-management relations should be fixed at a high level in the jurisdiction or organization. The person with that responsibility must have the ear of the top policymakers, be reasonably expert in labor management relations, have good political sense, and ideally be someone who can win the respect of union leadership. In smaller municipalities, this responsibility can be taken on by a mayor, deputy mayor, city manager (or assistant), or perhaps by the head personnel officer. However it is arranged, the person with primary responsibility for labor-management relations ought to be a substantial observer, if not a participant, in overall policy making.

Fourth, it is helpful to have a labor-relations philosophy and strategy. Ranking the importance of each prospective issue can serve well in carrying on day-to-day relations and can make for more successful bargaining. A bargaining strategy that tries to do too much may end up doing nothing. Is it most necessary, for example, to improve communications channels prior to bargaining, or is it more important to develop a better grievance system or medical benefits? Should management concentrate this year on reforming the pension system? Rarely can many complex issues be resolved in one bargaining round. Management will do best if there is some overall sense of what kind of labor relationship and operating results are most desired—and possible—and what actions are most crucial to bring that about. Taking a long view, over several bargaining rounds, far more can be accomplished.

Fifth, day-to-day actions of managers and supervisors should be consistent with the philosophy, strategy, and policies set forth for labor-management relations. This requires from management a combination of internal communication and training about labor policy, and internal channels which allow labor policy and bargaining to reflect the problems and needs of programs and employee welfare. Such channels make it more likely that the policies will fit well with the needs and problems encountered in day-to-day operational activities.

Sixth, to begin to improve the relationship between management and labor, managers should look for opportunities to work on problems whose solutions are in the mutual interest of labor and management. To do so, one must not only look at issues, but also at personalities and other factors that may present opportunities or barriers for beginning such work.

In seeking to solve specific problems or generally to alter or improve the relationship, it is important to remain focused on the problem and how the problem may be impeding the organization's work. Frequently, pride and other factors become dominant and one party or the other loses its focus on the reason why the problem should be solved. Joint committees present one mechanism for working out such problems and to begin to improve a previously contentious relationship.

Seventh, management should plan for bargaining. It should anticipate issues that are likely to arise and formulate and analyze possible positions and their effects. Management should also anticipate the needs of the other side and look for possible or necessary trade-offs. It should be sure that the relevant decision-makers on the management side are in agreement on goals, positions, and intentions. Poor bargaining outcomes can often be traced to disorganized management and a divided approach, including legislative-executive rivalry and confusion.

Eighth, bargaining and dispute settlement methods imposed by local statutes and traditions greatly influence the capacity to deal with local labor and management issues. Usually, the most significant laws are passed at the state level. Therefore, the political and legislative actions of state-level management and labor leaders will be important. Individual managers cannot influence state-level behavior, but state-level organizations of city managers, mayors, or labor relations professionals can make a difference in the sort of labor laws that arise. Capacity can be improved both by developing better bargaining laws and through labor laws that are generally supported both by labor and management. Where one side is unhappy, lobbying and litigation only divert attention from resolving bargaining and operational problems at the local level. Enmities of labor and management at the state-level can only exacerbate the mistrust between local management and labor.

Conclusion

Contract bargaining is a culminating event in a series of both conscious and unwitting actions that take place all year. The more management perceives and attempts to rationalize those actions to marshal a productive work climate and successful program delivery, the more likely it is that contract bargaining will reflect organizational priorities. Bargaining outcomes are shaped not simply by what happens at the table but by events all year long that affect working conditions and worker attitudes. Managers will also do well to remember that bargaining, by definition, is a give-and-take process, in which each side has certain rights and powers.

An appropriate labor relations structure can help greatly to make bargaining more productive and day-to-day management more stable. By eliminating confusion and focusing management on priorities and problem solving, a structure can eliminate the unnecessary bitterness that often arises between labor and management. While differences will always be present, unnecessary impediments can be minimized. Energy is then reserved for productive work and resolution of the central issues of concern to both management and labor.

In seeking to build capacity in labor-management relations, each manager should be practical and realistic and avoid ideology, prejudice, or impatience with the pace of change. It takes time to get competent and qualified people into positions of responsibility for labor-man-agement relations. It takes time to alter the way policy decisions are made. It takes time to develop ways of forming and communicating labor relations policy up and down the line and throughout the jurisdiction or organization. It also takes time to develop a constructive bargaining relationship and other channels for labor-management interaction.

Choosing a proper strategy for building capacity in an individual municipality or department depends on the history of the relationship, traditions of the municipality, organizational structure of municipal departments, and on peculiarities of municipal politics. Pre-existing personal relationships between key management and labor people can make a large difference in what progress is possible. Labor relations experiences in surrounding and related towns will color the views of both labor and management on how to behave and what to expect. The number of bargaining units, the personalities of leadership on both sides, and the effect of state laws and politics will influence the behavior of the major actors and the possibilities for improvement in local labor-management relationships. All of these factors must be considered in trying to apply any of the thoughts or concepts presented in this chapter.

Energy devoted to capacity building, however, should take precedence over simply reacting to or dealing with crises or seeking particular positions at the bargaining table. Resolution of crises and mutually successful bargaining can result from calmer and more constructive labor relationships and structures. Better bargaining outcomes, more employee satisfaction, and more effective service delivery is possible if labor relations is dealt with systematically, seen as more than bargaining, and handled with the priority that it deserves.

Notes

1. For a more complete discussion of these issues, see Jonathan Brock, *Managing People in Public Agencies* (Boston: Little, Brown & Co. 1984) chapter 1.

2. For a more elaborate discussion of these issues, see chapters 1 and 8, 206-207, in Jonathan Brock, *Bargaining Beyond Impasse: Joint Resolution of Public Sector Labor Disputes* (Boston: Auburn House Publishing 1982).

3. *Statistical Abstract of the United States* (Washington, D.C.: U.S. Government Printing Office, 1983).

4. As, for example, in the Professional Air Traffic Controllers' strike of 1982 against the Federal Aviation Administration. For a useful summary of the case, see "The Professional Air Traffic Controller," available from Harvard Business School Case Services, Soldiers Field, Boston, MA 02163.

5. This concept is more completely explored in John T. Dunlop, *Industrial Relations Systems* (Carbondale and Edwardsville: Southern Illinois University Press, 1977).

6. For example, see case studies "The Professional Air Traffic Controllers," HBS Case Services (Boston, 1982) and "Flextime Negotiations in the U.S. Patent and Trademark Office (A)," (John F. Kennedy School of Government Case Program, 1981) and "Police Negotiations in Barkfield, Massachusetts," in Brock *Managing People in Public Agencies*, (Boston: Little, Brown & Co., 1984).

7. For an example, see the case study "Labor Relations in the U.S. Employment Service (A)," in Brock, *Managing People in Public Agencies*.

8. Ibid.

9. See Fred K. Foulkes and E. Robert Livernash, *Human Resource Management*, (Englewood Cliffs: Prentice Hall, 1982), 121 and 122 and the case "Grievance Date," 125.

10. Research material from the Ontario Quality of Work Life Centre is especially valuable for understanding the usefulness and dynamics of joint labor-management committees. For a more general discussion of the use of joint labor-management committees, see chapter 14, "Labor-Management Committees: Functions and Experience," 227-241, and chapter 15, "The Work of Labor-Management Committees," 242-251, in John T. Dunlop, *Dispute Resolution: Negotiations and Consensus Building*, (Boston: Auburn House Publishing Company, 1984).

11. See Dunlop, *Industrial Relations Systems*, 247-251, for a recent example in a private context.

12. Ibid., p. 247.

13. See descriptions and evaluations in chapters 21 and 25, respectively, in John M. Greiner et al., *Productivity and Motivation: A Review of State and Local Government Initiatives* (Washington, D.C.: The Urban Institute Press, 1981).

14. The literature on quality of work life experiments is replete with these and similar themes. See Pehr Gyllenhammer, "How Volvo Adapts Work to People," *Harvard Business Review* (July-August, 1977) and Jacquie Mansell, "Dealing with Some Obstacles to Innovation in the Work Place," (Ontario Quality of Work Life Center, Occasional Paper 7, November, 1980).

15. An excellent recent example may be found in the bargaining laws developed for public safety bargaining in Massachusetts. See *Bargaining Beyond Impasse*, chapters 2 and 3.

12
Improving Local Government Competence: Strategies For Human Resource Development

WALTER BROADNAX

Managers and scholars interested in improving the overall quality of organizations in the public and private sectors have begun to refocus their attention on the fundamental importance of developing human resources.[1] "People management," although quite possibly the most difficult aspect of any managerial position, is arguably the most critical component to achieving overall organizational and managerial success. However, the scholarly and practitioner support for human resource development, as a means of increasing overall organizational and/or jurisdictional capacity, often exceeds available political and financial support.

Many political leaders in both large and small local governments are concerned about the cost and measurable impact of human resource development programs or are skeptical about their benefits. Those who see few short-term, visible impacts are inclined to demand that local employees simply "do their jobs"; they argue that training and development programs have limited benefits for the individual or organization. This is particularly true when the human resource development activity is not specifically technical, e.g., computer programming, accounting, typing, personnel procedures, and book-keeping.

The assumption of this chapter, however, is that human resource development is directly related to the issue of competence, and that the development of competent managers is a prerequisite for the development of competent local governments. The manager is the critical link between the local jurisdiction's desire to improve its competence and the employees of that jurisdiction who will be called upon to design and implement procedures, processes and programs for the purpose of improving services and increasing the efficiency and effectiveness of local government efforts.

Clearly, the terrain is uneven when we speak of local government. Local governments in the United States range from jurisdictions the size and complexity of New York City with a population of nearly eight million people to jurisdictions the size of Ipswich, Massachusetts, with a population of several hundred, or to even smaller communities.

Small local governmental jurisdictions, such as small cities and towns, are most dependent upon their managers' competence because of the limited amount of skilled labor available to them. There are many small towns and communities which depend greatly upon appointed and part-time elected officials to conduct their public business. These individuals, in most instances, are highly dedicated but are often untrained, inexperienced and suffer from the necessary fragmentation of their energies between their chosen job or profession and the affairs of their communities. Such conditions do not provide a mechanism or an opportunity for developing expertise and coherence in the management and direction of jurisdictional affairs. Moreover, the fragmentation of energies and the lack of a force to provide a coherence to the efforts of these local units often leave them with limited capacity to address the many problems they commonly must confront.

If we desire competent local governments, we must develop viable and practical strategies for improving their capacity. This can be achieved by promoting human resource development for managers. By increasing the competence of management, we can provide the necessary propellant and guidance for the overall improvement of governmental competence.

Competent managers and increased local governmental capacity are central, conceptually, to the arguments developed here. Therefore, a brief definition of these concepts is in order. Competence is the ability to function or develop in ways that lead to greater effectiveness and efficiency. For the manager, greater competence involves the development of intellectual and behavioral skills that will enable him or her to elicit greater effectiveness and efficiency from subordinates which will result in the increased ability (capacity) of an organization or jurisdiction to deliver products and services. These skills include policy, political, and people management skills.

Policy skills are those acquired intellectual abilities that enable the manager to analyze data (quantitative and qualitative) and develop inferences relevant to solving public problems. The fact that there may be periods of terrible traffic congestion which virtually bring movement along certain routes within the city to a halt is a problem for the public manager. Knowing how to conceptualize that problem and develop options for resolving it, requires an understanding of policy analysis techniques and some substantive understanding of transportation.

Once the problem has been analyzed and options developed, the manager must be able to discern the most politically efficacious approach within the context of his or her available options. This may entail a careful study of the potential impact on certain neighborhoods, if traffic routes are changed, and may require negotiating trade-offs between business, neighborhood and other interests.

While gathering and analyzing data, developing political strategies for implementation, and guiding the development of alternate work plans, the manager must help others set goals, design work teams, reward excellence, evaluate performance, and motivate subordinates. Managing the people who perform certain tasks for the manager is equally as important as the other skills needed to manage competently.

The requisite skills for developing competent managers can be taught and learned. The teaching and learning of these skills can take place in the workplace as well as in the classroom. Preferably, the development process would include both off-site classroom training and on-site, hands-on learning and developmental opportunities for managers.

Human Resource Development Strategies for Local Government

Given the variance in size and managerial talent across local governmental jurisdictions, it is necessary that several strategies for human resource development be examined. These strategies range from those initiated by other levels of government to those initiated internally and shaped specifically to accommodate the character of a particular jurisdiction.

Federal Initiatives

During the New Deal the federal government began to initiate manpower and human resource development programs. This continued in various guises through the early 1970s.[2] Both the New Deal initiatives and those of the 1950s and 1960s tended to rely heavily on the federal goverment for development and implementation activities. Local governments were asked for advice but were not often full players in the formative stages of program development.

The 1970s brought a revised approach in the form of the Nixon New Federalism, which emphasized increased discretion for local governments.[3] Therefore, it was now the responsibility of local government to initiate and implement human resource development activities. The Comprehensive Employment and Training Act (CETA), for example, gave local jurisdictions more discretion in their utilization of training and development funds.

The 1980s have brought an expansion of the Nixon New Federalism. With the election of Ronald Reagan to the presidency came renewed emphasis on a devolution of authority and responsibility to the local level, which included a proposed enhancement of responsibility for raising the necessary revenues.[4] Against this backdrop there has arisen a concern for how local governments will manage complex programs effectively and efficiently. It therefore behooves us to examine the strengths and weaknesses of a federally initiated approach to managerially focused human resource development (education and training in policy, political and people management skills) for local governments.

The positive case for a federally initiated approach hinges on the following perceived benefits: (1) a national focus, (2) potential coherence in management development across the nation, (3) the ability to adjust and modify models for delivery based on changes in national priorities, and (4) a broader revenue base from which to finance the human resource development effort.

During the 1960s and 1970s, the federal government was deeply involved in efforts to address the needs of disparate groups across the nation: the poor, the malnourished, blacks, hispanics, and others. This effort was successful to a certain extent. In the case of the poverty programs, poverty was reduced, hope was renewed, and upward mobility was achieved for thousands. Clearly, a national focus brings greater attention and resources to bear on any perceived problem. It is true for environmental protection, public health, conservation of natural resources and a plethora of other issues perceived as related to the general welfare of the nation. It is true as well for human resource development for local government managers.

The ability to provide coherence to management development across the nation is clearly most possible through the development of a nationally initiated program. Discerning those managerial competencies that may be necessary for addressing various problems within jurisdictions of different sizes and complexities is very important in terms of providing national coherence.

A nationally initiated program, moreover, would provide an ability to assess and adjust human resource development models as conditions and national priorities shift. For example, policy changes in energy, environment, natural resources or urban affairs have direct impacts on local governments and their management. Typically, these policy shifts are initiated by the national government but often require local actions to be achieved.

We must also appreciate the benefits to be derived from a broad revenue base for financing human resource development efforts. If we accept the thesis that competent management is a problem for the nation, then the financing and development of such a program might best be carried out at the national level. This would enable thousands of smaller jurisdictions to benefit more fully from a managerially oriented human resource development program.

On the other side, a federally initiated human resource development program raises the following issues: (1) targeting programs to the needs and conditions of various local jurisdictions; (2) usurpation of local initiative, and (3) too much federal involvement in local affairs.

As discussed earlier, the recent trend in American public affairs has been one of withdrawal of federal participation in and financing of local activities and programs. In light of this trend, the arguments for leaving human resource development activities at the discretion of local governments and their officials seem to make sense.

Within the context of current developments at the national level and public opinion regarding the national government in local affairs, it seems that a potentially fruitful approach would be to pursue federal involvement with careful attention to maximizing local participation and initiative in the overall design and management of the effort. Recognizing the diversity among local governments, it would be beneficial to create a national council composed of representatives from local governments of varying sizes, complexities, and regional location. For example, education and training in public policy management could be developed based on regional and local concerns. In some regions and locales the major policy concern may be water conservation and energy supply. This concern would be articulated within the national planning body and built into developmental activities for those jurisdictions with such policy and management needs. The policy and political dimensions would vary based on perceived regional and local needs. However, within regions there would be a coherent thrust to developmental activities.

State Initiatives

A state-initiated approach to human resource development would afford governors an opportunity to increase the capacity of local governments to provide services to their citizens. For those states that have offices of state planning, the planning office might be a good place to generate a state-led, state-based and locally oriented human resource development program for local government managers. The planning office stands out because its focus includes statewide development concerns and a statewide perspective is desired in this instance. Therefore, such an approach would afford states an opportunity to: (1) assess managerial needs in the state from a local government perspective, (2) develop strategies for curriculum development and training programs, (3) target intellectual resources needed for training and educational activities, (4) utilize various contractual and purchase of service arrangements for the delivery of training, (5) create and develop on-the-job rotational assignments between state agencies and local governments which might broaden the horizons of local government managers, and (6) develop on-the-job exchanges between various local governments and nonprofit organizations.

Such an approach would take advantage of economies of scale in managerial development and education. The state contains many local government jurisdictions within its borders, all of which would benefit from such an initiative. The state's revenue-raising ability, moreover, would afford all jurisdictions within its boundaries an opportunity to participate. Furthermore, the state's chief executive is necessarily dependent on the quality of local government management for the effective and efficient delivery of various services. Therefore, opportunities for improving the competence of local government managers would redound positively to the state administration, i.e., increased productivity and overall local governmental competence.[5] Political support could well be won for such an initiative. For example, the state association of cities and towns would have a great deal to gain and would most likely become strong supporters.

Recently, however, many states have experienced significant revenue shortfalls, large-scale relocation of industry, unemployment, and general economic reversal. Many governors have had to address the problem of reducing the size of state government in the face of shrinking revenues and citizen discontent with what is perceived as steady and, to some extent, rapid increases in their taxes. In the face of such economic difficulties many governors may find it very difficult to pursue politically the issue of human resource development for local government managers. Therefore, why should they wish to expend scarce resources for managerial development and education? Furthermore, why should the states be concerned about managerial capacity at the local level? Others could argue that states have a difficult enough time developing their own managerial talents.

It might also be argued that there are too many differences in the scope and nature of responsibilities in local government in any given state. Some might argue that it would be difficult to address the managerial needs of small local governments while simultaneously trying to address the human resource needs of medium- and large-sized jurisdictions.

Overall, though, states are in a good position to develop and manage educational and training activities for local managers. The thesis that in times of shrinking resources enlightened leadership will recognize the benefits of enhanced managerial capacity is very compelling, given private sector responses in times of crisis. States could position themselves to realize some of these benefits, such as greater local government efficiency, improved quality of life for citizens in various communities, and enhanced opportunities for state-local collaboration in problem solving, e.g., on toxic waste, drinkable water, water conservation, flood control, and highways.

State governments are greatly dependent upon local managerial talent to achieve state objectives. Once state leaders recognize that the key to improving general governmental competence is to improve *managerial* competence, the states would see that the investment of resources in achieving this objective could generate much larger benefits for the state and its communities.

State and Local Partnerships

Yet another approach to human resource development for local governments would be the creation of state and local partnerships for management training. A council composed of state and local officials could be responsible for developing human resource programs and creating management development opportunities. Furthermore, the council could be very helpful in discussing priorities; it would be able to develop an agenda for training and educational services throughout the state.

Under the leadership of the council, a series of rotational and cross-utilization assignments between various state agencies and local governments could be developed. For example, if a local manager needed experience in police and public safety, that manager could undertake a rotational assignment with the state public safety authority. Another approach would be to cross-utilize managers from the state authority with managers from a set of local governments.

The aforementioned council would clearly have an opportunity to develop rotational and curriculum development opportunities between the state-local partnership and selected nonprofit organizations as well as between state agencies and local governmental jurisdictions. There are many nonprofit organizations, such as the United Way, which play a fundamental role in maintaining the quality of life in cities and towns. The managerial policy perspectives of these organizations have a tremendous impact on local governments, as do local governmental policies on nonprofit organizations. Such an approach would maximize the strengths of both state and local government to improve managerial capacity statewide. This approach would also afford the jurisdictions an opportunity to share costs based upon the fiscal capacity of each participant.

Clearly this approach would develop a greater appreciation on the part of state managers, local managers, and nonprofit managers for the problems each confronts in their particular domains. Exchanges, rotations, and cross-utilizations would greatly improve the perspective of the managers operating within each of these sectors and in turn improve their competence in terms of dealing with problems that directly affect each other's sphere of operation. Moreover, such an approach would facilitate the development of a general management cadre which would be familiar with issues and problems across sectors. This increased familiarity would bring about an increased capacity to address and resolve problems which often do not lend themselves to resolution in the local or state level or in the nonprofit sector alone.

An argument against state and local partnerships involves the velocity of exchanges and rotations among state, local and nonprofit organizations and the risk that such exchanges might cause a drain of managerial talent from the local level. Typically, state managerial salaries are greater than those for many of the smaller local governmental units. If managers were to rotate into state agencies, they might become very interested in positions available at the state level; and state managers might be motivated to attract the best talent away from local governments. Moreover, depending upon the number of managers to be afforded development opportunities in a given fiscal year, the movement of large numbers of people back and forth between agencies and jurisdictions could be extremely complex and cause serious dislocations within each of the sectors involved.

One could argue also that there would be little interest in the development of general managerial and public policy talent at the state and local level. The preference might very well be for specialists. This argument hinges on the idea that the world of the public manager has become progressively more technical. These managers must contend with problems such as hazardous waste, acid rain and highway planning and location. The posture, then, is that it is the specialist who is required and the general manager has little to offer in a jurisdiction's need to resolve such technical problems.

Last, one could argue that local politicians may see the entire arrangement as a device for gaining greater control over local initiative and control of the operations of local government. Here again, the concern would be that now the state, as opposed to the federal government, would be intervening in those affairs best left to locally elected and appointed officials.

By following a state-local partnership approach, the enhanced managerial talent available statewide would increase the pool of talent available to each local jurisdiction. Therefore, no one jurisdiction should greatly benefit at the expense of another. Each state and, in turn, each locality would become progressively richer in terms of its existing pool of competent managerial talent.

Local and Private Partnerships

Creating local and private partnerships for human resource development places the emphasis on what local governments can do by using resources within their own boundaries. The major thrust of such an approach is that local governments could reach out to corporations in their area that possess relatively large management cadres and that may have an interest in enhancing the capacity of the local government. This approach would offer the local government, in conjunction with private entities within its jurisdictional boundaries, an opportunity to develop rotational assignments between corporate entities and local government. Pursuing such a strategy would entail targeting various managerial roles within companies that have the potential of providing a set of broadening experiences for local managers. Also, managerial opportunities for corporate managers within the local government could be targeted and provide learning opportunities for corporate managers. A committee composed of local leaders, both public and private, would provide the vehicle for developing an educational and training agenda and for setting meaningful priorities for human resource development.

The committee could establish joint training opportunities where costs could be shared by business and local government. Such an approach could constitute a range of activities jointly provided and delivered by the local-private partnership and range from activities such as seminars, field trips, lectures, personnel exchanges (short-term and long-term), contractual arrangements or consulting.

What then are the benefits to be derived from such an approach? Clearly such an approach is one where local initiative is unfettered by involvement at the state or federal level. Such an approach would also provide an opportunity to focus more sharply on specific local concerns. It is also important to point out here that corporations have a stake in the efficacy and viability of local governments. If the local government is inefficient and ineffective, then tax dollars are wasted or poorly used by the local government. It was through the efforts of private businessmen at the turn of the century that the movement to bring professional managers into local government was initiated. Therefore, it seems appropriate that corporate leaders would understand the importance of competent local government.

However, one might ask why the corporation should engage in such a joint venture? One might contend that such a venture would create unnecessary overhead for the company and that there would be little opportunity for it to benefit equally from the collaboration proposed here. Moreover, strong local managers could eventually be drained off from service with the local government into managerial positions with local corporations. Last, there is the perception that the difference between public and private managerial roles is great. In this regard, then there would be little benefit for either the corporation or the local government to engage in exchanges or collaboration. On balance, though, corporate managers understand the importance of this relationship and could be encouraged to engage in collaborative efforts with local government officials in the pursuit of improved competence and overall capacity of local governments.[6]

Local Initiatives

Local initiatives would rely on the local government drawing upon its own financial and managerial resources without collaboration from federal, state, and nonprofit, or private entities. Each local government would be totally dependent upon its own resources in carrying out such an initiative. The activities foreseen in such initiatives would include cross-utilization of local managers in various functions of the local government, such as fire, police, streets, sanitation, and sewers. Furthermore, cross-utilization efforts could take place within departments. For example, housing and economic development could initiate cross-utilization activities with community development. In addition, local governments could develop contractual arrangements for short-term seminars and workshops taught by consultants, and in certain instances they might be able to develop local academies and institutes for ongoing human resource development activities. The development of academies or quasi academies might be particularly attractive for large jurisdictions.

Following the local initiative approach, there would be no need to negotiate with other jurisdictions. This would reduce the problems of complexity and the probability of competent managers being attracted away from the local government in question. Furthermore, programs focused specifically on general management and locally oriented could be developed through such a single jurisdictional strategy because each manager participating in the human resource development program would be gaining experience and competence in areas of particular concern and interest to the local jurisdiction. The cost for such a program would be clearly targeted on and driven by the perceived needs of the local government, without the additional overhead costs generated by larger collaborative efforts.

Larger local governments (cities such as Los Angeles, New York, and Chicago) could readily undertake many of these management development efforts and provide meaningful human resource development opportunities for local managers. Within these larger jurisdictions, the agencies and departments are of such a magnitude that cross-utilization and rotational opportunities across structures would clearly be possible and meaningful because of the size, complexity and diversity of management challenges. Rotating managers between the police and fire departments, for example, might have tremendous potential for developing strong general managerial competence within the broader realm of public safety in a city the size of Chicago. This is true, particularly, when these functions are seen as competitors for local government resources and constitute such large proportions of the cities' employees.

On the negative side, it is clear that smaller local governments may lack the necessary resources and talent to conduct effectively such a human resource development program. Very small local governments'

Table 1. Human Resource Development Strategies: Pros and Cons

Locus of Initiative	Pro	Con
Federal	Provide a national focus for human resource development Coherent national management development design and structure Design flexibility based on national priorities Broaden revenue base for financing initiatives	Difficulty targeting local needs and understanding local conditions Perceived usurpation of local initiative Extends federal involvement in local affairs
State	Provides ability to assess local management needs from a statewide perspective Statewide perspective in developing curricula for education and training programs Ability to target resources in areas of greatest perceived need Facilitate activities between state and local government and nonprofit organizations	Constraints on availability of state resources State lack of concern for local problems Autonomy of local governments would be reduced Differences in scope and nature of responsibilities between state and local governments
State-Local	Enhanced opportunities for cross-utilizations and rotational assignments between state, local and nonprofits Access to developmental sites and opportunities on a statewide basis Increased understanding of intersectoral issues, problems and potential solutions	Frequency of exchanges between jurisdictions Potential drain of talent from smaller jurisdictions Political concerns regarding local autonomy General management development v. specialists Resistance to perceived complexity of rotational assignments and exchanges
Local-Private	Clearly targeted local government and corporate rotational assignments Cost sharing of developmental activities	Divergent corporate/local government interests Cost to corporation Potential drain of local talent by corporations

Table 1 *(continued)*

Locus of Initiative	Pro	Con
	Cost sharing of developmental activities	Dissimilarities between corporate and local government managerial roles
	Unfettered by federal or state involvement	
	Corporate stake in community's capacity	
Local	Eliminates cross-jurisdictional negotiations	Resource shortages (fiscal and human)
	Reduced complexity	Scarcity of management experience within smaller jurisdictions
	Eliminates concern about loss (drain) of local talent	
	Focus on general management development	Limited number of managers in smaller communities to participate
	Reduced overhead costs	
	Costs driven by local needs	

managerial staff, with minimal background and training, may be hard-pressed to reap the benefits of rotational and cross-utilization assignments. Where these entities may only possess one to ten individuals who could be considered managerial staff or where most individuals functioning in managerial roles do so as part-time appointees, the difficulty of carrying out such an initiative, strictly at the local level, could be overwhelming. Even the chief executive will often have tremendous difficulty removing him or herself from the job for external developmental opportunities.

Of the strategies discussed here, the least promising is local initiatives for human resource development. This is less true when we are speaking of larger jurisdictions such as New York, Chicago, and Los Angeles. However, most local governments are much smaller. In fact, there are thousands of local governments composed of very few management trained employees which rely upon the strengths and endure the weaknesses of citizens who serve in part-time capacities.

Conclusions

The question of capacity building revolves around the issue of enhanced local governmental competence. Local governmental competence is fundamentally related to local government's ability to develop and retain competent managerial talent. In this regard, the several approaches outlined in this chapter and summarized in Table 1 would afford local governments (with varying degrees of effectiveness and complexity) an opportunity to engage in managerially oriented human resource development programs.

If our nation is to improve its general capacity to deliver services to its citizens, it is critically important to focus our attention on the central role of human resource development. No institution or organization can progress without having available to it the best managerial talent possible.[7]

It would be possible to initiate various managerially oriented human resource development programs for achieving that objective independent of any involvement by the federal government. However, because the problem is national in scope, it is hoped that future actions will include federal participation.

Notes

1. Thomas J. Peters and Robert A. Waterman, Jr., *In Search of Excellence: Lessons from America's Best-Run Companies* (New York: Harper and Row, 1982).

2. Walter D. Broadnax, "Policy Planning for the Poor" in *The State and the Poor*, Manuel Carballo and Mary Jo Bane, eds. (Cambridge, MA: Auburn House, 1983).

3. Walter D. Broadnax, "The New Federalism: Hazards for State and Local Government," *Policy Studies Review*, 1, 2 (1981):231-235.

4. *Ibid.*

5. Several governors have recognized the relationship between competent local governmental management and the overall competence and viability of their states. Governor Bob Graham of Florida and Governor Mark White of Texas represent what is hopefully a developing trend among governors in this regard.

6. James L. Perry and Kenneth L. Kraemer, *Public Management: Public and Private Perspectives* (Palo Alto, CA: Mayfield Publishing, 1983).

7. Richard E. Boyatzis, *The Competent Manager: A Model for Effective Performance* (New York: John Wiley and Sons, 1982).

13
Building Capacity to Govern

GRAHAM S. TOFT

A time of turbulence is a dangerous time, but its greatest danger is a temptation to deny reality.

Peter F. Drucker

For public and private sectors alike, governance is undergoing a quiet revolution. "Board development," as it is called in the business literature, and its public sector equivalent, "governance capacity building", are being spurred by a common set of forces: turbulent environments in which "doing the right things" (picking winning strategies) is as important as "doing things right" (managing day-to-day operations). Governing assemblies are being called upon to be more accountable for long-term survival and growth. This calls for movement away from a passive/reactive mode to a more proactive mode through improved representation, participation, democratization and strategic planning.

Corporate boards, in particular, have been displaying increased planning activity[1], which entails articulating the mission, setting goals, formulating strategies, and overseeing performance. This "strategic" aspect of governance is the integrating theme of this chapter.

Capacity-building efforts for elected officials are not new. Tailor-made training programs are available in most states and through such organizations as the International City Management Association and the National League of Cities. What is relatively new are capacity-building efforts directed at the legislative assembly as a whole. In this chapter the training of elected officials is viewed as one of a larger constellation of approaches aimed at strengthening the performance of local legislative bodies. According to the 1982 Census of Governments, there were 82,688 units of government in the United States in 1982. Most of these are governed by appointed or elected assemblies of civic-minded volunteers, i.e., city councils, county councils, school boards, and planning commissions. Because of the part-time and transient nature of service on such assemblies, they become particularly stressed in times of rapid social, technological, and economic change when a collective vision and long-term outlook are required.

The challenge of the eighties in governance capacity building is on every front: theory development, conceptual frameworks for planned interventions, technical assistance and consultation tools, and consultation styles. This chapter surveys the state of the art, beginning with a brief introduction to trends in governance and a definition which stresses the strategic aspects of governing in turbulent times. The main body of the chapter comprises three sections addressing desirable qualities for strategic governance, intervention approaches and techniques, and the role of the third-party consultant. The chapter concludes with an attempt to integrate the popular notion of civic entrepreneurship with that of strategic governance.

Trends In Governance

During the post-World War II era of abundance and world economic dominance, American organizations become preoccupied with how to manage. It was the era of the "organization man." In the eighties, with a more "malarial" economy (repetitious chills and fevers) and more limited resources, organizations are becoming concerned with how to govern, with positioning and alignment. It is the era of the "strategic man."

Parallel trends between corporate and civic governance are striking. Governing assemblies of both types are becoming more proactive. They want to be "co-planners" with the chief executive. Their members are becoming more sophisticated and informed. They are increasingly concerned about broader issues of survival and performance. The most recent Korn/Ferry study shows that priority issues for corporate boards are finance and strategy[2]. Governing assemblies are also becoming more open to self-evaluation and self-improvement efforts in order to fulfill their expanding roles. It is this latter trend that provides the demand for consultation and programs in "board development" and "governance capacity building." The principal actors in such efforts are the council members, the chief executive, and their respective support staffs.

Governance Defined

Governance is the formulation of policies, the establishment of broad guidelines as to how policies are to be implemented, and the routine oversight of administrative execution and environmental change. In short, governance is organizationwide strategy formulation, system orchestration, and performance navigation.

The purpose of governance capacity building in the eighties is to smooth and accelerate the transition towards more local self-reliance. It is an empowerment approach: helping governmental decision-making bodies acquire systems, processes, and behaviors that advance local abilities to solve complex problems constructively and creatively and in such a way as to increase the likelihood that policies will be executed and desired outcomes realized.

"Capacity to govern" is a megaconcept, the meaning of which can be more clearly understood by articulating its component capacities. Table 1 displays a categorization of governance capacities under three broad headings: capacities for making policy, capacities for implementing policy, and capacities for networking. The first group is subdivided into capacities of information systems and capacities of problem solving and strategy development. The former includes access to adequate data sources, abilities to scan the changing external environment, keeping up-to-date with technological change and tools of governance, and access to sound technical studies. The latter, referred to in this chapter as "strategic governance," deals with the effectiveness of both the governing group and its individual members to conceptualize problems, generate alternatives, and formulate winning strategies.

The second group of capacities, those for implementing policy, is also subdivided into two categories: capacities for policy control and capacities for policy planning. Policy control mechanisms include legal authority, fiscal and descretionary powers, and program oversight. Policy planning mechanisms are those available for translating broad goals and strategies into implementable plans, such as procedures for documenting policies and linking planning to budgeting.

Table 1. Governance Capacities

Capacities For Making Policy

Capacities of Information Systems

1. Data Acquisition and Retrieval
2. Issues Management and Environmental Scanning
3. Awareness of Technological Developments
4. Expert Analyses and Technical Studies
5. Comparative Studies
6. Knowledge of the Tools of Governance

Capacities of Problem Solving/Strategy Development (Strategic Governance)

1. Group Capacities: group processes for problem solving, including conflict management, negotiation, consensus building, reconciliation, and brainstorming
2. Individual Capacities: creativity, determination, strategic thinking
3. Group Self-Evaluation

Capacities For Implementing Policy

Capacities for Policy Control

1. Legal Authority
2. Fiscal Powers
3. Influencing Strategies
4. Program Evaluation, Oversight, and Sunset

Capacities for Policy Planning

1. Documentation of Policy Statements
2. Breakdown of Policy Statements into Policy Objectives, Operational Strategies and Time-Action Plans
3. Linkages Between Policy Planning and Budgeting

Capacities For Networking

1. Information-Sharing Among Units of Government
2. Shaping External Environments Through Federations and Alliances

The third group of capacities concerns the federations and alliances a unit of government has with other units in order to improve its policy development through shared information or through coalitions for mobilizing support.

Strategic Governance—Priority for the Eighties

While all of these capacities are important, strategic governance is singled out as being central to strengthening capacity to govern in the eighties. Strategic governance is defined as the decision tasks of ensuring that the organization is aligned with the demands and forces of its changing environment; of ratifying statements concerning mission, goals and strategies; of allocating appropriate resources in accordance with these goals; and of routinely reviewing organizational performance. The processes of strategic governance include: collective interaction for creative problem solving, individual strategic thinking, and routine evaluation by the governing board of its own operational effectiveness. Strategic governance also includes imparting vision, direction, and enthusiasm to the organization.

"Strategic governance" is used in this chapter in the sense that "strategic management" is used in management terminology, i.e., one element of a larger constellation of functions. While strategic management may be performed by specialists in larger firms, it is an ingredient of all management positions, albeit in varying degrees. Equally, strategic governance is one of a number of governance functions required of local legislators and governing assemblies.

There are at least four reasons for focusing on strategy as the key to local governance capacity building in the eighties. First, the environment in which local governments must make decisions has become more turbulent due to a shrinking federal and state government presence. In recent decades, the federal and state governments have acted as buffers for local governments by protecting them against the full impact of the forces of economic change and by acting as universal change agents. Presently, stability and predictability in the policy environment facing local governments are being removed, and local officials must become their own pace-setters. Just as firms lose their expertise in competitive strategy in regulated environments[3], local self-reliant behaviors may have been weakened by thirty years of federal protectionism. Local officials must reacquire and strengthen their capacities to understand, channel, and manipulate change so as to achieve a viable present and promising future for their communities.

Second, local community leaders must find ways of removing themselves from the "firehouse" environment of day-to-day crises and special-interest concerns to look at the big picture. The greatest challenge facing local officials is to rise above immediate concerns, to retreat, to ask basic questions concerning "where are we going" and "what business must we be in to get there". Many local elected officials are dedicated to making an impact on their community, to leaving something worthwhile behind. To accomplish this in a fast-paced, volatile environment demands a long-range, strategic outlook.

Third, one of the major concerns of the commentators of federal capacity to govern is a weakening of the forces of coherence and unity. The social reforms of the sixties and seventies emphasizing liberation, community control, participation, and equal rights have contributed to an evermore pluralistic America. Power is more diffuse and democracy more adversary. Jane Mansbridge points out that a heterogeneous polity requires both adversary and unitary democratic processes[4]. A strategy development approach strengthens unitary democracy through its emphasis on solidarity, areawide perspective, and mutual goals.

Fourth, the art of statecraft is being rediscovered. Given the fiscal constraints and continuing pressure for services at all levels, governments are turning to off-budget and nonfiscal mechanisms to achieve public purposes[5]. At the local level this translates into a smorgasbord of "nonservice" alternatives[6]: contracting out, franchises, load shedding, consolidation, neighborhood association delivery, vouchers, user fees, and regulated markets. To address such alternatives, local governments must distinguish between their traditional service-provision role and their policy-making role[7], the latter having the potential to benefit from recent developments in corporate strategy.

Scholars of contemporary American governance, such as James Sundquist and the late Stephen Bailey, are inclined to believe that solutions to the crisis of federal capacity to govern lie in institutional, political, legal, and structural reforms[8]. From the local perspective, Yates similarly cautions that cities are inherently incapable of strategic responsiveness[9]. In this chapter, it is assumed that we can move beyond this institutionalist view. We know enough about the local policy-making process, about group dynamics, and about the tools of strategic management to modify governance by the design and incorporation of "technologies of strategic choice." These decision aids, both substantive and procedural, offer the potential for near-term improvements in policy judgment as well as the stimulus for the longer run institutional adjustments that Sundquist, Bailey, and Yates have considered desirable.

Key Factors for Success in Strategic Governance

As a first step toward the design of deliberative interventions in local governance, the qualitative differences between good and poor governance must be identified. This can be achieved by a process of observing winners and losers in a competitive setting. Through a synthesis process of intuition and peer review, certain key factors for success are identified, the logic underlying the management best-seller *In Search of Excellence* by Peters and Waterman.

By such a process, four hard-core qualities of good governance are proposed. The following can form the basis for both the design of intervention strategies to improve the strategic elements of governance and the evaluation of governance capacity-building efforts: policy leadership, strategic thinking and policy judgment, legislative organization and management, and governance information systems. Similarities can be observed between this list and Graham's predictive index for measuring capacity to govern: goals, doctrines, rational structures, authority and leadership[10]. "Goals and doctrines" corresponds with strategic thinking, "rational structures" with legislative organization and management, and "authority and leadership" with policy leadership.

Policy Leadership

"Policy leadership" is the word most commonly equated with local governance capacity. However, to avoid confusion, its meaning should be restricted to fit with the widely accepted notion of leadership, i.e., actions involving human interaction and influence directed at group goal achievement. Some characteristics associated with the common use of the term "policy leadership" are: a sense of public or community responsibility beyond special-interest and personal ideology; a desire to hear and aggregate citizen demands and concerns; a flexibility to anticipate change; a willingness to participate in and mobilize for change; a quiet self-confidence in the face of uncertainty and turbidity; and a breadth of vision. In short, policy leadership is being gutsy with, and on behalf of, the whole community. Heroic acts of policy leadership are considered to be "civic entrepreneurship" and are addressed later in this chapter.

Based on the functional approach to the study of leadership[11], policy leadership would be defined as actions of elected officials which (1) move the governing board and the community toward the clarification of common purposes, goals and strategies and (2) enlist and maintain follower commitment and collaboration toward defined goals and strategies. This definition highlights the two functional types of "leadership acts": the task function of mobilizing for goal and strategy formulation and the group maintenance function of inspiring others to become part of the city's future. The key ingredient in both functions is influence[12].

Strategic Thinking and Policy Judgment

While policy leadership is concerned with influencing skills for the common good, strategic thinking and policy judgment deal with the cognitive skills of solution making. The ability to impart vision or concern and to marshal human resources is different from that required to search for, organize, and test ideas.

Kenichi Ohmae describes strategic thinking as "a combination of rational analysis, based on the real nature of things, and imaginative reintegration of all the different items into a new pattern, using nonlinear brainpower"[13]. Strategic thinking, then, is a form of problem solving, basically creative and intuitive rather than rational, although up-front reality testing and analysis is essential. A second aspect of strategic thinking is that it is highly selective: it necessitates dealing only with the salient issues, the "high ticket" items. The localization, selection, and ranking of salient issues is, again, largely intuitive. A third aspect is that of thinking in terms of relative superiority. There are no absolutes, no ideal or perfect strategies. Strategy is about finding comparative advantage, sustainable edges, and taking advantage of these for survival and growth.

Strategic thinking pertinent to local governance includes:

(1) Getting the critical issues on the table.

(2) Developing a legislative agenda for the term of office.

(3) Regularly reviewing priorities on the legislative agenda so as to keep on the "high ticket items".

(4) Using priority areas and goals to drive the budget.

(5) Following through to ensure thresholds are reached so that change will occur.

(6) Encouraging city administrators to think in a businesslike manner—the wise management of public resources.

Strategic thinking is relevant and applicable to local governments and civic organization for several reasons. First, it does not require major planning and analysis capacities. Some of the most outstanding corporate performers have relatively small planning staffs. Second, strategic thinking can be learned: "There are ways in which the mind of the strategist can be reproduced, or simulated, by people who may lack a natural talent for strategy"[14]. Third, strategic thinking is a constructive response for dealing with the new competitive environment facing local governments in the eighties.

Legislative Organization and Management

The view of policy leadership presented earlier is largely concerned with the behavioral variables of group members. Bass suggests that leadership is also a function of providing structure within an organization or group which facilitates goal attainment and enables participants to overcome barriers to those attainments[15]. In this sense legislative organization and management might be viewed as part of policy leadership.

The path an issue takes through the public decision-making process may significantly affect the policy outcome. For example, the content of a draft bill or ordinance may be flavored by the legislative committee to which it is assigned. In addition, the procedures for dealing with public issues have become more complex in the past twenty years. This is partly due to the very complexity and interdependence of contemporary problems and partly due to equity concerns for citizen participation, open meetings, and freedom of information.

In this context, productivity improvement in local government should move beyond a concern for how the work gets done in the street-level and support departments. The entire local decision-making process of city councils, planning commissions, county commissioners and councils, regulatory and advisory boards is a major area for procedures productivity improvement and organization reform. Listed in Table 2 are some key areas for productivity improvement in local legislative operations.

Governance Information Systems

Recent research on the operations of corporate boards suggests that information is a most critical factor in board development[16]. Control of information is recognized as a very effective method by which chief

Table 2. Areas for Productivity Improvement in Local Legislative Operations

Agenda Setting—What is the procedure for ranking issues?

Agenda Management—How is time allocated among agenda items? How much coverage do the "big issues" get versus the routine and the trivial?

Legislative Committee System—Are committees doing their homework? Are they providing initial policy formulation and data collection prior to hearings by the whole council?

Information Flow Between Legislature and Executive—Is there regular interchange between council and mayor or manager, such as briefing sessions before council meetings, over lunch, and so on?

Brainstorming or Work-Study Sessions—Are there provisions for regular informal work sessions of the council to clarify issues, throw out ideas, dream, and so on?

Policy Documentation—Does the council get goals and plans out in the open with municipal policy statements, supplementary statements to the budget, ordinance preambles, and so on?

Legislative Oversight—Is there routine feedback to the council on the progress of administrative departments, agencies, boards and commissions?

Span of Control—How many independent boards, commissions, task forces, and so forth report to the council? Is this realistic and are the separation of powers and accountabilities clear?

Group Self-Evaluation—Does the council meet occasionally to review its own performance?

executives keep their boards in a passive/inactive mode. The availability of information and its open discussion tends to direct boards away from largely legal and routine matters to future-oriented, strategic, and oversight issues.

Boards often suffer from information overload. The problem is not supply but the pertinence, quality and organization of data. Considerable thought must be given to a governance information system (GIS) linked with the inhouse management information system. Particular design features of a GIS are thorough indexing for ready access; focus on critical variables that indicate changing external and internal environments; trend monitoring of organizational performance using key indicators; and methods of display readily interpretable by the non-expert (such as issue diagrams, decision trees, product-market matrices, life-cycle diagrams, portfolio matrices).

Technologies of Strategic Choice

The nature and purpose of practical efforts to improve local governance depend upon the relative importance given the previously mentioned four key factors for success. This section compares and contrasts five different approaches to governance capacity building.

Concerning their work in urban planning governance, Friend and Jessup asked: "How can those who are elected to exercise choice on our behalf preserve and extend their capacity to choose discriminatingly, when the sheer complexity of the issues facing them tends all the time to make them increasingly dependent on the skills and judgments of their professional advisors?"[17]. They saw their challenge as reconciling the basic principle of democratic control with the use of techniques that match the complexity of contemporary planning problems. These they called "technologies of strategic choice." In a similar vein, Carver calls for a "technology of governance" for nonprofit and governmental boards, a need "to do for governance what precision management techniques have done for operations"[18].

Technologies of strategic choice are the approaches, methods, and techniques employed to arrive at strategic decisions. Technologies of strategic choice are embedded in all social organizations. They vary from being highly rigorous and manipulated by experts to being loosely structured, unsophisticated "inner logics" acquired through socialization.

The five approaches briefly described in this section survey the state of the art, which is largely an integration of operations research/decision sciences and the applied behavioral sciences. The immediate challenge is to develop techologies, both social and analytical, that address the following considerations:

(1) How to get long-range thinking in the quick-response world of the elected official.

(2) How to build holistic thinking (civic trusteeship) among delegates representing different interests.

(3) How to strengthen conflict management in a fragmented and suspicion-filled decision environment.

(4) How to build trust so that individual policy judgments and novel ideas can be shared openly.

(5) How to minimize additional time required of the elected official. Most importantly, how to incorporate new technologies of strategic choice into the regular decision-making process.

(6) How to reduce the resistance of elected officials to new decision-making techniques.

Management Training Approach

Management training focuses on building the competencies of individuals. In the form of elected-official-training programs, it is the most widespread and long-standing effort at governance capacity building. These programs are of three main types: basic knowledge—the legal, fiscal and institutional framework; personal competencies—skill development, such as time management, conflict management, and media relations; and options awareness—choices in nonservice alternatives and the tools of governance.

Difficulties with the training approach are: (1) it assumes that the nature of the capacity problem is understood; (2) it focuses on the individual and therefore does not adequately address the task interdependence of most governance choice making; and (3) there is no guarantee of knowledge transfer to the organization. These drawbacks are highlighted in Table 3 by comparing the traditional training approach with organization-specific approaches.

With organization-specific approaches, it is assumed that each local governance system is unique. On-site diagnosis leads to prescribed technologies of strategic choice most appropriate to enhancing local policy-making activities. The goal with all these approaches is common, that of building whole solutions and cultivating commitment, tailored to the problems and needs of each governing assembly. This assumes that consultants bring with them a repertoire of organization-specific approaches, such as:

The Organization Development Approach

Probably the most widely used organization-specific approach is organization development (OD). Organization development is concerned with the system-wide change of human and social variables through the use of applied behavioral science techniques. The key variables for change are social processes, values, and attitudes.

Table 3. Traditional Training Versus Organization-Specific Approaches

Program Design Variables	Elected Official Training	Organization-Specific Approaches
Client	The individual	A particular local governing body
Goals	Improving individual performance	Improving task inter-dependence and governance effective-ness
Learning Group	Unrelated	Intact work group
Content	Knowledge acquisition and skill develop-ment	Knowledge, skills, roles, attitudes, values, substantive issues (i.e., content and process)
Specificity	Generalized material	Organization-specific material
Transferability to the local jurisdiction	Little guarantee	High probability
Program Format	Structured	Guidelined, flexible
Prelearning Input	Usually very little	Interviews to tailor-make the inter-vention
Learning Method	Primarily didactic	Didactic, experiential, topical
	(lecture-discussion method)	(group activities around common problems)
Degree of Turbulence	Well-suited to stability	Well-suited to change

The National League of Cities' Council Policy Leaders Program is a prominent example of governance capacity building using this approach[19]. The initial phase of the project involved a survey-feedback technique. This was followed by tailor-made training programs for each of the six cities. For three of the cities, this second phase focused on council organization and procedures. Typical areas addressed were committee organization, agenda and report format, and coordination between legislature and executive.

The other three cities chose a training effort directed at council decision making and interpersonal communications. Particular assistance was provided in consensus building, role clarification, effective communication and team building.

The Strategy Development Approach

In strategy development the key variables for change are strategic planning and problem solving. Strategy development technologies draw heavily from both the strategic management and organization development literature. They have a substance/task focus rather than the relational/group maintenance focus of traditional OD and are particularly suited to organizations in transition[20].

The author has field-tested the open-systems-planning technology (OSP) with four city councils with moderate success, using improved group planning and problem solving as the criteria of evaluation[21]. The primary goal of OSP is to stimulate the unconstrained exchange of ideas, enabling those who govern to improve their group strategic thinking and trust. By providing a structured workshop comprising core mission definition, environmental scanning, performance appraisal, and action planning, ideas are "managed" in such a way as to lead to constructive and realistic solutions.

The Social Judgment Theory Approach

Social judgment theory focuses on the cognitive sources of disagreement among decision-makers. The cognitive process by which an individual integrates items of information into a single judgment is called judgment policy. Self-knowledge of the implicit characteristics of one's judgment policy help in understanding why one makes certain judgment calls and provides a systematic basis for negotiations with policy-makers of differing judgment policies. The social judgment theorists point out that as a problem becomes more complex, conflict resulting from cognitive differences, as opposed to self-interests and interpersonal differences becomes more pronounced. They believe that the externalization of the basis for a decision-maker's judgment alongside the technical analysis of a policy problem become a powerful "symmetrical decision aid"[22].

With the aid of interactive computer graphics, social judgment theory uses mathematical and pictorial descriptions to portray a decision-maker's underlying values and priorities. This is achieved through a four-part process. First, the decision-makers must jointly agree on a set of criteria common to their judgments concerning a particular issue. Second, each is asked to judge a set of hypothetical alternatives. Third, a regression model for each person is run using the hypothetical judgments as the dependent variable and the selected criteria as the independent variables. Fourth, the coefficients and structure of each regression equation are interpreted to indicate the weights being assigned to various criteria and the way in which criteria are being aggregated into a composite judgment call. While the analytical procedures are quite complex, "canned" programs are now available.

Experiments with social judgment theory in local governance have been conducted by the Center for Research on Judgment and Policy at the University of Colorado[23]. Applications include budgeting, land use and criminal justice. One interesting application was a study carried out for the Denver City Council to aid the council in selecting appropriate handgun ammunition for the Denver Police Department[24]. This involved a three-phase process: (1) obtaining the social policy of the city council, (2) obtaining the technical judgments of ballistics and medical experts, and (3) combining social policy judgments with technical judgments.

In the first phase the council was required to determine what weights would be given to three agreed-upon selection criteria: amount of injury, stopping effectiveness, and threat to bystanders. Council members were asked to make their best judgment as to the relative desirability of each of thirty hypothetical bullet configurations. After thirty judgments were made, they were shown pictorial displays of their judgment policies, that is, the relative weights (importance) they were giving injury, stopping effectiveness, and threat to bystanders. In the second phase, ballistics and medical experts provided ratings of the potential severity of injury, stopping effectiveness, and threat to bystanders relative to eighty real bullets. Average ratings were analyzed by regression techniques. The third phase involved graphical displays on which trade-off decisions could be made using both the social policy and technical judgments.

The Systems Analysis/Operations Research Approach

Systems analysis technologies are used primarily to model the technical/substantive aspects of policy issues. However, some can be used as decision/strategy aids. Interpretive Structural Modeling (ISM), for example, is an interactive computer graphics technology used to structure elements and relationships between elements in a complex system where participants are working collectively on a problem[25]. It has been used to aid goal structuring and budget ranking in local governments. In the latter case the elements were units of cutback. The city council as a group was required to choose between pairs of elements and ISM was then used to arrange these cutback units into a priority order that represented the group's consensus[26].

Operations research techniques also have potential application in the study of work flow and productivity in legislative operations.

Comparison of Organization Specific Approaches

In Table 4 these four organization-specific approaches are compared using as criteria the key factors for success discussed earlier and targeted variables for change. Variables for change are subdivided according to process variables, i.e., those that are human, social or behavioral, and substance variables, i.e., those dealing with tangible plans, resource allocations and formal structures.

As a coarse approximation, OD and strategy development approaches are concerned with the generation of ideas, commitments, and enthusiasm. They focus attention on a conducive social environment in which elected officials are able to creatively interact on critical problems. On the other hand, social judgment theory and systems analysis approaches are largely concerned with the clarification of ideas, data needs to test ideas, and the bases for selection among ideas. This dichotomy somewhat parallels the two-pronged prescription from Ellis for cultivating "responsive management"[27]. He suggests that to solicit and guide appropriate responses in a turbulent environment senior management must (1) stimulate initiatives and (2) support initiatives. The former is concerned with the generation of pools of ideas and initiatives through a free atmosphere, supportive climate, and loose structure. The latter deals with arriving at closure for action and is assisted by organizational and informational arrangements. Since both qualities are desirable, governance consultants would do well to be familiar with complementary capacity-building approaches.

The Third Party In Governance Capacity Building

Organization-specific approaches frequently call for a third-party consultant/technical assistance provider. Third-party intervention at the strategic apex of public organizations is unique in a number of respects. The presence, energies, and expertise of a third-party consultant can be

Table 4. Comparison of Organization-Specific Approaches

Targets	Organization Development Approach	Strategy Development Approach	Social Judgment Theory Approach	Systems Analysis/Operation Research Approach
Key Factors for Success (ranked)	1. Policy Leadership 2. Legislative Organization and Management	1. Strategic Thinking and Policy Judgment 2. Policy Leadership	1. Strategic Thinking and Policy Judgment 2. Governance Information Systems	1. Governance Information Systems 2. Legislative Organization and Management
Variables for Change: Process (human/social/behavioral)	Team cohesion Interpersonal relations Group communication Role clarification	Group planning and problem solving Brainstorming and creative thinking Conflict management	Individual cognition Exchange of subjective information Group openness	Group problem structuring Consensus building
Variables for Change: Substance (plans/resource allocations/structures)	Committee organization Coordination Agenda management	Environmental scan Appraisal of strengths and weaknesses Mapping opportunities and threats	Weighting of individual preferences Decision criteria	Goals Priorities Legislative work flow analysis Information needs assessment

viewed as an obstruction of traditional political processes. Furthermore, in keeping with a kind of Jacksonian mind-set, elected officials are inclined to feel that governing, somewhat akin to parenting, comes naturally. To call in policy-making assistance may be interpreted as admission of failure.

On the other hand, elected officials are frequently heard airing frustrations about their inability to effect constructive and creative change. Considerable potential for improving the workings of governing boards exist, but the credibility of the consultant is crucial. Both prestige and style of consultation are important.

The selection of a consultation style centers around two issues: technical expertise versus process consultation and interpersonal process consultation versus instrumental process consultation.

Process consultation addresses the problem-solving activities of the client system as opposed to the substances of the problems per se. When local elected officials gather to resolve issues, they respect those who can provide technical input. Pure process consultation does not appear to have a great deal of appeal. A mixed content/process style is preferable. At least one of the consultants must have a good working knowledge of the problems facing local governments, including a repertoire of possible solutions and factual information about approaches being taken by similar communities.

Elected officials do value the contribution of process consultation where it addresses concrete work flow problems, i.e., instrumental process consultation. Lipshitz and Sherwood distinguish between interpersonal and instrumental process consultation as follows:

> The focus of instrumental process analysis is on the person as doer of work. How he perceives his role, how he prefers to conduct his activities, and what is their impact on others. The purpose of an instrumental intervention is to change work relationships. Frequently, that involves bargaining and negotiating for mutual adjustments. The focus of interpersonal process analysis goes beyond the person as a role incumbent. To use a tired cliche, the focus is on the person as a *human being*. Interpersonal process analysis is concerned with feelings, attitudes, and perceptions that organization members have about one another.[28]

There appears to be little place in governance capacity building for T-group-type training. The "specificity proposition" appears to hold very strongly: consultative intervention is more likely to succeed where it is problem-specific, time-specific, concrete, and practical. Problems can be substantive or procedural/relational, but should be addressed from the perspective of "how can this group get its job done better." In short, it requires a human resources, rather than a human relations, perspective[29].

Civic Entrepreneurship Capacity Building

Underlying the preceding discussion is an emphasis on rationality, creativity, and good will as the basis for strengthening strategic governance. In addition, there will always be the continuing need for the heroic act, what some are calling "civic entrepreneurship"[30]. The civic entrepreneur is the leader of exceptional personal vision, ability to mobilize resources, and strategic intuition. He or she is the civic equivalent of the company founder or company former: not necessarily the conceiver of the idea, nor the inventor, nor owner[31], but the mover and shaker. The civic entrepreneur is one who is able to make quantum jumps in the ways of organizing resources in order to meet changing demands with creative responses under contradictory or ambiguous circumstances[32]. In the words of Theodore White: "The Legend of La Guardia was most important. It takes only one such commanding personality per generation to change a city, state or nation."[33]

Cultivating civic entrepreneurship is one of the unmet challenges in governance capacity building. While programs to advance private entrepreneurship through new business institutes are burgeoning, we have not found ways to equally bring forth nonutilized entrepreneurial potential for the collective good. Growth economists argue that innovation and entrepreneurship are two of the few expandable resources in an economy[34].

Civic entrepreneurship education/capacity-building is hampered by a sluggishness on the part of local officials to accept the challenge of community-based growth. While they complain of insufficient legal and fiscal powers and of intergovernmental interference, many appear reticent to more aggressively exploit the powers and capacities they already have. Due to a preceding era of federal intervention in local affairs, it is possible that impoverished (subordinate) policy roles have led to impoverished motives and skills. In his recent book, *The Leader*, Michael Maccoby points out that throughout American history, ideal leadership expressed vision and values that brought out the best in the social character[35]. He believes no vision has yet inspired the new social character of the eighties. Perhaps civic entrepreneurship education could begin by rekindling and nurturing visionary thinking.

Conclusion

In this chapter governance has been approached from an open-systems-theory perspective with emphasis on the interaction between an organization and its environment. Governance is a complex sociotechnical system comprised of elected officials, chief executive(s) and their advisors, their motivations and feelings of control, their creative thinking, their powers to act, governance information systems and work flows, the repertoire of governance tools, and so on. The bottom line for assessing the performance of such a system is how well a community adapts to its changing sociopolitical and economic environment. Thus, in turbulent times, the bottom line for assessing the effectiveness of governance capacity-building efforts is how well they put in place systems, processes and behaviors that facilitate creative and transformational policy and their orchestration for change.

Strategic governance has been proposed as the focal concern in the design of such capacity-building interventions for the eighties. It targets the problem-solving, goal-setting, planning, resource-allocating, and oversight functions of governing assemblies with the intent of forcing local officials into a generalist mode. This entails trying to move governing assemblies away from partisan, factional, and piecemeal thinking to looking at the big picture on a long-term horizon.

John Naisbitt describes the shift from centralization to decentralization in the United States as follows:

> For example, we have no national urban policy because the old top-down, master-plan approach is completely out of tune with the times. It is inappropriate to ask: "Are we going to save our cities?" We are going to save some of our cities and we are not going to save others. We are going to save parts of some of our cities and allow other parts to decline. And the whole process is all going to turn on local initiative. The only "national urban policy" that is in tune with the times is one that is responsive to, and rewarding of, local initiative.[36]

The laissez-faire realities of the "new localism" are upon us: "the willingness of some leaders to tackle their own problems aggressively will leave more reticent communities at a needless disadvantage."[37] Communities and their leaders who want to formulate and implement winning strategies will need to take a hard look at their governance systems.

Local self-government has always been the product of deliberately exercised capacities. While the field of governance capacity building is still in its infancy, recent social and technical innovations indicate promise for sustaining democratic control in an increasingly complex and turbulent decision environment.

Postscript—The Personal Challenge

At the personal level the challenge of governance capacity building is at least twofold. First, there are the sociocultural barriers between academics and management consultants on the one hand and part-time elected officials and local government chief executives on the other. Second, the work is filled with paradoxes and ambiguities; facts versus interpersonal relationships, analytics versus intuition, substance versus process, and political power versus common sense. For those who enjoy sociotechnical puzzles, who can cross disciplinary boundaries with ease, who are patient, who are themselves strategic thinkers and who believe democratic government is viable but not necessarily assured, there are abundant challenges for the eighties.

Notes

1. Ahmad Tashakori and William Bolton, "A Look at the Board's Role in Planning," *Journal of Business Strategy* (Winter 1982): 64-70.

2. Korn/Ferry International, Board of Directors Tenth Annual Study (New York: 1983).

3. John F. Mahon and Edwin A. Murray, "A Strategic Planning for Regulated Companies," *Strategic Management Journal* 2 (1981): 251-262.

4. Jane J. Mansbridge, *Beyond Adversary Democracy* (New York: Basic Books, 1980).

5. Frederick C. Mosher, "The Changing Responsibilities and Tactics of the Federal Government," *Public Administration Review* (November-December 1980): 541-548.

6. Steven A. Waldorn et al., *Rediscovering Governance* (Menlo Park, CA: SRI International, 1980).

7. Committee for Economic Development, *Public-Private Partnership: An Opportunity for Urban Communities* (Washington, D.C: 1982) 2.

8. James L. Sundquist, "The Crisis of Competence in Government," in *Setting National Priorities*, ed. Joseph A Peckham (Washington, D.C.: The Brookings Institute, 1980): 531-562).

9. Douglas Yates, *The Ungovernable City* (Cambridge, MA: MIT Press, 1978).

10. George A. Graham, *America's Capacity to Govern* (University: University of Alabama Press, 1960).

11. James E Spotts, "The Problem of Leadership: A Look at Some Recent Findings of Behavioral Science Research," in William R. Lassey and Richard R. Fernandez, *Leadership and Social Change* (La Jolla, CA: University of California, 1976).

12. William R. Lassey, "Dimensions of Leadership," in Lassey and Fernandez, *Leadership and Social Change*.

13. Kenichi Ohmae, *The Mind of the Strategist* (New York: McGraw-Hill, 1982) 13-15.

14. Ibid. 5.

15. Bernard M. Bass, "Some Observations about a General Theory of Leadership and Interpersonal Behavior," in *Leadership and Social Challenge*, 68.

16. Tashakori, "A Look at the Board's Role in Planning."

17. J.K. Friend and W.N. Jessup, *Local Government and Strategic Choice* (London: Tavistock, 1982).

18. John Carver, "Business Leadership on Nonprofit Boards," Monograph 12 (National Association of Corporate Directors: 1980).

19. Stephen W. Burks and James F. Wolf, *Building City Council Leadership Skills: A Casebook of Models and Methods* (Washington, D.C.: National League of Cities, 1981).

20. Richard Beckhard and Reuben T. Harris, *Organizational Transitions: Managing Complex Change* (Reading, MA: Addison-Wesley, 1977).

21. Graham S. Toft, "Evaluation of an Open-Systems Planning Approach to Collective Problem Solving and Planning among City Officials." Paper presented to the 1982 National Conference of the American Society for Public Administration (March 1982).

22. Kenneth R. Hammond, Jeryl L. Mumpower and Thoams H. Smith, "Linking Environmental Models with Models of Human Judgment: A Symmetrical Decision Aid," in IEEE Transactions on Systems, Man and Cybernetics SMC-7, 5 (May 1977) 359-367.

23. Thomas R. Stewart and Linda Gelberg," Analysis of Judgment Policy: A New Approach for Citizen Participation Planning," *American Institute of Planners Journal* (January 1976): 33-41; and Derick O. Steinmann et al., "Application of Social Judgment Theory in Policy Formulation: An Example," *Journal of Applied Behavioral Science* 13, 1 (1977) 69-88.

24. Kenneth R. Hammond et al., *Report to the Denver City Council and Mayor Regarding the Choice of Handgun Ammunition for the Denver Police Department*, Report 179 (University of Colorado: Center for Research on Judgment and Policy, 1975).

25. George G Lendaris, "Structural Modeling—A Tutorial Guide," *IEEE Transactions on Systems, Man and Cybernetics.* SMC-10, 12 (December 1980): 807-810.

26. James G. Coke and Carl M. Moore, "Coping with a Budgetary Crisis: Helping City Council Decide Where Expenditure Cuts Should Be Made," in Burks and Wolf, *Building City Council Leadership Skills.*

27. R. Jeffrey Ellis, "Improving Management Response in Turbulent Times," *Sloan Management Review* (Winter 1982).

28. Kaanan Lipshitz and John J. Sherwood, "The Effectiveness of Third-Party Process Consultation as a Function of the Consultant's Prestige and Style of Intervention," *Journal of Applied Behavioral Science* 14, 4 (1978) 495.

29. Raymond E. Miles, "Human Relations or Human Resources?" *Harvard Business Review* (July-August 1965).

30. Committee for Economic Development, 2.

31. Albert Shapero, "The Role of Entrepreneurship in Economic Development at the Less-Than-National Level," in *Expanding the Opportunity to Produce,* Robert Friedman and William Schweke (Washington, D.C.: The Corporation for Enterprise Development, 1981) 28.

32. Eugene Lewis, *Public Entrepreneurship* (Bloomington, IN:Indiana University Press, 1980) 9.

33. Theodore White, *America in Search of Itself* (New York:Harper and Row, 1982).

34. H. Liebenstein, "Entrepreneurship and Development," *American Economic Review* (May 1968) 77-79.

35. Michael Maccoby, *The Leader* (New York: Simon and Shuster, 1981) 52.

36. John Naisbitt, *Megatrends* (New York: Warner, 1982).

37. Committee for Economic Development, 6.

Bibliography

Ansoff, Igor H. 1965. *Corporate Strategy: An Analytic Approach to Business and Policy for Growth and Experience*, NY: McGraw-Hill.

Bailey, Stephen K. 1980. "Improving Federal Governance," *Public Administration Review*, Volume 40, No. 6, November/December, pp. 548-552.

Bass, Bernard M. 1976. "Some Observations About a General Theory of Leadership and Interpersonal Behavior," in William R. Lassey and Richard R. Fernandez, *Leadership and Social Change*, La Jolla, California: University Associates, p. 68.

Beckhard, Richard and Reuben T. Harris. 1977. *Organizational Transitions: Managing Complex Change*, Reading, Massachusetts: Addison-Wesley.

Burks, Stephen W. and James F. Wolf. 1981. *Building City Council Leadership Skills: A Casebook of Models and Methods*, Washington, D.C.: National League of Cities, February.

Carver, John. 1980. "Business Leadership on Nonprofit Boards," *Monograph 12*, National Association of Corporate Directors.

Chandler, Alfred. 1962. *Structure and Strategy: Chapters in the History of American Industrial Enterprise*, Cambridge, MA:MIT Press.

Coke, James G. and Carl M. Moore. "Coping with a Budgetary Crisis: Helping City Council Decide Where Expenditure Cuts Should Be Made," in Burks and Wolf.

Committee for Economic Development (CED). 1982. *Public-Private Partnership: An Opportunity for Urban Communities*, Washington, D.C., February, p. 2.

Ellis, R. Jeffery. 1982. "Improving Management Response in Turbulent Times," *Sloan Management Review*, Winter.

Friend, J. K. and W. N. Jessup. 1982. *Local Government and Strategic Choice*, London:Tavistock.

Graham, George A. 1960. *America's Capacity to Govern*, Alabama:University of Alabama Press.

Hammond, Kenneth R., Thomas R. Stewart, Leonard Adelman and Nancy E. Wascoe. 1975. "Report to the Denver City Council and Mayor Regarding The Choice of Handgun Ammunition for the Denver Police Department," Center for Research on Judgement and Policy, *Report No. 179*, University of Colorado.

Hammond, Kenneth R., Jeryl L. Mumpower and Thomas H. Smith. 1977. "Linking Environmental Models with Models of Human Judgment: A Symmetrical Decision Aid," *IEEE Transactions on Systems, Man and Cybernetics,* Volume SMC-7, No. 5, May, pp. 259-367.

Korn/Ferry International. 1983. "Board of Directors Tenth Annual Study," New York, February.

Lassey, William R. 1976. "Dimensions of Leadership," in Lassey and Fernandez.

Lendaris, George G. 1980. "Structural Modeling - A Tutorial Guide," *IEEE Transactions on Systems, Man And Cybernetics,* Volume SMC-10, No. 12, December, pp. 807-810.

Lewis, Eugene. 1980. *Public Entrepreneurship,* Bloomington, IN:Indiana University Press, p. 9.

Liebenstein, H. 1968. "Entrepreneurship and Development," *American Economic Review,* May, pp. 77-79.

Lipshitz, Kaanan and John J. Sherwood. 1978. "The Effectiveness of Third-Party Process Consultation as a Function of the Consultant's Prestige and Style of Intervention," *Journal of Applied Behavioral Science,* Volume 14, No. 4, P. 495.

Maccoby, Michael. 1981. *The Leader,* NY:Simon and Schuster, p. 52.

Mahon, John F. and Edwin A. Murray. 1981. "Strategic Planning for Regulated Companies," *Strategic Management Journal,* Volume 2, pp. 251-262.

Mansbridge, Jane J. 1980. *Beyond Adversary Democracy,* New York:Basic Books.

Miles, Raymond E. 1965. "Human Relations or Human Resources," *Harvard Business Review,* July-August.

Mintzberg, Henry. 1973. "Strategy Making in Three Modes," *California Management Review,* 16(2), pp. 44-53.

Mosher, Frederick C. 1980. "The Changing Responsibilities and Tactics of the Federal Government," *Public Administration Review,* November/December, pp. 541-548.

Naisbitt, John. 1982. *Megatrends,* New York: Warner.

Ohmae, Kenichi. 1982. *The Mind of the Strategist,* New York:McGraw-Hill, pp. 13-15.

Salamon, Lester M. 1981. "Rethinking Public Management:Third-Party Government and the Changing Forms of Government Action," *Public Policy,* Vol. 29, No. 3, Summer, pp. 255-275.

Shapero, Albert. 1981. "The Role of Entrepreneurship in Economic Development at the Less-Than National Level," in Robert Friedman and William

Schweke, *Expanding the Opportunity to Produce*, Washington, D.C.:The Corporation for Enterprise Development, p. 28.

Spotts, James E. 1976. "The Problem of Leadership: A Look at Some Recent Findings of Behavioral Science Research," in Lassey and Fernandez, pp. 44-63.

Steinmann, Derick O., Thomas H. Smith, Linda G. Jurdem and Kenneth R. Hammond. 1977. "Application of Social Judgment Theory in Policy Formulation: An Example," *Journal of Applied Behavioral Science*, Volume 13, No. 1, pp. 69-88.

Stewart, Thomas R. and Linda Gelberg. 1976. "Analysis of Judgment Policy: A New Approach for Citizen Participation Planning," *American Institute of Planners Journal*, January, pp. 33-41.

Sundquist, James L. 1980. "The Crisis of Competence in Government, " in Joseph A. Peckman (ed.), *Setting National Priorities*, Washington, D.C.: Brookings, pp. 531-563.

Tashokori, Ahmad and William Bolton. 1982. "A Look at the Board's Role in Planning," *Journal of Business Strategy*, Winter, pp. 64-70.

Toft, Graham S. 1982. "Evaluation of an Open-systems Planning Approach to Collective Problem-Solving and Planning Among City Officials," paper presented the 1982 National Conference of the American Society for Public Administration, March.

Waldhorn, Steven A., et al. 1980. *Rediscovering Governance*, Menlo Park, CA:SRI International.

Warfield, John N. 1976. *Societal Systems: Planning, Policy and Complexity*, New York:John Wiley.

White, Theodore H. 1982. *America in Search of Itself*, NY:Harper and Row.

Yates, Douglas. 1978. *The Ungovernable City*, Cambridge:MIT Press.

VI
Federal Effects on Municipal Management Capacity

14

The Federal Role in Capacity Building: Lessons In Energy and Financial Management

CHARLES R. WARREN AND KATHLEEN D. WARREN

Is There a Federal Role?

Most people agree that there is a need to strengthen the management capacity of state and local government, but there is little consensus on where the responsibility for management improvement lies. Some would contend that state and local management is like "state's rights" and "home rule," or to paraphrase an old dictum—"government heal thyself!"

The public administration and "good government" community has consistently supported federal programs to strengthen state and local managerial capacity. Such prominent bodies as the Office of Management and Budget and the National Science Foundation have advocated a federal commitment to capacity building and have documented the need for such programs.[1] Despite their arguments, federal support in this area has virtually disappeared. The 701 general planning assistance program has been eliminated, as has the Office of Personnel Management's Intergovernmental Personnel Program. One is hard-pressed to find any significant program among the 500 plus intergovernmental grant programs designed explicity to build management capacity at the state and local levels.

The arguments against a federal role are fairly straightforward. One can point to the principles of federalism and suggest that state and

271

local management is properly a state and local responsibility. The Constitution does not assign any federal rights or obligations regarding the quality of administration in governmental units below the national government. Indeed, one can argue that the wide variations in state laws, constitutional requirements, and administrative structures would preclude any meaningful national involvement. An argument against federal involvement could also be made on budgetary grounds. That is, federally funded management improvement programs confront unlimited needs. Essentially, it is a "bottomless pit."

The arguments for a federal role rest upon four major assumptions:

(1) State-local implementation of national policy objectives.

(2) Federal origins of state-local management problems.

(3) Necessity of federally funded support in developing increased management capacity.

(4) Economies of scale possible at the national level.

The first assumption is that the effectiveness of nationally legislated programs depends almost entirely upon the performance of state and local governments, which are the primary deliverers of public services. After all, grant-in-aid programs, which in 1982 totaled approximately $90 billion in federal expenditures, are the chief mechanisms for achieving domestic policy objectives. If we are to secure national goals, we must have capable state and local governments.

The second argument is based on the contention that the management problems of states and localities are partly a result of the requirements and conditions that the federal government imposes upon them. The Advisory Commission on Intergovernmental Relations reported that the federal government has imposed roughly 1,600 mandates on local units through direct orders and conditions of aid. OMB has identified some fifty-nine cross-cutting requirements, which accompany federal aid to states and localities. Thus, the federal government, having created some of the management problems of states and localities, should assume some obligation in helping to correct those problems.

The third argument relates to the necessity of federal support. The fiscal problems facing states and local governments often prevent them from undertaking the kinds of essential management improvement activities required to solve the problems they face. The funding of capacity-building programs by local governments might have to come at the expense of providing basic public services. Modestly funded national programs are much easier to support and maintain than would be possible at lower levels of the federal system.

The final case for a national effort in capacity building is perhaps the most persuasive and revolves around the efficiencies and economies that are possible if such efforts are undertaken on a national scale. Among these advantages are the economies gained when reports and materials are produced for a nationwide audience, rather than having each state or region "reinvent the management wheel" or duplicate the innovations of others. Federal involvement also allows for the national identification and dissemination of effective management techniques, rather than limiting the effort to certain states or regions. In fact, some argue that this point should be extended to encompass transnational capacity-building exchange programs. One point is clear and irrefutable: expertise and innovation, like dirty or clean air, are not confined within political boundaries.

Financial and Energy Management Programs

The federal government has been engaged in two programs in recent years to assist state and local governments in improving their capacities in energy conservation and financial management. This chapter reports on those experiences and attempts to distill and compare the lessons learned. The two programs are the Financial Management Capacity Sharing Program (FMCS), sponsored by the U.S. Department of Housing and Urban Development (HUD), and the National Community Energy Mangement Center (NCEMC), sponsored by three federal departments: Energy, HUD, and Transportation.

These programs were designed to include what were deemed to be the most successful techniques utilized in other federal capacity-building efforts. They also were intended to provide both a unified and yet a multidisciplinary approach to complex, cross-cutting problems. Each program gathered information from "user-groups" to define needs and required areas of assistance. Both considered information dissemination and consciousness-raising activities as highly important. The programs developed training packages. And both programs attempted technical assistance and "peer-match" approaches within budgetary limitations. The "success" of each program was largely beyond the control of its managers. Departmental budgets, changing administration priorities, and the difficulty (in the case of the NCEMC) of managing a program funded by multiple agencies were significant environmental factors affecting program management.

In 1977 HUD's Office of Policy Development and Research developed the FMCS program in response to the growing fiscal problems numerous local jurisdictions faced and the acute financial emergencies in a few large cities, most notably New York City. FMCS continues to this date as a HUD-sponsored activity, albeit at a much more modest level. The NCEMC was conceived during the last year of the Carter administration in response to the energy crisis and to the fact that, for most local governments, energy costs were the second largest line item in their operating budgets (after personnel costs).[2] NCEMC was funded by the Reagan administation on January 22, 1981, and operated until November 1982.

The descriptions and conclusions in this article are based on third-party evaluations of the two programs conducted by the authors for the sponsoring federal departments.[3] The Financial Management Capacity Sharing program was evaluated by a panel of the National Academy of Public Administration consisting of twelve persons with expertise in state and local finance. The panel included state and local officials, private sector financial managers and consultants, and members of academia. This evaluation provided continuing advice on program direction and content to the program managers. The panel and staff participated in FMCS-sponsored workshops and conferences as observers; reviewed FMCS reports, publications and handbooks; and interviewed staff of the national public interest groups. The academy staff conducted a survey of a sample of FMCS program users by mail and telephone to determine user satisfaction and program effectiveness. A sample of 175 users was surveyed from a known universe of 956. The survey sample was stratified based on two variables: user affiliation and type of assistance received.

The energy management program was evaluated by one of the authors and was also conducted continuously. The evaluation was performed by using the following methodologies: (1) interviews with key persons involved in NCEMC activites and operations (federal sponsor representatives, officers and staff of the Academy for State and Local Government (formerly the Academy for Contemporary Problems), advisory council members and staff of the national associations); (2) review of NCEMC documents, materials, and files; (3) direct

observation of NCEMC conferences and workshops; and (4) a telephone suvey of twenty-eight local government jurisdictions identifed as
NCEMC technical assistance recipients (a 50 percent sample of the
universe).

Program Philosophy

The energy and financial management programs were based on the
same philosophy and relied on essentially the same approaches for the
delivery of management assistance. This philosophy was termed
"capacity sharing" to distinguish it from the more standard approach of
"capacity building." The principles of capacity sharing were developed
under the FMCS program and subsequently used to design the energy
management program.

The adoption of the phrase "capacity sharing" by the FMCS
program designers was an important semantic distinction. The logic
behind this distinction was explained in an internal HUD memorandum
dated September 1978 (author unknown):

> As far as sharing vs. building is concerned, I think we should rely
> on past federal experience and stick to more modest "sharing" of
> available financial management solutions. Other approaches (dem-
> onstrations, funded or promulgated innovations) run the risk of
> becoming the arrogant federal "solutions" we are trying to avoid.

The sharing concept was meant not only to avoid a "top-down"
approach which might denigrate local capacity, but also to bring
expectations for the program more in line with the available resources.
More importantly, capacity sharing denotes that local governments are
capable and innovative and that they need not be treated as underdeveloped, but rather should be assisted in transferring and sharing the
best practices and proven management techniques found among their
members.

During the evolution of the FMCS program, a coherent methodology for providing management assistance and encouraging the
adoption and use of improved practices was developed. The capacity-
sharing approach combined many of the most effective techniques of
previous federal management assistance efforts. More importantly, it
developed several new ways to identify needs and practical solutions or
methods and to disseminate information and materials to the target
audience. The federal role was that of a convenor and facilitator.
Because of the program philosophy and the well-articulated approaches

used in the financial and energy management programs, these federal assistance efforts represent unique contributions to the long and varied history of capacity building.

Capacity-Sharing Principles

FMCS and NCEMC were designed on the basis of four management principles:

(1) Allow users to define program priorities.

(2) Employ varying levels of management assistance.

(3) Work through the associations of state and local government.

(4) Build a capacity-sharing network.

These principles were based on knowledge of successful practices in previous capacity-building programs, the need to respond to a sizable and diverse audience, and to budget limitations. Each of these four principles is explained below. In both programs, the universe of aid recipients was at least 39,000 general purpose local governments and fifty states. The FMCS program had a total budget of just over $6 million for the 1978-1982 period, and the Energy Center was allotted $1.7 million for its two years of operation. While both programs were relatively well funded, the demand greatly exceeded the resources available.

USER-DEFINED PROGRAM PRIORITIES. FMCS and NCEMC conducted needs assessments to determine the priority topics and areas of assistance that would be offered to states and localities. Under FMCS, needs assessment was an extensive and lengthy process, which included surveys and solicitation of local government views, forty-nine workshops with user groups, and a national conference. In all, over 900 local and state officials were involved. The needs-assessment process conducted by the energy program was more modest, based largely on a review of the literature and interviews with local officials and the staffs of Washington-based public interest groups.

The principle of allowing users to shape program priorities is a valid and important element of capacity sharing for two reasons. First, it helps ensure the relevance of the topics addressed by the assistance program, and, second, it establishes the credibility of a federally sponsored effort. Our survey of FMCS users revealed that 88 percent judged the program to be highly relevant to their financial management concerns. Involving users in program design also overcomes some of the traditional skepticism held by local officials toward the federal bureaucracy, publicizes the activity, and thus helps to develop a constituency for it. However, elaborate needs-assessment activities, as in the case of FMCS, can divert resources from the actual delivery of management assistance.

LEVELS OF MANAGEMENT ASSISTANCE. FMCS and NCEMC capacity-sharing programs offered assistance at various levels of intensity and through a variety of approaches. The application of this principle permitted broad coverage and flexible response to user requests. The mechanisms for delivering assistance ranged from (1) funding the development of substantive materials; (2) distribution of publications; (3) information and referral services (telephone or written); (4) national and regional conferences; (5) topical or geographical workshops; and (6) on-site technical assistance.

Publications, information services, and conferences are useful and cost-effective mechanisms for reaching a sizable number of persons, particularly those with an initial or general interest in the management topic. Workshops and direct technical assistance, by contrast, are appropriate methods for transmitting jurisdiction-specific management reforms. The workshop format is an economical way of providing detailed information to a group of officials who share a common concern or have similar assistance needs.

Our evaluations of the two programs demonstrated much greater satisfaction among users who participated in smaller workshop sessions than among those who attended the larger regional or national conferences. We also concluded that in order for workshops to be effective, at least two conditions should be met: the group should be fairly homogenous (for example, city managers from smaller jurisdictions), and the topics should be highly focused.

Direct or on-site technical assistance, the most intensive level of management aid, has the highest payoff in inducing change or gaining implementation of reforms. It is, however, the most costly method of transferring innovations from one locality to another, because the number of communities that can be reached is limited. Our survey of FMCS users revealed that those officials who had received direct technical assistance were two to three times more likely to initiate or adopt new practices than were those who had received less intensive forms of aid.

It should be noted that the FMCS program reached a wide variety of local governments, ranging in population size from under 10,000 to over 500,000, and that users were evenly distributed among officials representing small, medium-sized and large jurisdictions.

The concept of capacity sharing includes the provision of different levels of assistance to respond to a diverse audience and varying needs for information and aid. It also encompasses a technical assistance process which can be charted as follows:

(1) Determination of the need for assistance

(2) Initiation of a request for aid

(3) Assessment or refinement of request

(4) Provision of information (materials or people)

(5) Development of recommendations or action steps

(6) Implementation

(7) Evaluation of the results

The Energy Center operated with an awareness of this continuum and shaped its services and activities to respond to users at any point along it. For example, the conferences and workshops it sponsored might be helpful in enabling a local official to become aware of a new approach to energy conservation and lead to the generation of a request for further assistance. There were other examples of telephone inquiries for information about specific techniques that were used by local officials in a self-help approach. In the cases where on-site technical assistance was provided, the NCEMC and individual communities became involved in each step of the continuum.

Working Through Associations. Both the FMCS and NCEMC relied on the national- and state-level associations of state and local government as the primary method of reaching their target audiences. This was done in a variety of ways — by providing grants or contracts to the associations for the production of publications or handbooks, by providing financial support for workshops or training sessions arranged by the associations, by funding association staff to provide technical assistance or manage other program activities, and through cosponsorship of conferences with consortia of national and professional associations.

Intermediary organizations play a critical role in technology or innovation transfer. One survey of this process concluded:

A process of "intermediation" between the adopter and the supplier of technological innovations characterizes the adoption processes of state and local governments. This intermediation occurs through channels such as professional associations, consultants, manufacturers, federal agencies and universities. These channels serve to convey information about the existence of an innovation, to test and certify the acceptability of innovations, to facilitate communication between adopters and nonadopters and to establish professional norms of best and standard practices.[4]

A number of studies have found that individuals and public officials most often turn to their professional colleagues for advice and information. In fact, one of the principal reasons for the existence of an association is to provide a structured means of communication among its members. The role was confirmed by the Stanford Research Institute whose interviews with decision-makers at the local and state levels revealed that they frequently turned to the following for advice:

Publications of organizations they know and trust

National conventions sponsored by these organizations

Regional, state or sub-regional workshops where there is an opportunity to exchange information and register feedback[5]

The use of the national associations of state and local government to deliver program services by FMCS and NCEMC produced considerable benefits and had obvious advantages in reaching the target audience. The associations have well-established lines of communication with their members, offer considerable experience in providing training and technical assistance, and can tailor program materials to meet member interests.

Because of the diversity of the state and local audience, HUD consciously adopted a guideline of designing technical assistance responses that would meet the specific needs of various FMCS subgroups. This was clearly an appropriate principle to follow with respect to a number of the activities supported. For instance, the obvious primary audience for model state legislation is elected state legislators and their staffs. Few can quarrel with this kind of targeting. The decision to support specific activities targeted to diverse audiences was justified in principle, but was flawed in its application. The major shortcoming was equating targeted audiences with single constituencies. Audiences were not defined generically (e.g., chief executives), but by interest groups such as mayors. This arrangement largely restricted the utilization of individual FMCS products to the membership of the sponsoring grantee organization.

For example, the U.S. Conference of Mayors was funded to produce a "Mayor's Handbook on Financial Management." It is a comprehensive, readable, and well-written document that would be equally relevant to county executives, city council members, city managers, finance directors, and other senior managers. Yet, by terming it a "mayor's handbook" and including repeated reference to the mayor in the text, its potential audience was limited to a single constituency group. In other cases, workshop attendance was limited to members of the sponsoring association.

Another difficulty is that not all local governments are members of the national groups and thus are not reached through this approach. For this reason, and because the travel costs associated with attendance at national meetings precluded smaller and rural jurisdictions from participating in most FMCS activities, we recommended that greater emphasis be placed on the use of state-level organizations to disseminate information and sponsor training and technical assistance.

A SUPPORT NETWORK. The fourth management principle of the capacity-sharing concept requires the creation of a support network or organizations and individuals that can help state and local managers learn where they can readily locate management aid, which organizations have expertise in specific areas, and what publications and handbooks are available. If capacity sharing is to take place, there must be a focal point or clearinghouse for assistance activities. Such a network enables a local official seeking assistance to understand the aid options available and to link different sources of expertise together.

Under the FMCS program, the support network was somewhat attenuated and activities were not as well integrated as they might have been. HUD did not exercise strong, central coordinating authority, but instead vested responsibility for program marketing and coordination in the individual associations which were grantees. As a result, most of those who participated in a FMCS activity were unaware of the larger program. Our conclusion was that a key function of the federal funding agency should be program coordination, particularly if capacity-sharing activities are to be delegated to possibly competing interest groups. HUD did assign the Municipal Finance Officers' Association a coordinating and central dissemination role, based on our recommendations.

In an attempt to overcome the problems encountered during the

FMCS experience, the federal departments interested in funding an energy center entered into a cooperative agreement with the Academy for State and Local Government (ASLG) to establish the center. ASLG serves as a joint research and advisory organization for the seven national associations of state and local government. The Academy, in turn, entered into subcontracts with the four major associations of local government (International City Management Association, National Association of Counties, National League of Cities, and U.S. Conference of Mayors). The Energy Center was to provide some services directly with its own staff, but also to direct and coordinate the programs and activities of the associations with those of the Energy Center. As a result, the energy management capacity-sharing program was potentially better integrated than FMCS. Yet, the management difficulties that arose in this interorganizational milieu were formidable. NCEMC had to be responsive to the distinct and varied interests and missions of three federal agencies as well as to four national associations of state and local governments which also served as grantees.

The Peer-Practitioner Network

Another significant component of the energy management program and its support network was the creation of a Peer-Practitioner Network. As originally conceived, the center's delivery of technical assistance was to be accomplished primarily through a group of 200 local government officials and consultants with energy management expertise. These individuals were identified largely with the help of the four local government associations and were categorized by subject matter expertise and geographic location. The center, thus, had the capability to match a community's request with an individual skilled and experienced in the topic and proximately located.

The peer-practitioner concept was a unique service offered by the center and was a function central to the concept of capacity sharing. Those interviewed during the course of the evaluation shared the view that this network filled a major gap in energy management assistance and was very useful. The promise of the peer-practitioner network was demonstrated by the Energy Center, but its potential was not realized because of the decision to discontinue federal funding. However, the promise inherent in this feature of the center's program demonstrates a rationale for federal support of capacity sharing. A peer network of this type cannot operate without a subsidy. It is essentially based upon one local government official volunteering to share time and expertise with another. Yet for the network to be effective, there must be a central dispatch office that can match a community's needs with an expert individual, and there must be a source of funds available to enable local officials to travel to other jurisdictions.

Evaluation Results

Our evaluations of the FMCS and NCEMC capacity-sharing programs were generally positive. The FMCS evaluation was conducted by a panel and staff of the National Academy of Public Administration which concluded:

> the FMCS program is addressing a critical need of local and state governments; the program philosophy of capacity sharing is sound; and the activities undertaken to date have been reasonably effective in helping selected local and state officials initiate needed financial management reforms.[6]

The NCEMC evaluation concluded:

> The record of the performance of the Center has demonstrated that the basic concept is sound; there is a need for the services it is providing; it is filling an important gap in energy management assistance; and has done so effectively.[7]

Despite these endorsements, both programs had a number of weaknesses. There were tendencies in both efforts to overemphasize large national conferences and programs intended to attract attention and build constituencies for the effort. In both cases, too much time elapsed between these efforts and the actual delivery of intensive technical assistance in the form of focused workshops and on-site visits. There were also too many attempts to produce quick successes and payoffs by amassing anecdotal data about dollars saved or reforms implemented.

Beyond these issues, the most serious deficiencies in the early stages of the programs were managerial: activities were not always well coordinated, teamwork among subgrantees was often missing, and program events were not well publicized beyond immediate constituency groups. These management problems tended to lessen as the effort matured. So while the management principles of capacity sharing are sound, their application requires considerable skill and demands that program managers have an astute understanding of the environment in which public interest groups operate and be familiar with the context of state and local government.

One of the major problems faced in an on-going evaluation of a capacity-sharing program is to demonstrate that the sponsored activities and management assistance produced tangible results (i.e., to show a cost-benefit ratio for the investment of federal funds.) First, the programs we evaluated were in their initial stages, it takes time to go through the awareness, acceptance, and adoption stages of innovation transfer. Second, it is hard to prove causality and show that the reform would not have occurred without the assistance provided. Third, the quality of management assistance may be high, but implementation may fail to take place because of external factors (for example, financial or economic barriers, changes in priorities, or political or personnel factors). Finally, there are times when the nature of the request simply does not lend itself to implementation. For example, a city may decide, for a variety of reasons unrelated to the technical assistance it receives, not to change its practices or invest in new technologies, In many cases, management assistance may simply produce increased understanding or knowledge on the part of the recipient, which may or may not lead to improved practices at some later date.

Conclusion

The two programs we evaluated were either terminated or reduced substantially. The FMCS program was scaled back primarily as a result of the Reagan budget cuts and partly because of the new administration's priorities. While financial management remains important to HUD, other topics—for example, enterprise zones, privatization, and contracting out—are stressed more. The Energy Center program was a victim of budget cuts, the oil glut, and a drastically different perspective on the role of the federal government in energy conservation. The present status of both programs does not discredit the capacity-sharing concept nor does it lessen the potential effectiveness of similar efforts.

In the final analysis, the decision about whether the federal government should or should not be involved in capacity building comes down to a judgment of whether national purpose is at stake. Abstract considerations have little consequence in making this determination. We suspect that if the capacity of state and local governments to manage their finances, or if their capability to deal with a new and dramatic energy crisis were contributing to a national calamity, the justification for federal action would come quickly and persuasively.

If there is to be a federal role, one other lesson from these two examples should be learned. It takes time for a national program to determine state and local needs, build a constituency for specific federal responses, develop appropriate materials and approaches which can assist state and local governments, and demonstrate that credible assistance can be obtained through a federal program. We would suggest that future capacity-building efforts attempt to build in continuing funding for at least a five-year period. It is not only unrealistic, but impractical to expend federal funds on programs that are not given a fair chance to prove their worth to their state and local government partners.

Notes

1. See the following: Special Task Force on Intergovernmental Management, *Strengthening Intergovernmental Management: An Agenda for Reform*, (Washington, D.C.: American Society for Public Administration, 1979); Study Committee on Policy Management Assistance, *Strengthening Public Management in the Intergovernmental System*, (Washington, D.C.: U.S. Office of Management and Budget, 1975; and Intergovernmental Science, Engineering and Technology Advisory Panel, *A Joint Federal Research and Development Process to Meet State and Local Needs*, (Washington, D.C.: National Science Foundation, 1981).

2. Steve Hudson, "An Assessment of Local Government Energy Mangement Activities," *Urban Data Service Reports* 12, 8 (Washington, D.C.: International City Management Association, August 1980), 1.

3. See the following reports and articles: Charles R. Warren and Leanne R. Aronson, *Improving Financial Management in State and Local Government: An Assessment of a HUD Capacity-Sharing Program* (Washington, D.C.: National Academy of Public Administration, November 1980). Charles R. Warren and Leanne R. Aronson, "Sharing Management Capacity: Is There A Federal Responsibility?" *Public Administration Review*, (May/June, 1981). Charles R. Warren, *Third Party Evaluation of the National Community Energy Management Center*, (Washington, D.C.: Academy for State and Local Government, September 1982).

4. Irwin Feller and Donald C. Menzel, *Diffusion of Innovations in Municipal Governments*, Report to the National Science Foundation (The Pennsylvania State University: 1976).

5. George Barbour et. al., "Productivity Assessment and Packaging Activity: Interim Report to the U.S. Department of Housing and Urban Development," (December 1977).

6. Charles R. Warren and Leanne R. Aronson, *Improving Financial Management in State and Local Government:*, 56.

7. Charles R. Warren, *Third-Party Evaluation of the National Community Energy Management Center*, 28.

15

Capacity-Building Policy for Local Energy Management

BEVERLY A. CIGLER

Few issues rival energy in their fundamental relevance to the success or failure of both domestic and foreign policy. The mid-1970s demonstrated the role that efficient energy use could play. Energy conservation is now recognized as the country's largest and cheapest near-term source of additional energy.[1]

Although the value of energy efficiency is undisputed, the means of achieving it are unsettled. Many conservationists advocate a strong government role, including regulations, incentives, and direct assistance to both individuals and among levels of government. Others prefer to rely on the market, believing that high prices will reduce consumption. While the nation has debated how to achieve energy efficiency, the effects of inefficient energy use, rising energy prices, and fluctuating energy supplies are acutely felt at the local level.

The Arab oil embargo of 1973-1974 marked energy as a significant cause of the rising cost of public service delivery and an obstacle to local governments' meeting public needs and demands. Later events—natural gas interruptions, gasoline shortages, gasoline price increases, an Iranian oil shutdown, the near-disaster at the Three Mile Island nuclear plant in Pennsylvania, double-digit inflation and a war in the Persian Gulf—contributed to making energy policy a key concern of local officials.[2] A 1979 survey of more than 1,000 mayors and city council members, for example, found that 87 percent of those city officials rated the cost of energy as their most serious community concern.[3]

By 1980, energy had grown from a minor budget item ten years before to the second largest item in the budgets of nearly 60 percent of our cities and more than 40 percent of our counties.[4] Studies of energy consumption, cost, and expenditure patterns of communities revealed that about 85 cents of every dollar spent on energy leaves the local economy.[5]

If energy purchase and investment decisions were based solely on considerations of cost, one would expect that energy conservation programs would have quickly been added to the agendas of local governments in the mid-1970s. Because energy markets are imperfect, however, the level of energy conservation investment being made by local governments was far less than the economic optimum, despite high prices. In response, a proliferation of capacity-building activities[6] by the federal and state governments, as well as public interest groups and professional organizations representing local governments, occurred between 1973 and 1980. No local government should have been bypassed by the widely disseminated capacity-building materials.

Community energy management (CEM) stands at an important juncture. There has been clear documentation of local energy strategies as significant factors in achieving cost savings, often without the use of new revenues.[7] On the other hand, several studies reveal that the most significant energy activities, in terms of financial and/or energy savings, have not yet been undertaken by cities and counties.[8] And the Reagan administration's policies have ended the flow of capacity-building materials and pilot projects. Most programs have been eliminated or had their funding cut.[9] At the same time, of course, local governments' own abilities to consider new programs have decreased.

If local governments are to realize the opportunities afforded by energy options, they are in need of cost-effective, politically and administratively feasible strategies to slow down the flow of dollars out of their communities and to help reduce fiscal stress. This chapter is designed to fill some of the obvious information gaps in assessing progress toward community energy management and in developing and implementing programs.

The chapter begins by: (1) outlining the roles that local governments might play in energy conservation; (2) summarizing CEM progress to date, along with the capacity-building efforts aimed at enhancing local government energy roles; and (3) examining empirical research findings that help explain the barriers to development and implementation of community energy management strategies. Next, the potential organizing models for CEM are analyzed in light of how capacity-builders have influenced local organization. Finally, the chapter offers research and policy recommendations that flow from empirical research findings and the analysis presented.

Central to this chapter is the argument that those who developed materials to aid local government energy efforts (capacity-builders)[10] failed to utilize a "users' perspective"[11] in assessing their clients' needs when developing and disseminating information. This resulted in unworkable organizational structures at the local level that, if corrected, may still yield useful energy-as-cost-savings programs.

Local Government Energy Roles

There are a number of compelling reasons for local government interest in energy conservation and renewable resources:

First, energy conservation programs are, in effect, cost-savings strategies that alleviate the energy price spiral for operating local government itself.

Second, energy conservation is the functional equivalent of the production of energy. Thus, local government promotion of conservation slows down the flow of energy dollars leaving a community, allowing more disposable income for businesses, industries and families to invest.

Third, energy conservation can have immediate payoffs. Reductions in current energy consumption enhance the local area's ability to withstand future curtailments of fuel without rapid price increases, decreasing vulnerability to outside events.

Fourth, energy conservation can create more jobs per dollar spent, especially in high unemployment areas, than most alternative energy strategies. It is an equity-centered energy approach.

Fifth, energy conservation offers the least insult to the safety and health of a community and its citizens, compared to other energy sources such as coal and/or nuclear power.

Sixth, unlike many other energy sources, conservation is relatively unhampered by technological barriers.

Seventh, local energy conservation programs contribute to national energy policies by strengthening the nation's ability to coordinate strategies for operating in the international energy arena.

Eighth, energy conservation programs offer one of the few energy policies individuals can affect at the community level. In addition to the democratic virtues of such policies, the attitudinal and institutional barriers to conservation in general may be ameliorated through the leadership of local officials.

Ninth, the unique differences among local communities in climate, geography, economic and political institutions, as well as physical development, also suggest locally created policies as a wise route to pursue.[12]

A framework for examining the energy-related roles of local government can be derived from the five areas cited by Henderson as potential energy-related roles for local government.[13] These include the roles of consumer, producer, planner, policy-maker and regulator. Of course, not every local government performs every role, and many responsibilities are shared with other levels of government and the nonprofit sector.

The local government's role as energy consumer spans two major responsibilities to citizens: using as few tax dollars for energy as possible in providing goods and services and encouraging adequate supplies of fuel in case of emergencies in order to protect public health, safety, and welfare. Local governments can increase their energy productivity in several ways: by developing energy consumption and cost statistics on municipal service units to aid in decision making; by identifying essential operations, establishing service priorities and maintaining auxiliary supplies of fuel; and by planning and developing alternative fuel sources, such as fuel from waste and methane- or propane-powered vehicles.

As producers of energy, local governments are active in owning and operating over 2,000 electric utilities in the United States and in developing renewable energy resources. Examples are co-generation and district heating, wind and geothermal energy, and alternative fuel such as ethanol and methanol for vehicle fleets. Direct solar energy, with both active and passive applications, is used extensively by many communities.

The areas of housing, transportation, and economic development, as well as planning for fuel emergencies, demonstrate the local energy-planner role of local governments. Communities have required coordination of new developments with mass transit routes, for example, as well as requiring landscaping for passive solar cooling.

Empirical studies of the land use strategies with the greatest potential for achieving energy-efficent development suggest the following activities as key concerns: (1) promoting compact development (which reduces transportation energy consumption, providing more energy-efficient housing, and reducing the embodied energy required for new development); (2) focusing on transportation policies to reduce energy consumption for work trips; (3) implementing strategies that will reduce household operating energy; and (4) reducing excessive development standards.[14]

The local government roles of energy regulator and policy-maker are especially important. Community leaders can help focus attention on energy problems and solutions. Local energy policies and programs can help in achieving citizen consensus and lead to even greater energy savings for a community.

As energy administrators, local officials can incorporate energy concerns into every phase of government, both internal operations and external, communitywide concerns. Wise fiscal management demands the need for energy budgets for departments, life-cycle-costing in purchasing decisions, and reward systems for energy and dollars saved. Community development, as discussed earlier, can be affected through incorporation of energy concerns into zoning and building code implementation as well as capital-improvement projects that affect the location and type of sewer, water, street and lighting projects. Local governments can also influence the rate of investment in energy efficiency communitywide by innovative tax administration that rewards energy efficiency.

I have offered another way of viewing the local energy role by dichotomizing the types of energy opportunities available and/or utilized by local governments as those internal to government operations and those activities that are external or communitywide.[15] For each dimension, a continuum of activities ranges from technical, hardware activities to those that affect life-style or attitudes. Thus, on the internal dimension, weatherizing public buildings and improving vehicle fleet maintenance are the most technical and least involved with people, while restricting employee travel or changing employee conservation behavior, though limited to internal operations, do involve a broader potential scope of conflict.

Similarly, on the external dimension, public education/awareness campaigns are the least controversial operations, followed by appointment of citizen committees. Any attempts to incorporate energy efficiency into land use or zoning policies, building codes or transportation plans are both the greatest sources of energy and finanical savings and the most related to changes in community life-styles and attitudes, heightening chances for conflict.

Table 1. Federally Funded Energy Capacity-Building Projects

Program Title	Sponsor	Description
Portland, Oregon Energy Program	HUD	Adoption of energy policies and ordinances in 1979.
Comprehensive Community Energy Management Planning Program (CCEMP)	Argonne National Laboratory	Development of methodologies for energy conservation by sixteen diverse communities.
Local and Municipal Renewable Energy Planning Support Pilot Program	Oak Ridge National Laboratories	Grants to three governments for renewable energy planning.
Solar Technology Assessment Program (TAP)	Oak Ridge National Laboratories	Development of energy future alternatives in pilot areas based on economic, social, and political criteria.
Energy Extension Service (EES)	Established by the National Energy Extension Service Act of 1977 (P.L. 95-39)	A ten-state pilot program to enable states to provide direct, personalized information and assistance on conservation alternatives to small-scale energy users, including local governments.
Development and Implementation of State Energy Conservation Policies	Energy Policy and Conservation Act of 1975 (EPCA) (P.L. 94-163)	Funded state comprehensive energy conservation plans if they contained five mandated provisions.
	and Energy Conservation and Production Act of 1976 (ECPA) (P.L. 94-385)	Augmented and expanded EPCA by mandating provision for public education, intergovernmental coordination, and energy audits for buildings and industrial plants.

Achieving Community Energy Management Through Capacity Building

There have been three stages of local energy involvement.[16] The first occurred between 1973 and 1979 and was a formative period of education, pilot projects, and examination of the local energy role.[17] The most important characteristic of the period was the domination of the federal government and its centralized approach to energy problems: mandatory standards for automobiles and thermostat settings and pricing mechanisms, such as decontrol of crude oil prices, dominated policy agendas.[18]

Although there were some state-initiated efforts[19], several federally funded capacity-building efforts were most notable in promoting a role for local governments in energy policy during this first period. See Table 1 for examples of these federal programs.

The 1973-1979 period led to a greater realization of the potential for local energy involvement but only a few widely publicized communities (Davis, California; Seattle, Washington; and Portland, Oregon) achieved highly successful comprehensive energy management. The country became complacent when oil supplies were reestablished after the Arab oil embargo and when the price of oil actually fell relative to the consumer price index between 1974 and 1978.

The second era of local energy involvement began in 1979 when Americans were exposed to the startling news of the toppling of the Shah of Iran, OPEC's ability to double world oil prices, the seizure of American hostages in Iran, and a serious nuclear accident in Pennsylvania.[20] A new terminology—CEM—emerged within hundreds of local governments as leaders and citizens mobilized to develop comprehensive community energy management programs.[21]

The greatest number of capacity-building activities occurred during this second period as federal and state governments, as well as public interest groups and professional organizations representing local governments, developed a wide variety of assistance programs aimed at the major energy management needs of local governments.[22] These are summarized in Table 2.[23]

Printed CEM materials intended for widespread dissemination were the most prevalent type of capacity-building assistance available to local governments in this second period of local energy management. They included background readings on energy conservation and renewable resources; existing community plans and studies; technical

Table 2. Capacity Building for Local Energy Management

Local Energy Management Needs	Examples
1. Increased Opportunities for Local Participation in National/State Policy Formulation	Formal representation for local governments in DOE policy making (1979) and on many state energy bodies.
2. Data Collection, Monitoring, and Evaluation Assistance	DOE's CCEMP, aimed at development of formal methodologies for systematic documentation of energy conservation.
3. Increased Technical Assistance	EES extended nationwide in 1980.
4. Increased Financial Assistance	Most programs.
5. Information Clearinghouses	The President's Clearinghouse for Community Energy Efficiency, operated by the International City Management Association (ICMA), the National Association of Counties (NACo), the National League of Cities (NLC), and the U.S. Conference of Mayors (USCM).

methods, procedures and models for developing programs; and bibliographies.[24]

In addition, each of the professional associations representing state and local governments, proven innovators at the municipal level,[25] developed energy materials and established energy projects. By late 1980 several states, including Pennsylvania, Massachusetts and North Carolina, had developed statewide associations of energy officials. Hundreds of guidebooks for CEM were produced and distributed in this era by governments at all levels, their professional organizations, and public interest groups.[26]

Many local governments appeared ready to embark on serious efforts toward using energy programs as cost-avoidance strategies. Enthusiasm for community energy management escalated with the signing of a cooperative agreement by three federal agencies (Department of Energy, Housing and Urban Development, and Transportation) in January 1981. This led to the opening of the National Community Energy Management Center (NCEMC) the following autumn. The center, however, was a creation of the Carter administration during the transition to the Reagan presidency and closed in autumn 1982, a victim of budget cuts, oil gluts, and the Reagan administrations's philosophy of federal noninvolvement in energy conservation.

The center was unique in several important ways. Its design and organizational structure had few counterparts in the history of inter-governmental relations, and it developed a national network of expertise in the energy field to diffuse cost-effective measures among local governments. Its small core staff cooperated with the four local government associations (ICMA, NACo, NLC and USCM) as well as a wide spectrum of experts from the public and private sectors. A consulting network of peer practitioners was available to local com-munities for information on such energy topics as financing, multifamily dwelling retrofit, program development, and contingency planning.[27] Despite its demise, NCEMC's enthusiastic reception by local com-munities demonstrated the heightened levels of interest in local community programs in the early 1980s.

The election of Ronald Reagan in 1980 brought to a close the second era in local energy management. A third era has since emerged, marked by a dramatic shift in national priorities. Fiscal constraints at all levels have forced governments to eliminate, postpone, and reduce energy activities. The Reagan administration's energy policies favor market forces, at the expense of most technical and financial assistance programs for development and implementation of community energy programs.[28] Local governments must now rely on their own initiative and resources to develop and implement CEM programs.

Despite the obvious advantages of community energy strategies and the amount and diversity of capacity-building efforts aimed at enhancing local roles, all of the CEM monitoring studies document the slow progress of most local governments in responding to oppor-tunities for energy management. A 1980 survey by the ICMA and several single state studies show significant energy programs, in terms of financial and/or energy savings, in only a few hundred American cities.[29] A 1981-1982 survey by the NLC of communities belonging to their Conference of Local Energy Officials (CLEO) found that even those cities most interested in CEM have not yet mounted aggressive energy programs in their communities nor taken the necessary steps toward major savings in internal operations.[30] A state-of-the-art survey published in 1980 of 1,426 local-, regional- and state-planning agencies found that only thirteen American communities had enacted land use and development regulations explicitly to accomplish energy savings goals.[31]

The monitoring studies show that local governments, regardless of population, have not developed extensive internal or external energy programs, except for some low-cost, low-risk, usually technical operations within local government. Three separate studies in North Carolina —of small governments, the state's largest cities, and county governments, respectively—found that, despite weak energy programs, most governments did not plan on any additional energy activities.[32]

Follow-up surveys of community progress toward CEM by the California Office of Appropriate Technology in that state and in North Carolina[33] do show increases in community activities by 1981, suggesting that CEM captured local officials' attention after the initial studies in 1979-1980 and before the Reagan administration cutbacks took effect. Still, a nut-and-bolts approach to energy programs dominates with uncontroversial internal operations efforts most prevalent and activities affecting attitudes or life-style changes rarely attempted.

Inefficient energy use, cyclical rises of energy prices, and fluctuating energy supplies will continue to have important fiscal, social, environmental and political impacts on local communities. A major need is the identification of the limits of market forces in encouraging energy conservation. The next sections of this chapter review research findings on the institutional, informational, technical, social, and economic barriers to local energy programs; analyze the organizing models for CEM advocated by capacity-builders; and offer arguments and policy suggestions to enhance local program success.

Empirical Research

The CEM monitoring studies have provided answers to such questions as, What are the options for local energy programs? and Which Programs are most frequently pursued? The local government preference for nuts-and-bolts programs parallels other research findings on individual conservation behavior, which suggest that the most convenient, least costly, and least threatening to life-style practices are most popular.[34]

Very few empirical research efforts, however, have addressed the obstacles to organizing and/or implementing energy programs. Such information is fundamental, especially as the federal government continues to decrease its capacity-building roles in CEM. The systematic attempts in examining CEM fall into two broad categories: (1) a few research efforts examining selected obstacles to organizing for energy programs as well as policy implementation, and (2) studies of those communities most successful in community energy management, especially those participating in federal government capacity-building projects.

Systematic studies of CEM in a single state (North Carolina) examined the linkage between energy program development and financial resources, technical assistance, and public opinion.[35] There is mixed evidence on the role of financial resources, especially since conservation goals may be achieved without high levels of investment. Certainly, the most successful and diverse local energy programs often occur in communities with good in-house resources or those that have received financial assistance from the federal or state government. On the other hand, a wide range of low-cost/no-cost conservation options exists that is not being tapped by most governments.

The three North Carolina energy program development studies—covering 59 percent of the state's counties, 72 percent of its municipalities with populations greater than 10,000, and 119 smaller communities—concentrated on the administrative role of government in community energy management. The lack of substantial local energy innovation might be related to the perception of decision-makers that outside interest and assistance from other levels of government and the public were necessary to the development of local energy policies. Whether such support is necessary is not the point. By perceiving outside support as a prerequisite, decision-makers voluntarily limited their pursuit of policies. A key set of findings, for example, suggested that a perceived lack of public support served to inhibit energy innovation by local officials, with public support ranking higher than technical assistance as the communities' "most pressing need" in *developing* energy programs.[36]

Research findings on weak local energy programs and the perceptions by local officials that public support is lacking for their energy efforts are supported by numerous studies on individual citizen conservation efforts[37] and a wealth of public opinion research.[38] Most important, since significant energy/cost savings come from external programs dealing with heating and cooling, automobile transportation, land use, zoning, building construction, and other factors affecting lifestyle, socioeconomic status is a major determinant of conservation actions, with education, occupation, and age also closely related.[39]

Interestingly, the North Carolina studies found that most of the communities had demonstrated enough interest in energy programs to attend state workshops. However, the most energy-active communities used outside capacity-building efforts least. High workshop participation and low levels of meaningful energy programs in force for most communities suggest that the workshop materials may not have been directed to the most important energy management needs of the local communities.[40] State leadership in California, on the other hand, does demonstrate successful capacity building, although local communities in the state have been reluctant to use available outside funds for energy audits.[41]

A more recent North Carolina study sought local energy coordinators' perceptions of the key obstacles to program *implementation*. On the internal dimension, employee attitudes were cited most frequently by respondents that had attempted internal programs. And those few respondents with experience in communitywide energy programs cited citizen opposition and lack of interest and expertise by local elected officials as the major obstacles to program implementation.[42]

Despite these obstacles to community energy management programs there are a substantial number of success stories. Several case studies[43] and other examinations of successful communities nationwide[44] have attempted to uncover factors leading to program success. The most-examined communities are those participating in the federally funded Comprehensive Community Energy Management Program (CCEMP) (e.g., Boulder, Colorado; Greater Bridgeport, Connecticut; King County, Washington; Los Angeles; Knoxville, Tennessee; Janesville, Wisconsin; Portland, Maine; Richmond, Indiana; Seattle, Washington) and a few other communities with unusually good in-house resources or help from state government (e.g., Ann Arbor, Michigan, and Austin, Texas). Most of these communities attempted wide-ranging comprehensive energy programs, beginning with an analysis of energy consumption and development of a wide range of alternatives.

It is difficult to generalize on the varying successes of the communities studied. However, several common factors dominate the program development and implementation processes, leading some commentators to term these the "preconditions" for successful community energy management.[45] One set of preconditions relates to the local environment:

(1) Shortages of energy supply and price increases have led some communities to debate nuclear power, have prompted ratepayers' revolts and have set the stage of comprehensive energy programs;

(2) The presence of an energy constituency (e.g., in university towns such as Austin, Ann Arbor, Chapel Hill or Boulder, or an active citizenry as in Seattle) is related to program

success. On the other hand, in Knoxville, where the TVA has played a paternal role, the effect has been a complacent energy citizenry and a comparative lack of program success;

(3) The local economy may be related to program initiation (e.g., growing communities can more easily integrate energy into land use planning);

(4) Supportive state programs, such as California's solar and conservation tax credit legislation and solar access laws may also help determine local success.

The other category of preconditions for successful community energy management relate to the organizational process itself. Again, generalizations are difficult, but several analyses attribute the following factors to successful community energy management:

(1) Early and continued support by local officials, especially elected mayors and council members and city managers;

(2) A clear linkage of energy strategies to the economic self-interest of community leaders and citizens;

(3) An early focus on program implementation and selected activities that are highly visible and cost-effective (i.e., attention-grabbers)

(4) Skillful program management, with a formal implementation process involving detailed work programs, reports, consultant studies and widespread citizen participation, as well as participation and support from local utilities;

(5) An emphasis on expanding existing programs or activities that support agreed-upon community objectives;

(6) Housing of the energy personnel in an agency with the capability of implementing plans (e.g., in the office of the mayor or manager).

A number of U.S. communities have developed successful, energy programs. That is, they bypassed the costly process of detailed technical reports on community energy consumption and attempted to adopt programs incrementally. Examples include Davis, California's early focus on integrating energy concerns into zoning and building policies;

the municipal solar utilities (MSU) in Carbondale, Illinois, and Santa Clara, California; the residential audit programs in Greensboro, North Carolina, and Austin, Texas; the strong regulatory programs in San Diego County and Berkeley, California; creative financing programs in Fort Collins, Colorado, and Hartford County, Maryland's tax incentive programs. These incremental programs all appear to have been supported by committed elected officials interested in energy programs, a solid foundation of technical support from planning/consultant staffs and an interested and supportive local energy constituency consisting of citizens, developers, realtors and others affected by resulting policies. It must be concluded, then, that a truly rational, comprehensive approach to energy management is not a precondition to program success.

Potential Organizing Models for CEM

Energy policy presents a particularly complex challenge to the American political system in that success relies on the actions of millions of individuals and thousands of governmental units. For local governments it is a relatively new agenda item that has received only sporadic attention as concern rises only when prices rise or supplies fluctuate. In addition, just as the time was ripe for local energy involvement, local governments were hard-hit with fiscal stress brought on by a sluggish economy, the taxation/expenditure limitation movement, and other factors that lowered revenues. The incentives to undertake energy programs were undercut by conflicting demands for more traditional services not perceived to be linked to energy.

It would be easy to simply add local energy programs to the long list of options that offer great potential for aiding local governments but pose seemingly intractable problems in implementation. The social and political obstacles to energy programs cannot be underestimated. And it is unlikely that local governments will incur costs (by developing energy programs) in order to provide benefits (saved energy) for the nation unless they perceive definite and tangible benefits for themselves.[46]

This economic reality suggests that an important factor has been overlooked, both by researchers trying to explain the relative failure of CEM (compared to its potential) and, more importantly, by those who attempted to build the capacity of local governments for energy management. The neglected issue is the way local governments have been prompted to organize for energy management.

Community energy programs have not been viewed or promoted as cost-reduction strategies to be incorporated into every phase of local government.[47] The pilot and demonstration projects offered by the federal and state governments, as well as the voluminous writings on "how to do" CEM, present energy programs primarily as energy strategies, not ways to save money. Placing energy issues apart from other local concerns depended on who took responsibility for local capacity building and the organizing strategies promoted by those groups.

DOE and the state energy agencies took the lead in giving advice to local governments for organizing for CEM, not HUD or state community development/assistance agencies. Even the capacity-building project administered by HUD was labeled "Local Government Approaches to Energy Conservation."[48] "Energy projects" were created at each of the national associations representing local government— USCM, NLC, NACo, and ICMA. Energy was not incorporated into existing capacity-building programs. In 1981, the NCEMC opened its doors to provide local governments technical assistance, training, and information about local energy programs.

All of these projects, while presenting information on energy cost savings, set energy apart from other local issues in both a symbolic and organizational sense. Local governments have been urged to appoint "energy coordinators" to be responsible for their communities' overall energy programs. "Comprehensive community energy management" has been the espoused goal of programmatic energy efforts.[49] And local officials have been sent handbooks, workbooks, and other materials that contain all of that "comprehensiveness" between two covers.[50]

This centralized, comprehensive and rational approach to energy management is unlikely to be realized in the same form as the ideal. Few local governments can afford to hire a full-time energy officer with energy expertise or establish an energy office with additional staffing. The comprehensive model may even serve to intimidate smaller governments who do not seek out energy program information because they feel they lack the necessary resources. But local governments *can* appoint someone in their organization to serve as a part-time energy coordinator. In fact, the advice of federal and state capacity-builders, along with that of their professional associations, *has been taken* by local officials. The 1980 ICMA survey[51] found that 54 percent of the cities and 71 percent of the counties in the national study reported that a specific employee had been assigned responsibility for handling energy matters. (As expected, only 5 percent of the cities and 18 percent of the counties having energy coordinators had hired a full-time energy officer.) The North Carolina studies[52] also found high interest in energy programs as most communities had appointed energy coordinators.

It is not surprising that the capacity-building efforts have promoted a centralized, comprehensive approach to energy management, with the designation of energy coordinators. Those preparing the materials are energy experts, and most materials were developed following the approaches of the early innovators—Portland, Seattle, and Davis. These communities may be unique in that their elected officials are among the few who had extensive interest in energy programs. A users' perspective that first examines the typical local government's need and ability to pursue a centralized, comprehensive approach was not used.

Considering the range of responsibilities suggested for an energy coordinator—data collection, policy and program development, budgeting governmental energy use, intergovernmental coordination, contingency planning, liaison work with the community, and monitoring and evaluation—and the likelihood that part-time coordinators have not been given the authority to perform their roles, it may be that this organizational variable is a key to understanding local progress toward CEM. If the existing group of local energy coordinators has neither the authority nor interest, for example, in fulfilling the necessary comprehensive energy management role, any flow of information to them may fail.

There is an alternative approach to organizing for CEM that, ironically, builds on an understanding of the comprehensiveness of energy topics to bypass the temptation to designate a comprehensive energy coordinator. Rather that calling for a comprehensive, centralized approach through the creation of new issues, programs, or personnel, this little-used alternative would seek to integrate energy concerns into every phase of local government operations and policies, using existing staff and systems. In effect, the organizing strategy would be a fragmented, decentralized effort to incorporate energy concerns into ongoing programs. The organization would not even need a designated "energy coordinator" as the benefits of energy programs would be merged into every organizational role. Capacity-building materials would be developed for specialized audiences and sent to relevant organizations.[53]

Interestingly, the energy options available to local communities span *all* of the options currently being debated in the contemporary literature on productivity improvements for local governments—

whether dealing with economic, industrial engineering/technological, or behavioral science techniques.[54] However, energy programs are a major, unrecognized tool. The energy management materials prepared by the federal and state governments, as well as professional and other organizations, are replete with linkages of energy management to other issues and concerns, such as productivity improvement and economic development.[55] However, the materials are disseminated primarily to those who have been designated as "energy coordinators" and others keyed to hearing about "energy" strategies.

On the other hand, the voluminous literature on productivity improvements for local governments is conspicuously lacking in its treatment of energy concerns. The best examples are the *Productivity Improvement Handbook for State and Local Governments* and the Urban Institute publication, *Linkages: Improving Financial Management in Local Government.*[56] The first offers separate chapters on a variety of techniques for productivity improvement, but energy options are nowhere recognized as cost-reduction strategies. The latter book shows how to link local budgeting, accounting, performance management, and auditing. Clearly, energy concerns should be integrated into these systems and linkages, as they are as fundamental as land, labor, and capital to the overall managerial process.[57]

What may be a flaw in the capacity-building efforts on energy management is the adherence to treating energy as a separate issue in need of its own bureaucratic framework at the local level. It is not surprising, however, to find state energy offices and DOE and/or "energy projects" of any type reluctant to dismantle their efforts and, instead, work more quietly for integration of energy into the overall management process. This would entail the abandonment of the production of massive and comprehensive energy manuals and workshops for local officials and, instead, dissemination of specialized materials to personnel in such functional positions as budget officer, finance officer and building supervisor. It might mean having only one production agency to try to integrate energy into the overall management framework by working with specialized professional line associations such as the Government Finance Officers Association or American Planning Association, not the many separate energy projects now in operation.[58] And it would certainly mean less talk about energy and more talk about cost savings from energy.

Because a users' perspective was not used in developing or disseminating energy materials, or in designing model approaches to energy management, there appears to be a glaring need for such research. Early research efforts bypassed examination of the energy coordinator's role in achieving CEM, largely because overall levels of program commitment were so low that differences among communities did not exist. Now, however, such research can be undertaken as hundreds of American communities have attempted energy programs, using an organizational approach accepted several years ago.[59] We need to know if the dominant ways of organizing for CEM and disseminating information for local energy involvement are effective.

Conclusions and Recommendations

The central thesis of this chapter is that energy capacity-builders may have ignored user needs in the development of local energy materials, resulting in severe organizational obstacles to program implementation. First, the capacity building surrounding local energy management has too often treated "energy" as an issue separate from other local concerns, placing too much emphasis on the need for new organizational structures and personnel. Rather than incorporating knowledge of the cost savings from energy into the basic management process, local officials have been beckoned to address a new issue and incorporate it into their organizations. Second, since so many local governments designated energy coordinators to fulfill comprehensive roles, the position of such part-time personnel may have been overlooked both in developing informational materials and in assessing the obstacles to CEM. If local officials who designate energy coordinators are themselves confused about the comprehensive nature of energy potential, they may have hampered their own progress by appointing individuals ill-equipped for the energy role.

Local governments *may* have bright prospects for success in instituting and implementing energy programs, despite slow progress to date. Local officials have demonstrated interest in energy savings by appointing energy coordinators. However, the efforts of capacity-builders who have neglected a users' perspective in dealing with local governments may have led to the use of an organizing model unsuited to most local governments.

I have several policy suggestions relating to capacity building for community energy management, especially information dissemination:

(1) The dominant way of organizing for CEM—appointment of a part-time energy coordinator—may not work well because the position of the coordinator in the normal

organizational setting has not been recognized as a possible "precondition" to success either by those appointing coordinators or the capacity-builders who have promoted the appointment of energy coordinators.

(2) Communities may not need energy coordinators to achieve cost savings from energy. Generalist officials, such as city managers, may be well equipped to fulfill the role of heightening interest in integrating energy concerns into the overall management process. They should be targeted for energy information on the potential for local opportunities to use energy strategies. More technical, specialist officials are perhaps less interested and qualified to fulfill a comprehensive energy role, but may be very receptive to specialized energy information targeted to their interests and needs. This piecemeal approach might yield greater chances for integrating energy concerns into the overall management process.

(3) Local energy involvement has been hampered by the tendency to "reinvent the wheel" by approaching energy as a concern to be set apart from other types of productivity measures by calling for new structures and personnel. A more fruitful approach may be to integrate energy concerns into existing organizational systems through alternative approaches to information flow in the organization and greater use of energy examples in the literature on productivity improvement. Finally,

(4) A users' perspective is a useful early step in the development of capacity-building materials for local government energy management.

Local governments may indeed have the "capacity" for dealing with energy management. However, the skills and resources needed to develop, implement, and evaluate energy management programs must be incorporated into the overall management process.

Notes

1. The major studies documenting this conclusion are: Daniel Yergin and Martin Hillenbrand, eds., *Global Insecurity: A Strategy for Energy and Economic*

Renewal (Boston: Houghton Mifflin, 1982); Solar Energy Research Institute, *A New Prosperity: Building A Sustainable Future* (Andover, MA: Brick House Publishing, 1981); Marc Ross and Robert William, *Our Energy: Regaining Control* (New York: McGraw-Hill, 1981); John H. Gibbons and William U. Chandler, *Energy—The Conservation Revolution* (New York: Plenum Press, 1981); Roger Sant et al., *The Least Cost Energy Strategy* (Pittsburgh, PA: Carnegie-Mellon University Press, 1979); Henry Kendall and Steven Nadis eds., *Energy Strategies: Toward a Solar Future* (Cambridge, MA: Ballinger, 1980); Hans H. Landsberg, et al., *Energy: The Next Twenty Years*. Report by a study group sponsored by the Ford Foundation and administered by Resources for the Future (Cambridge, MA: Ballinger, 1979); National Research Council, *Energy in Transition: 1985-2010*. Final Report of the Committee on Nuclear and Alternative Energy Systems, National Academy of Sciences (San Francisco: W.H. Freeman, 1979); Robert Stobaugh and Daniel Yergin, eds., *Energy Future*. Report of the Energy Project at the Harvard Business School (New York: Random House, 1979).

2. David Morris, *Self-Reliant Cities* (Washington, D.C.: Institute for Local Self-Reliance, 1982) and Jon van Til, *Living With Energy Shortfall* (Boulder, CO: Westview Press, 1982) offer longer histories of these energy events as they affect local government.

3. National League of Cities, *Problems, Programs and Needs: A Report on the National League of Cities Survey of Municipal Officials* (Washington, D.C.: National League of Cities, 1980).

4. Steve Hudson, "An Assessment of Local Government Energy Management Activities," *Urban Data Service Reports*, 12, 8 (Washington, D.C.: International City Management Association, August 1980).

5. For examples, see: Annette Woolson, *The Energy Production Handbook* (Washington, D.C.: National Association of Counties Research Foundation, 1981) and David Morris, *Self-Reliant Cities* (Washington, D.C.: Institute for Local Self-Reliance, 1982).

6. On capacity building, see: Beth Walter Honadle, *Capacity-Building (Management Improvement) for Local Governments: An Annotated Bibliography* (Washington, D.C.: U.S. Department of Agriculture, 1981) and Beth Walter Honadle, "A Capacity-Building Framework: A Search For Concept And Purpose," *Public Administration Review*, 41, 5 (September/October 1981): 575-580.

7. Good examples are found in: David Pomerantz and Steve Hudson, *Energy Management in Municipal Organizations: A Framework for Action* (Washington, D.C.: International City Management Association, 1981) and Annette Woolson, *The County Energy Production Handbook* (Washington, D.C.: National Association of Counties Research Foundation, 1981).

8. Steve Hudson, "An Assessment of Local Government Energy Management Activities," *Urban Data Service Reports*, 12, 8 (Washington, D.C.:

International City Management Association, August 1980) is a national survey. There have also been several single-state studies. On North Carolina, see: Beverly A. Cigler, "Organizing for Local Energy Management: Early Lessons," *Public Administration Review*, 41, 4 (July/August 1981): 470-479; Beverly A. Cigler and J. Kent Crawford, "Energy Programs: Untapped Cost Savings for Small Governments," *Municipal Management: A Journal*, 5, 1 (Summer 1982), 39-47 and Beverly A. Cigler and J. Kent Crawford, "Organizing for County Energy Programs: Early Lessons," *Current Municipal Problems*, Winter 1984, vol. 10 (No. 3), 298-319. On Texas, see: James L. Franke and Ann Bowman, "Energy Conservation in a Pro-Consumption Environment." Paper presented at the Annual Meeting of the Southern Political Science Association (Atlanta, Georgia, 6-8 November, 1980).

9. For a discussion of specific activities and programs, see Beverly A. Cigler, "Intergovernmental Roles in Local Energy Conservation: A Research Frontier," *Policy Studies Review*, 1, 4 (May 1982): 761-776. For an excellent overview of market-oriented energy conservation strategies, such as those pursued by the Reagan administration, see Marc Ross and Robert Williams, *Our Energy: Regaining Control* (New York: McGraw-Hill, 1981).

10. See note 6.

11. On a "users' perspective" see the literature on knowledge creation, diffusion, and utilization. An excellent and comprehensive reference is: Robert F. Rich, ed., *The Knowledge Cycle* (Beverly Hills, CA: Sage, 1981), which includes an extensive set of bibliographies on the knowledge cycle.

12. See, especially: "Energy in the Cities Symposium," edited by Joel T. Werth, for the *Planning Advisory Service*, Report 349 (April 1980), including the article by William H. Lucy, "Politics and Energy Conservation: The Role of Local Government," 5-10. Also see: Steve Hudson, "Managing the Impact of the Energy Crisis: The Role of Local Government," *Management Information Service*, 12, 2 (Washington, D.C.: International City Management Association, August 1980) and Beverly A. Cigler, "Directions in Local Energy Policy and Management," *The Urban Interest*, 2, 2 (Fall 1980): 34-42.

13. Lenneal Henderson, "Energy Policy and Urban Fiscal Management," *Public Administration Review* 41, Special Issue (January 1981): 158-164.

14. Especially useful references are: Raymond J. Burby et al., *Saving Energy in Residential Development* (Chapel Hill, NC: The Center for Urban and Regional Studies, 1982); Robert W. Burchell and David Listokin, eds., *Energy and Land Use* (Piscataway, NJ: Center for Urban Policy Research, Rutgers University, 1982); and Carla S. Crane and Joseph D. Steller, Jr., eds., *Energy-Efficient Community Development Techniques* (Washington, D.C.: The Urban Land Institute, 1981).

15. Cigler, "Intergovernmental Roles," 761-776. The internal-external distinction parallels the system-maintenance services (such as water and sewer functions) and life-style services (planning, zoning, housing) categorization of

local government activities developed by Williams. See: Oliver P. Williams, "Life-Style Values and Political Decentralization in Metropolitan Areas," *Southwestern Social Science Quarterly*, 48 (December 1967): 299-310.

16. Beverly A. Cigler, "Implementing Community Energy Management Strategies," in Max Neiman and Barbara J. Burt, eds., *The Social Constraints of Energy Policy Implementation* (Lexington, MA: Lexington Books, 1983), 155-170.

17. A review of the first-generation literature on the topic is Beverly A. Cigler, "Community Energy Planning and Management," *Journal of the American Planning Association*, 48, 2 (Spring 1982): 245-248.

18. The Energy Policy and Conservation Act of 1975 (EPCA, P.L. 94-163) included phased decontrol of crude oil prices and automobile fuel efficiency standards. Phased deregulation of natural gas prices was part of the Natural Gas Policy Act of 1978 (P.L. 95-621).

19. Research studies of state programs include: James L. Regens, "State Policy Responses to the Energy Issue: An Analysis of Innovation," *Social Science Quarterly*, 61, 1 (June 1980): 44-57; Common Cause, *The Path Not Taken* (Washington, D.C.: Common Cause, October 1980); Patricia K. Freeman, "The State's Response to Energy Crisis: An Evaluation of Innovation," in Robert M. Lawrence, ed., *New Dimensions to Energy Policy*, (Lexington, MA: Lexington Books, 1979), 201-207; Hanna J. Cortner, "Developing Energy Policy Within New Sociopolitical Realities," in Gregory A. Daneke and George K. Lagassa, eds., *Energy Policy and Public Administration*, (Lexington, MA: Lexington Books, 1980), 263-273; Thomas R. Dye and Dorothy Davidson, "State Energy Policies: Federal Funds for Paper Programs," *Policy Studies Review*, 1, 2, Nov. 1981 255-262; and Charles S. Perry, "Energy Conservation Policy in the American States: An Attempt at Explanation, *Social Science Quarterly*, 62, 3, Sept. 1981 540-546.

20. Morris, *Self-Reliant Cities*, 129, 130, and 189.

21. An excellent case study explaining CEM is Marion L. Hemphill, "Energy Management from A Community Perspective," *The Urban Interest*, 3, 2 (Fall 1981): 66-75.

22. A description of local government energy management needs is found in Cigler, "Directions in Local Energy Policy and Management," 34-42.

23. See Michael J. Meshenberg et al. *Guidebook for Establishing a Local Energy Management Program* (Argonne, IL: Argonne National Laboratory, 1982) for good examples of programs.

24. See, for example, Werth, "Energy in the Cities Symposium," 5-10; Los Angeles Energy Management Advisory Board, *The Energy/LA Action Plan* (Los Angeles: Office of the Mayor, 1981); City of Portland, *Energy Conservation Choices*. (Springfield, VA: National Technical Information Service, 1977); Hittman Associates, Inc. *Comprehensive Community Energy Planning* (Washington, D.C.: U.S. Department of Energy, 1978); Alan Okagaki and James Benson,

County Energy Plan Guidebook (Fairfax, VA: Institute for Ecological Policies, 1979); and Sizemore and Associates, *Methodology for Energy Management Plans for Small Communities* (Washington, D.C.: U.S. Department of Energy, 1978). The most comprehensive bibliography is Michael J. Meshenberg, *Community Energy Management: An Annotated Bibliography* (Argonne, IL: Argonne National Laboratory, 1982).

25. Richard D. Bingham et al., *Professional Associations and Municipal Innovation* (Madison, WI: The University of Wisconsin Press, 1981).

26. See notes 7 and 24 for examples.

27. See Beverly A. Cigler, "Energy Center Assists Local Officials," *Public Administration Times*, 5, 9 (1 May, 1982): 4.

28. For a review of Reagan policies through 1982, see Cigler, "Intergovernmental Roles in Local Energy Conservation: A Research Frontier," 761-776. For FY 1983 the Reagan administration made a budget request of $22 million for energy conservation and $79 million for solar and other renewable energy programs. Congress appropriated $410 million for conservation and $253 million for solar. For FY 84 the Reagan administration has asked for $101 million for conservation and $102 million for solar and renewables.

29. See note 8.

30. Reported in mid-1982 in a memorandum to members of the National League of Cities Conference of Local Energy Officials. The survey data were reported by Mike Phillips of the Office of Policy Analysis and Development, National League of Cities.

31. Duncan Erley et al., "Energy-Conserving Development Regulations: Current Practice," *Planning Advisory Service*, Report 352 (Chicago: American Planning Association, August 1980).

32. Cigler, "Organizing for Local Energy Management," 470-479; Cigler and Crawford, "Energy Problems: Untapped Cost Savings for Small Governments," 39-47; and Cigler and Crawford, "Organizing for County Energy Programs."

33. California Office of Appropriate Technology, *Local Energy Initiatives: A Second Look. A Survey of Cities and Counties* (Sacramento: California Office of Appropriate Technology, December 1981) and Cigler, "Implementing Community Energy Management Strategies," 155-170.

34. For one example, see: Paul P. Craig, Joel Darmstadter and Stephen Rattien, "Social and Institutional Factors in Energy Conservation," In Jack M. Hollander et al., eds., *Annual Review of Energy*, 1 (Palo Alto: Annual Reviews, Inc., 1976): 535-551.

35. See notes 32 and 8.

36. Cigler, "Organizing for Local Energy Programs: Early Lessons," 470-479.

37. William H. Cunningham and Sally C. Lopreato, *Energy Use and Conservation Incentives: A Study of the Southwestern United States* (New York: Praeger, 1977). Also see note 34.

38. See van Til, *Living with Energy Shortfall;* Marvin I. Olsen, "Public Acceptance of Energy Conservation," in Seymour Warkov, ed., *Energy Policy in the United States: Social and Behavioral Dimensions* (New York: Praeger, 1978); and on public opinion, see Barbara Farhar et al., "Public Opinion About Energy," in J.M. Hollander et al., eds., *Annual Review of Energy*, 5 (Palo Alto: Annual Reviews, Inc., 1980), 141-172.

39. Max Neiman and Barbara J. Burt, "The Political Constraints on Energy-Conservation Policy: The Case of Local Citizen Receptivity," in Max Neiman and Barbara J. Burt, eds., *The Social Constraints of Energy Policy Implementation,"171-188.*

40. *See notes 32, 8 and 35.*

41. *California Energy Commission, Energy Tomorrow, Challenges and Opportunities for California: 1981 Biennial Report* (Sacramento: California Energy Commission, 1981).

42. Cigler, "Implementing Community Energy-Management Strategies," 155-170.

43. The most important is: John L. Moore et al., *The Comprehensive Community Energy Management Program: An Evaluation* (Argonne, IL: Argonne National Laboratory, December 1981). This examines the communities that participated in a federal government CEM capacity-building effort. An intensive look at obstacles to program implementation in the twelve most energy-active North Carolina communities is reported in Cigler, "Implementing Community Energy Management Strategies," 155-170. An evaluation of the Solar Technology Assessment Program is S. Carnes et al., *Community-Based Assessment and Planning of Energy Futures: Final Report of the Decentralized Solar Energy Technology Assessment Program* (Oak Ridge, TN: Oak Ridge National Laboratory, 1982).

44. See John Randolph, "Implementation of Community Energy Plans and Programs," in National Association of Counties and National League of Cities, eds., *Community Energy Strategies* (Washington, D.C.: National Association of Counties, 1982), 3-25; Moore et al., *Comprehensive Community Energy-Management Programs;* and Cigler, "Implementing Community Energy-Management Strategies," 155-170.

45. Cigler, "Implementing Community Energy-Management Strategies," 155-170.

46. Mancur Olson, *The Logic of Collective Action* (New York: Shocken Books, 1971) is the source from which this conclusion is drawn. David Rosen, "Local Energy Options and National Policy: A Changing Environment," *The Urban Interest*, 3, 2 (Fall 1981), 57-65 makes this point about individual conservation behavior in his skeptical view of the local role in energy involvement. He overlooks, however, the possibility of promoting local energy involvement on the grounds of cost savings, not energy savings.

47. This conclusion is made after reviewing over 400 separate publications and other capacity-building materials directed toward local energy involvement, as well as examining the literature on productivity improvements in government. Interesting is the new local government trend of "organizing for productivity improvement" by creating special positions or units solely to deal with productivity. See: W. Maureen Godsey, "Productivity Improvement in Small Governments," *Urban Data Service Reports*, 14, 7 (Washington, D.C.: International City Management Association, July 1982). Most of these efforts utilize existing personnel such as the city manager's office.

48. See: U.S. Department of Housing and Urban Development, *Capacity Building: Local Government Approaches to Energy Conservation* (Washington, D.C.: U.S. Department of Housing and Urban Development, 1979). There have been attempts, however, to promote the use of community development block grant funds for energy programs, but this has not been extensive and the terminology used is still "energy." See: U.S. Department of Housing and Urban Development, *Block Grant Energy Conservation* (Washington, D.C.: U.S. Department of Housing and Urban Development, 1980).

49. See Meshenberg, *Community Energy Management: An Annotated Bibliography* for a compendium of the literature, including existing community plans and the national publications and models developed for CEM.

50. This author's review of 400 CEM materials shows that the typical approach has been to develop a single, comprehensive guidebook on CEM for distribution to local officials. An example is: North Carolina Energy Division, *Energy Management at the Local Level in North Carolina* (Raleigh, NC: North Carolina Department of Commerce, 1979). The book treats the energy issue with chapters on every phase of government involvement. It was used for six statewide workshops with local energy officials in 1979.

51. See note 8.

52. See notes 32, 8, 35, and 40.

53. The state of Florida began using this approach in mid-1981. Twelve separate volumes were developed on local energy programs, each treating a specialized topic and sent to officials in that specialty. The volumes treat such topics as procurement practices, street lighting, building management, em-

ployee programs and public utilities. See: State of Florida, Governor's Energy Office, *Energy Technical Assistance Series for Local Governments*, 12 Volumes (Tallahassee: Governor's Energy Office, Fall 1981). However, the Florida materials still separate energy from other issues in both a symbolic and organizational sense.

54. See: Jay M. Shafritz and Albert C. Hyde, *Classics of Public Administration* (Oak Park, IL: Moore Publishing, 1978); Gary A. Giamartino and Diane C. Hudgins, "Buttress or Bubble? Behavioral Science Approaches on Improving Public Sector Productivity." Paper presented at the annual meetings of the Urban Affairs Association, Philadelphia, April 1982); and John P. Topinka, "Integrating Energy: A Fiscal and Resource Management Strategy for Local Government—An Overview." Unpublished draft prepared for the National Association of Counties, April 1982.

55. Leslie A. Brook, "Integrating Energy Resources Management into the Public Management Process: A Strategy of Comprehensive Energy Management," *County Energy Management Notebook* (Washington, D.C.: National Association of Counties, 1981), demonstrates this point for Dade County, Florida.

56. George Washnis, ed., *Productivity Improvement Handbook for State and Local Governments* (New York: John Wiley & Sons, 1980) and Frederick O'R. Hayes et al., *Linkages: Improving Financial Management in Local Government* (Washington, D.C.: The Urban Institute, 1982).

57. The point is that the productivity improvement works are lacking an essential ingredient—the incorporation of energy into all systems—*because* the energy "experts" have not been successful in realizing linkages or, perhaps, disseminating their works.

58. The National Community Energy Management Center was a cooperative service of the professional associations representing state and local governments. Not surprising, these associations continue their own separate energy projects, which may be confusing to casually interested officials.

59. The author is currently completing such a project. The theoretical background used here is reiterated and tested in Cigler, "Implementing Programs: The Place of Position," manuscript in progress.

16

Capacity Building in an Intergovernmental Context: The Case of the Aging Network

ROBERT B. HUDSON

The concept of capacity building has considerable relevance to the network of agencies serving the elderly which has come into existence since passage of the Older Americans Act in 1965. In addition to the State Units on Aging created through the original legislation, there are now over 600 substate Area Agencies on Aging mandated by amendments passed in 1973. A major nutrition program for the elderly was authorized in the same year and has since been folded into the Title III social services program. Expenditures for social and nutrition services under the act have grown from $5 million in 1966 to over $600 million in 1981. More recently, however, budgetary constraints, the demands of the new federalism, and concern about meeting the social and health needs of a growing older population have placed new demands on these agencies. Concern with capacity building has mounted because these developments pose a significant challenge to the organizational integrity of aging agencies and to their ability to meet mandated objectives.

Conversely, the place and history of the state and area agencies on aging represent a useful application of concepts and strategies associated with capacity building. Agencies established and funded through federal grants-in-aid have characteristics that set them apart from general purpose and other indigenous governmental agencies. Agendas, funding, and support often originate in Washington and, depending on the proportions, make designated agencies of federal grants something of a breed apart. Furthermore, the unit in question may be a private nonprofit agency, a separate commission, a bureau, division, or, in the case of aging, a department unto itself. The formally designated beneficiaries in federal GIA programs may also differ from those that have been or would be highlighted in the state and substate decision-making process. This was most clearly the case in the War on Poverty programs, but the litany of grants-in-aid show it to extend well beyond these. Most generally, it is the vertical linkages and symbiotic relation-ships among corresponding federal, state, and local agencies that often differentiate the grant-in-aid supported programs from state and local ones.

This paper brings capacity-building issues to "the aging network": the Administration on Aging (AoA) in Washington, charged with administering the Older Americans Act programs (excepting the Senior Community Service Employment Program, administered by the De-partment of Labor with a 1981 budget of $288 million); the fifty-seven State Units on Aging (SUAs), serving as the designated state agencies; some 650 Area Agencies on Aging, which plan and coordinate service delivery in substate planning and service areas; and 1,200 congregate meal sites and an even larger number of social service providers.

The development of this network of agencies and the increase in federal appropriations by a factor of 120 is impressive. However, here the question of capacity becomes critical. Large numbers and high growth rates are not necessarily the result of demonstrated capacity nor do they necessarily mean that capacity has developed in their wake. Rather, one can argue that much of this growth took place largely independent of properties associated with organizational capacity. The question then becomes: What has been and can be done to build capacity given that it is now both needed and mandated? Following a brief definitional discussion of capacity building, these issues are discussed in turn in the context of this network of aging agencies.

Capacity Building in an Organizational Context

As demonstrated by Honadle[1], capacity and capacity building are used and understood in a number of ways. Some treatments stress programmatic accomplishments, others emphasize organizational at-tributes or states. As Honadle notes, neither those emphasizing public service nor those invoking organizational survival as end-states tell us about what capable organizations do.

This dichotomy is reminiscent of the long-standing debate in organizational sociology concerning how best to understand and measure organizational effectiveness. Goal-centered views emphasize outputs to the point where, as Etzioni remarks, "the fact that an organization can become more effective by allocating less means to goal activities is a paradox."[2] A systems resource approach, such as that of Yuchtman and Seashore, stresses the ability of an organization "to exploit its environment in the acquisition of scarce and valued resources."[3] The difficulty of stressing resource acquisition to the virtual exclusion of all else is captured by Hannan and Freeman:

> Organizations are social systems whose creation is accomplished through a public affirmation of goal-seeking behavior. This announcement of intention serves as a legitimating device and as a basis of the claim on resources including participation.[4]

Thus, neither of these two approaches taken alone is sufficient for understanding the interplay of goal-related activity and organizational needs. Goal-oriented approaches pay inadequate attention to organizational and political factors necessary to organizational well-being, and pure systems approaches weight organizational health to at least the partial exclusion of official goals and mandated objectives.

Capacity building becomes a useful concept in this context because it captures the need to bridge these perspectives. It is not simply that official goals must be pursued or that organizations have separate needs in the pursuit of such goals, but rather that means must be devised to make congruent the organizational goal of prosperity and the public expectation of goal attainment. As understood here, high-capacity organizations are those that perform the following four organizational functions.

(1) They are able to anticipate changing circumstances (an intelligence function), and they are able to move expeditiously in directions called for (an adaptive function).

(2) They are able to attract resources—personnel, dollars, public/elite support—on a secure and regularized basis.

(3) They use their resources to accomplish programmatic goals, but are able as well to transform or parlay both their "raw" resources and their programmatic accomplishments in such a manner that promotes further goal-seeking activity and organizational well-being.

(4) They are able to determine policies and implement program responses with considerable autonomy.

These imperatives meld the two perspectives above and do so by placing a particular emphasis on the importance of having in place organizations that can move in and draw from their environment.

Agencies that grew up under the Older Americans Act have not had to depend on their success in undertaking either of these subtasks, but are finding it increasingly in their organizational interest and in the interest of functionally impaired older persons to be able to do so. Such actions are made necessary by actual or threatened shifts in their sources of funding, demographic changes affecting both client and provider populations, and more demanding expectations of what they should be undertaking and accomplishing. In light of these changes, aging network agencies must structure their activities in ways designed to enhance their performance in line with this set of organizational functions.

Aging Network Development and Capacity Building

The history of the aging network is one of notable growth and the development of many services and some service systems. However, because of their historic dependence and reliance on Older Americans Act language and funding, the state and area agencies have not, for the most part, demonstrated high levels of organizational capacity. Why capacity has not developed in light of the very substantial growth of the network can be laid to three interrelated factors.

Most notable have been the appropriations increases which lessened the need for agencies to look elsewhere for both monetary and political support. Secondly, there has been a multiple and shifting programmatic mandate around what should be the services emphasis, priority clients, and appropriate agency roles. These substantive and temporal inconsistencies have made it difficult for network agencies to stake out their programmatic and organizational place and thus attract and develop the resources needed for capacity-building efforts. Finally, aging agencies have had limited success in attracting support from political and professional constituencies which might provide the multiple-support base critical to building organizational capacity. In generating and maintaining support from any given group, they have left themselves open to criticism or indifference from other potential supporters.

Origins and Appropriations

The aging network was largely the creation of federal initiative, and its funding base depends heavily on federal funding through the Older Americans Act. Only a handful of states had small commissions on aging prior to 1965. With passage of the Older Americans Act, all states had a designated agency on aging by 1969. The federal administrative allocations for these agencies were miniscule, being limited to $15,000 until 1969 and $25,000 until 1972. The bulk of the Title III funds were passed through to local communities where its principal uses were for senior center and recreational activities. In 1969, the federal/state matching ratio was increased from 1:1 to 3:1. By 1971, funding under Title III had still only reached $13 million, but serious questions had nonetheless arisen about how the program was being administered and what it was accomplishing. At the convening of the 1971 White House Conference on Aging, there was serious talk that the program should be fundamentally restructured or eliminated altogether.[5]

For a variety of reasons, the White House Conference resuscitated the Older Americans Act program. Agency capacities and program accomplishments were not among the reasons. Rather, they resulted from President Nixon's decision to announce a quadrupling of Older Americans Act appropriations to the 4,500 delegates as a means of distracting them from the fact that he was opposing a 20 percent increase in Social Security benefits being proposed by presidential candidate Wilbur Mills and his Democratic colleagues[6]. Nixon also endorsed creation of a nutrition program for the elderly which the Democrats had also been promoting. The result of all this was an increase in total Older Americans Act appropriations from the $32 million of 1971 to $196 million in 1973.

The ongoing concern that the Older Americans Act program was accomplishing little coupled with this enormous increase in funding and institution of a new categorical grant program, in turn, yielded a new substate planning strategy. The administration combined its interest in substate regional planning strategies with its belief that state aging agencies could not develop local aging services. From this emerged the 1973 amendments to the act, which created the Area Agencies to broker and develop services[7] and which now provided federal funds for services development on a 90:10 matching basis. By the late 1970s, Area Agencies blanketed the country, and steps had also been taken to bring the nutrition program under Area Agency control in the name of developing a comprehensive and coordinated service delivery system. Most impressive, however, have been the appropriation increases which, excluding the Title V Senior Community Service Employment Program, jumped from the $196 million of 1973 to $350 million in 1976, to $509 million in 1978, and $674 million in 1981, before falling off slightly during the last two years. In light of both the rate and size of this growth in federal financial support, capacity-building concerns were not critical to aging network agencies.

Programmatic Mandate

A second factor, more directly impeding development of organizational capacity in aging network agencies, has been the scope and variety of their mandate. They are, at once, charged with being advocates for older persons on a whole range of concerns—income, health care, employment, housing, transportation, among others—and with putting in place a variety of social services. No formal means testing is allowed, but state and area agencies are to give priority to the economically and socially disadvantaged. Within the spectrum of social services, certain ones are to be given priority, but which services and how much priority has been changed at least three times since the idea of priorities was first introduced in the 1975 amendments. Area Agencies are not intended to deliver services themselves, but that proscription has been unevenly invoked over the years as well. Finally, Area Agencies are expected to draw down, pool, tap, and mobilize local resources while developing coordinative relationships with other local agencies and providers.

The multiple mandates and expectations have also created dilemmas for state and Area Agencies which bear directly on capacity-building issues. A major one concerns the relative emphasis to be placed on services development and on more general advocacy efforts aimed at getting generic systems to better serve the elderly, or what Armour et al. refer to as the "direct delivery of services" versus the "institutional change" strategies.[8] While the ambiguity has been present all along, a reading of the legislative history strongly suggests that the state agencies set up under the original legislation in 1965 were to see to it that departments of welfare, mental health, etc., took greater cognizance of the elderly in their activities.

The amendments of 1969 also gave heavy emphasis to this function. However, it was difficult for these nascent organizations to take on such major entities, and they tended to develop (or fall back on) service activities. Studies addressing the place of the state agencies beyond their services development work found limited impact[9] and low salience with state influentials[10]. This trend was abetted by the high growth rates in funds directly under the agencies' control, by the creation of the Area Agencies, and in the increasingly generous federal financial participation formula. In these earlier years, the Area Agencies worked to solidify their relations with the state agencies (and they were by no means always tranquil) rather than working or being forced to reach accommodation with human service agencies and other political actors at their own level. That strategy made sense under one set of environmental circumstances, but not so much under the constraints seen more recently.

A second dilemma concerning organizational mandate centers on whom among the elderly the agency should give priority attention to and, more generally, how it wishes to conceptualize and view "the elderly" in the community. The ambiguities facing an Area Agency are seen in both the Older Americans Act language and in the local statutes by bylaws that govern their activities in the community. Should all older persons, regardless of their individual circumstances, be served equally, or should the predominant effort go towards the needs of poor, sick, isolated, and minority elderly? Means testing is not permitted, and the general legislative emphasis on disadvantaged status can be given more or less weight. The recent attention to public allocations to the aging[11] and among the aging[12] has heightened overall concern and especially the adequacy versus equity choices contained therein.

In political terms, the elderly have high standing[13], and the provision of visible services to such a legitimate group can generate much support. Congregate nutrition programs are the best example because they tend to attract older persons who are relatively mobile and are tied into the community, and the nutrition sites themselves are excellent political focal points. However, when resources are constrained and the frail population is growing (the number of Americans over eighty-five grew by more than 50 percent during the past decade), there are distinct pressures for choosing target populations and services.

The general question has clear capacity-building ramifications: do Area Agencies better meet their responsibilities and augment their own capacities by highlighting the needs and contributions of a community's senior citizenry (Nelson, 1982, plays out this option under the rubric of "veteranship")[14] or by concentrating their limited resources on the most disadvantaged subpopulations. The first option runs the risk of degenerating into cheerleading and "creaming" clients. However, the second can lead these modestly-sized agencies into confrontation with health and long-term care service systems, which could overwhelm them if they are not up to the task organizationally[15]. The degrees of freedom associated with the multiple mandates of earlier years are being supplanted by emerging fiscal and demographic pressures. The future appears to lie in areas where capacity will be a requisite of organizational strength and purpose.

Perceived Roles and Purposes

Also impeding organizational development have been the perceptions and expectations of different audiences of what the organizational place and purpose of Area Agencies should be. This can be seen in contrasting the perspectives and concerns of service providers with whom aging agencies contract, sister human service agencies with whom they deal on a less formal interorganizational basis, and oversight officials who are often negatively disposed toward categorical and client-oriented agencies.

As befits organizations that have had large budgetary increases, mainly for the purpose of contracting for services, aging agencies have frequent and positive relationships with service providers. In their study involving twenty-four Area Agencies, Newcomer et al. report that service providers comprised by far the largest category of "interorganizational partners" of Area Agencies and that services and program development have been emphasized much more heavily than "legitimation" activities, vis., those aimed at elected officials and public media.[16]

Because providing services dollars is a prototypical distributive activity from which all involved parties benefit, its being of high frequency is not surprising. Federal dollars are coming to agencies of recent creation which are charged with and have chosen to devote much effort to making social and allied services available to a well-regarded and visible constituency. Furthermore, this activity imposes virtually no constraints on the behavior of the other parties involved, such as would be the case in a more regulatory policy or a less legitimate constituency. So long as only minimal competition for the services dollars is present, as has often been the case, a very positive and nonthreatening set of relationships can be developed. These relationships, however, do not require or foster capacity-building efforts.

The perspective of other human service agencies with which Area Agencies engage on a nonfunding basis can be quite different. Where an Area Agency confines itself to funneling federal dollars through to service providers, there need not be a relationship of any kind. However, assuming a program development role may take the Area Agency into the province of other agencies, and assuming an advocacy role involves prodding other agencies into doing more on behalf of the elderly within their service population. A recent instance reported in several areas centers on the opposition of Visiting Nurses Associations to the involvement of Area Agencies in health-related case management.

Advocacy activities undertaken vis-a-vis other agencies, if meaningful, involve new priorities or allocations on the part of those agencies. As a result, a not-infrequent consequence of these activities is relatively high levels of goal displacement in the form of working agreements and joint agreements which, once in place, may generate little in addition. More substantive remedies have come where generic agencies, such as departments of public welfare, have spun off dollars and responsibility to state and area aging agencies, as in the case of federal Title XX funds. Moves of this kind may involve considerable dollars, but they do not necessarily lead to capacity building. Domains may be redefined without concomitant improvements in management or administration, on the one hand, or services and output effectiveness on the other. However, where new functions have been assumed in conjunction with such a transfer, as in the case of Massachusetts Home Care Corporations (the state's Area Agencies), increased organizational capacity can result.

The third audience with yet another perspective are the policy planners and legislative oversight bodies looking for measures of services effectiveness in the amelioration or prevention of problems among the elderly. Agencies throughout the aging network encounter skepticism here whether they are involved in service-oriented or advocacy-oriented activities or both. The services strategy lends itself to measurement in terms of output units, best exemplified by the nutrition program. However, the more pervasive problem in the social services, resulting from the fact that "all services are good"[17] often means that a broader, rather than a narrower, array of services is developed.

Program planners, among others, have a particular problem with advocacy efforts, primarily because it is difficult to document what, if anything, they have actually accomplished. And when supportive figures are generated—such as the Administration on Aging reporting that state and area agencies mobilized $437 million in fiscal year 1979—they may satisfy the policy planners[18], but there are skeptical reactions elsewhere, including some state and area agency officials. Overall, oversight pressures have inclined aging agency officials toward strategies that are quantifiable but which also may be insular. Without debating the programmatic issues in question, the larger point remains that these pressures may do more to concretize organizational outputs than to strengthen organizational capacity.

The origins of aging service programs under federal auspices and the marked increase in appropriations for services and allied activities over the years has meant that growth could take place largely in the absence of capacity-building efforts on the part of the agencies involved. The mixed programmatic mandates and multiple program constituencies made it difficult to put together effective capacity-building efforts while at the same time making it possible to avoid the risks and investments such efforts might entail. Thus, in important regards, the need preconditions for building capacity in aging network agencies have not been present.

The New Relevance of Capacity Building

Shifting trends and perceptions in the human services environment have generated a new need for and concern with organizational capacity. They are also creating new organizational and programmatic opportunities in the area of community-based, long-term care services and management toward which a number of aging network agencies are now moving.

Budgetary pressures and the New Federalism are clearly threatening to upset the world of the aging network as it has developed in its first fifteen years. Funding for Older Americans Act programs has held up better than in many human service areas, but level funding is the most that the Title III program can reasonably expect in the years immediately ahead. There also continues to be concern—that ebbs and flows with various grant consolidation proposals—that the Older Americans Act might be folded into the social services block grant and potentially the state and area agencies with it. The presence of this 700-plus agency network and the symbolic affirmation represented by the Older Americans Act has helped forestall this. However, with the HHS Office that houses the Administration on Aging and in analogous situations in state capitals across the country, there have been attempts to earmark funds and consolidate functions. The aging agencies generally see this as encroachment and in violation of provisions of the Older Americans Act. Hierarchical officals in the umbrella offices housing these agencies see this rather as needed coordination in the name of more comprehensive programming.

The aging of both the overall population and of the older population itself will exacerbate these budgetary and bureaucratic pressures. The population aged sixty-fifty and older will increase by 30 percent between 1980 and 2000, and the population over eighty-five by 84 percent. This growth in the "old-old" population has major policy ramifications in that 22.5 percent of persons aged over eighty-five have "extremely impaired" health status as contrasted with 6.3 percent for those aged sixty-five to sixty-nine. Adding further pressures is changing population ratios between younger and older groups. Thus, in 1950 there were 130 persons aged sixty-five or over for every 100 persons aged forty-five to forty-nine, by 1980 that figure had risen to 210. There are also fewer "older" children potentially available to care for aged parents: in 1950 there were thirty persons aged sixty-five or over for every 100 aged sixty to sixty-four; by 1980 the ratio had increased to 50:100. The volume of health and social needs among the elderly will grow significantly in the years ahead while the proportion of middle-aged and young-old persons available to assist in informal caregiving will decline. Since by far the greatest portion of informal caregiving has been undertaken by daughters and other women, the increased labor force participation of women will further limit the amount of informal caregiving available.

The logical, if extremely difficult, solution to these budgetary and demographic trends lies potentially in inexpensive, noninstitutional social/health services. Herein lies the principal substantive issue facing state and area agencies on aging. The demarcation point in long-term care between social and health services is often murky. Many older persons who have moderate functional incapacities are living alone or in settings where they cannot maintain themselves without some amount of outside assistance. A combination of social services (nutrition, housekeeping, transportation) and health services (bathing, therapy, self-medication) can assist such individuals in staying at home, an objective to which virtually all older persons, gerontologists, and policy analysts subscribe. The growth of a new paraprofessional, the homemaker-home health aide, embodies the mixing of these two worlds.

The question here becomes who should fund, organize, oversee, administer and staff the mix of community-based health and social services where so much attention is being focused. Public funding has most often come from Title XX and the Older Americans Act, but major modifications in Medicaid regulations in 1981 have opened up that very considerable source of funds to a much greater extent than was previously the case. Organizations involved in this arena have been from health and social work, have been professional and paraprofessional, and have been public, private nonprofit, and proprietary. The lack of coordination around assessment, screening, care planning, provision of care, and funding sources has been of increasing concern over the last decade[19].

Community-based, long-term care serves as the best current example of a problem area where high organizational capacity for those involved is not only needed, but also where such capacity can be generated. The potential importance of an area such as long-term care can be seen in the following discussion relating the Area Agencies on Aging to the four-part composite of capacity-building functions set forth earlier. It should also be noted that there is growing evidence of increased interest and concrete efforts on the part of network agencies in long-term care systems building, most notably in Massachusetts, Wisconsin, Arkansas, and Maine.

Capacity-Building Steps for the Aging Network

It is safe to say that Area Agencies on Aging need to be more concerned about capacity building today than they have at any point in their development. Historically, there has been a category of Area Agency that chose and was able to "low ball it"; i.e., they simply took the federal money, passed it out to service providers as extensively as possible, met the minimum reporting requirements, sat on the boards of a few other human service agencies, and generated a modicum of publicity for themselves. There may continue to be a small number that exist doing essentially this, but they come sufficiently close to Eisenstadt's category of "debureaucratization" as to warrant no further attention here.

The capacity-building and programmatic issues confronting the Area Agencies result from altered funding streams, heightened interest and expectations in their work, and a general uncertainty that has not beset this highly protected network until recently. In order to attain acceptably high levels of capacity, Area Agencies must engage in activities in line with the definition enumerated earlier. The discussion here is organized around those elements, with the material suggesting what must be done in light of the situation most Area Agencies find themselves in today.

Adapting to Changing Circumstances

In order to attain high levels of organizational capacity, the Area Agencies must increasingly identify with problem areas that are salient to the community at large, political elites, and the elderly and their families. In so doing, they establish the legitimacy of their claims to new resources and the potential for their own further development.

Organizations do not generate capacity if there is not a recognition that they need it. Whereas in prior years, social services for the elderly was considered a second-order agenda item, that arena today has a series of first-order functions associated with it: client-oriented tracking and monitoring, pre-admission screening, discharge planning, channeling and triage. It is not that these functions are new, but they and a variety of allied noninstitutional service/planning options for the elderly have taken on a currency that can serve a traditional social services organization that actively engages in them. The increasing concern among executive offices, legislative committees, and advocates may also serve Area Agencies in moving toward center stage in development of community-based health/social service systems. In past years, an aggressive stance would have been construed as moving where other agencies had well-established prior claims. Today, Area Agency initiatives in this direction can be more easily interpreted as their moving to assume a more central role in an area of very legitimate concern to them, the Visiting Nurses Association example notwithstanding.

While Area Agency adaptation involves assuming this new role, it does not necessitate giving up all that has gone before. In particular, engaging in major problem-solving efforts does not require that Area Agencies give up their fully legitimate (if also often underutilized) claims to institutional representation of the elderly as a constituency and all of the visions of senior power and voting blocs that may accompany it. That is a constituencywide orientation that no other public agency can realistically lay claim to, and it is one that continues to have clear political value. The Area Agency can symbolically represent the collective interests of older persons to the community, and it can give recognition to those leaders and others who have served that constituency well. Despite recent debate and alarms, there remains very considerable public support for old-age benefits[20]. To transform that kind of resource into needed benefits stands an appropriate use of the general support that exists for the elderly.

Resource Generation

Capacity building often carries with it the notion of self-sufficiency, as in Gamm and Fisher contending that communities should be assisted in their development with a minimum of outside assistance.[21] In the case of organizations, certainly as understood in open-systems terms, there is an unending need for attracting outside resources which can be transformed in ways valued by the larger environment. Critical to high-capacity organizations is their ability to attract resources on a regular basis, almost certainly from multiple sources. The importance of this last criterion is shown especially clearly in the case of the Area Agencies on Aging where ever-growing levels of resources from what had proved to be a remarkably secure funding source seem clearly to have impeded capacity-building inclinations and efforts.

Under the now-prevailing or impending circumstances, most Area Agencies must rethink past strategies on purely maintenance grounds if not capacity-building ones. Specifically, there is a utility function that Area Agencies must now consider. Put simply, to whom are they essential and to what extent can those parties provide them with requisite levels of support? Echoing the previous section, it will no longer do to have local actors acknowledging that Area Agencies provide a community service and that it is good to have them in place. When area nursing homes have sixty-plus day-waiting lists, when city mental health officials are trying to find alternative placements for a census that is both aging and being deinstitutionalized, when constituents want to know how a frail relative can be served, and when county budgets are being strained by an array of demands, the Area Agency that has answers and strategies will be in a favorable resource-attracting situation.

The particular effort many Area Agencies need to make in this regard centers on constituency building. Despite the presumed fact that the elderly stand as a natural and easily mobilized group, there have been very uneven efforts at the local level in doing this. To this point, state and area agencies have not been prominently featured in those instances of successful political mobilization reported[22]. Area Agencies that can identify a limited number of salient concerns that would generate interest and activity among older persons (who comprise over 30 percent of the population in some rural counties) could in turn set a number of forces into action. By identifying possible solutions, as well as problems, and by keeping key officials informed on both counts (surprising officials with constituency complaints generated by one's own actions is not a wise agency posture), the agency can become the focal point for a community response.

By joining reasonable solutions to problems that are pressing on both individual constituents and political officials, the Area Agency makes an initial claim to additional support. As new resources are drawn in, the development process can then build. Staff and monetary resources generate programmatic output which redound to the benefit of the agency in the form of a reputation for reliability and effectiveness. From this state can then come continued community support for the agency's role in the problem area at hand.

Parlaying Resources

The notion of parlaying resources presumes the ability of an organization to transform raw resources into valued organizational outputs, but also includes the idea that high-capacity organizations are able to bank or store some of these resources. Strictly in dollar terms, this might mean being able to create discretionary accounts to be used in the future or, even more desirable, being able to establish the equivalent of endowments. In the case of public funds and public agencies, however, such steps are not easily taken.

Less tangible but of at least equal value are resources that can be held and built upon. Skilled personnel and leadership are most notable here. Agencies that attract, hold, and develop skilled personnel are in an upward cycle of capacity building that can take a fledgling organization and fully institutionalize it. The importance of high-quality personnel and strong leadership need not be belabored here; the point in this context is that personnel represent the most important organizational resource that can be developed and employed without being directly expended.

A second organizational resource that can serve to build the organization does so as it is expended, this being of course the programmatic output of the organization. The agency that is demonstrably effective in meeting objectives, or just reputedly so, is one that is building on and recapturing the quality of its own product. This positive track record becomes a core resource in the form of the organization's effectiveness, legitimacy, and goodwill.

For relatively small, publicly supported human service organizations like Area Agencies, a skilled staff and positive reputation are the principal bankable commodities. The studies conducted on aging network agencies relating to organizational development issues consistently speak to the leadership and personnel variable. Marmor and Kutza determined that the well-known problem of lack of legislative clarity and mandate could be more than offset if certain organizational attributes were in place—the most important being agency leadership.[23] Lebowitz, in reviewing the findings of several early studies of Area Agencies, concluded that structural factors—often argued to impede effective interorganizational activity—were also of second-order importance where leadership, political savvy and local support were present.[24] Recent interviews conducted in four communities reinforce these conclusions. Thus in one community, county commissioners felt they would be morally obligated to allocate additional county funds to the Area Agency if Older Americans Act appropriations were cut because of the Area Agency's remarkable track record at attracting significant amounts of outside funding. The reputation for doing much with little seemed clearly to have generated future exchange value.

Autonomy in Goal Choice

Capacity building connotes more than anything else the organizational ability to embark on activities the organization has determined to be central to its mandate and purpose. This presumes the ability to move independently in its environment as contrasted with being buffeted and constrained by those around it. As environments become marked by more actors, limited resources, new problems, and increased outside attention, the ability to choose one's course becomes increasingly difficult. Under those circumstances, however, autonomy is a better indicator of high capacity than it is where categorical and funding protection lend the appearance of latitude and discretion.

Even in pressured circumstances, it should be possible for small agencies to develop goal strategies that help to establish their position and direction without immediately threatening them. Positive working relationships have developed between Area Agencies and mental health, public health, and welfare agencies where there are overlapping or dovetailing clienteles or concerns (e.g., the chronically mentally ill elderly). The size of the task in such cases is sufficient to induce agencies to pool their resources, and their exposure, as the volume of need arises faster than budgetary allocations. The collective mentality of public agencies may be further reinforced as interest among hospitals and nursing home chains in vertical integration into the community grows more pronounced. Environmental pressures may transform the goal-displaced and artificial interagency linkages of past years into decidedly goal-oriented coalitions determined to maintain their place and prerogatives.

The latitude and differentiation that Area Agencies may need will be in place at such time as organizational (or coalitional) goals are set and understood by the larger community. Goal choice is the principal means through which an organization deals with those around it, and the organization that is able to choose the course it wishes to follow has also developed a high level of organizational capacity.

Conclusion

Much of the above is about changing circumstances and emerging issues. Of greatest overall concern must be how to meet the needs of a population that is both growing and growing older during a period when resources for health and social service functions will not increase at past rates. Devising appropriate interventions will require high levels of both intellectual and organizational capacity.

What is most notable about the aging network perhaps is that the circumstances—demographic, budgetary, intergovernmental—that make capacity building important are the very ones that to some degree make it possible. Out of dislocations and pressures can come the openings that foster, as well as require, capacity-building efforts. The key to success will lie in recognizing and addressing these opportunities while retaining the more traditional functions and identities that have given agencies serving the elderly a positive standing.

From the perspective of both public administration and inter-governmental policy making, a question that looms throughout centers on the wisdom of maintaining and further developing what will continue to be in some measure a network associated with client recognition as well as problem solving. Whatever the negatives may be, a strong argument can now be made that, by chance as much as by design, there is a network of well-established agencies in place which can potentially perform key, long-term care functions and do so in a manner that can complement and supplement the health-related institutional sector. The history and modest size of these agencies leave many questions unresolved, but their particular place in the human services is such that, with increased levels of organizational capacity, they might prove very well suited to the task.

In its application to the aging network, the approach to capacity building used here has gone beyond the fairly straightforward notion that organizations must develop an ability to move with autonomy and direction in their task environments. The approach here has, first, emphasized that understanding the reciprocal relationship between goal activity and organizational well-being is critical. Thus, while organizations need to be strong enough to realize their mandated goals, the very choice of those goals and the activities directed toward them is an integral component in their developing organizational strength. Organizations that do not choose goals sanctioned by members of the larger community will be unable to attract and mobilize the monetary and staff resources essential for capacity-building purposes.

Second, organizations must devise means of storing and enhancing these resources rather than simply processing and funneling them. In fact, this concept of parlaying, when operationalized and in force, connotes a reversal of the unidirectionality usually associated with the systems model. Existing resources, including both staff and product, can generate an appeal and reputation which attracts resources to an organization independent of staff efforts to bring them in. Human service agencies that appreciate the reciprocity of public goals and organizational health and who use each for the enhancement of the other will attract resources and develop capacity while also serving a larger need.

Notes

1. Beth Walter Honadle. "A Capacity-Building Framework: A Search for Concept and Purpose," *Public Administration Review* 41 (September-October 1981):575-580; and Beth Walter Honadle. "Managing Capacity Building: Problems and Approaches." *Journal of the Community Development Society* 13 (1982):65-73.

2. A. Etzioni, "Two Approaches to Organizational Analysis: A Critique and a Suggestion." *Aministrative Science Quarterly* 5 (September 1960):257-278.

3. E. Yuchtman and S. E. Seashore. "A System Resource Approach to Organizational Effectiveness, " *American Sociological Review* 32 (1967):891-903.

4. M. T. Hannan and J. Freeman. "Obstacles to Comparative Studies," in *New Perspectives on Organizational Effectiveness*, ed. P. S. Goodman and J.M. Pennings (San Francisco:Jossey-Bass, 1977).

5. H. Sheppard. *The Administration on Aging—Or a Successor?* (Washington, D.C.: U.S. Senate Special Committee on Aging, 1971).

6. R.B. Hudson. "Client Politics and Federalism: The Case of the Older Americans Act." Paper prepared for the 1973 annual meeting of the American Political Science Association, New Orleans, LA.

7. B. Gold. "The Role of the Federal Government in the Provision of Social Services to Older Persons." *The Annals* 415 (September 1974):55–69.

8. P.K. Armour, C.L. Estes and M.L. Noble. "The Continuing Design and Implementation Problems of a National Policy on Aging: Title III of the Older Americans Act," in *The Aging in Politics*, ed. R.B. Hudson (Springfield, IL: Charles Thomas, 1981).

9. R.B. Hudson and M. Veley. "Federal Funding and State Planning: The Case of the State Units on Aging, *Gerontologist* 14 (April 1974):122–129.

10. R.J. Newcomer et al. *Funding Practices, Policies, and Performance of State and Area Agencies on Aging: Final Report, Executive Summary* (University of California at San Francisco, School of Nursing, 1982).

11. R.J. Samuelson. "Aging America: Who Will Shoulder the Growing Burden." *National Journal* 10 (1978) 1712–1717; and J.A. Califano. "The Aging of America: Questions for the Four-Generation Society," *The Annals* 438 (July 1978): 96–107.

12. B. Neugarten, ed, *Age or Need? Public Policies for Older People*. (Beverly Hills, CA: Sage, 1982).

13. R.B. Hudson, "The 'Graying' of the Federal Budget and Its Consequences for Old-Age Policy," *Gerontologist* 18 (October 1978):428–440.

14. Douglas W. Nelson, "Alternative Images of Old Age as the Bases for Policy," in Bernice L. Neugarten (ed.), *Age or Need?* Beverly Hills, CA:Sage, 1982.

15. R.B. Hudson, "A Block Grant to the States for Long-Term Care," *Journal of Health Politics, Policy and Law* 6 (Spring 1981): 9–27.

16. Newcomer. *Funding Practices*.

17. M. Mogulof, *Making Social Service Changes at the State Level: Practice and Problems in Four States* (Washington, D.C.: Urban Institute, 1973).

18. Office of the Assistant Secretary for Planning and Evaluation, Department of Health and Human Services, *Exploratory Evaluation of Administration on Aging Programs* (Washington, C.C.:ASPE, 1980).

19. J.J. Callahan and S. Wallack, eds., *Major Reforms in Long-Term Care* (Lexington, MA: Lexington Books, 1981); U.S. Congressional Budget Office, *Long-Term Care for the Elderly and Disabled* (Washington, D.C.: U.S. GPO, 1977); and U.S. General Accounting Office, *The Elderly Should Benefit from Expanded*

Home Health Care .... (Washington, D.C.: U.S. Government Printing Office, 19820.

20. F.L. Cook, *Who Should Be Helped?* (Beverly Hills, CA: Sage, 1979) and D.L. Klemmack and L.L. Roff, "Predicting General and comparative Support for Government's Providing Benefits to Older Persons," *Gerontologis* 21 (December 1981): 592–599.

21. L. Gamm and F. Fisher, "The Technical Assistance Approach" in J.A. Christianson and R.W. Robinson, eds., *Community Development in America* (Ames, Iowa: Iowa State University Press, 1980).

22. W.W. Lammers, *Public Policy and the Aging* (Washington, D.C.: Congressional Quarterly Press, 1983).

23. T.R. Marmor and E.A. Kutza, *Analysis of Federal Regulations Related to Aging: Legislative Barriers to Coordination Under Title III* (University of Chicago, School of Social Service Administration, 1975).

24. B.D. Lebowitz, "The Management of Research in Aging: A Case Study in Science Policy," *Gerontologist* 19 (April 1979): 151–157.

Bibliography

Armour, P.K., Estes, C.L., and Noble, M.L., "The Continuing Design and Implementation Problems of a National Policy on Aging: Title III of the Older Americans Act," in R.B. Hudson (ed.), *The Aging in Politics* (Springfield, Ill.: Charles Thomas, 1981).

Califano, J.A., "The Aging of America: Questions for the Four-Generation Society," *The Annals*, v. 438 (July, 1978): 96–107.

Callahan, J.J. and Wallack, S. (eds.), *Major Reforms in Long-Term Care* (Lexington, Mass.: Lexington Books, 1981).

Cook, F.L., *Who Should Be Helped?* (Beverly Hills, Cal.: Sage Publications, 1979).

Etzioni, A., "Two Approaches to Organizational Analysis: A Critique and a Suggestion," *Administrative Science Quarterly*, v. 5 (Sept., 1960): 257–278.

Gamm, L. and Fisher, F., "The Technical Assistance Approach," in J.A. Christianson and J.W. Robinson (eds.), *Community Development in America* (Ames: Iowa State University Press, 1980).

Gold, B., "The Role of the Federal Government in the Provision of Social Services to Older Persons," *The Annals*, v. 415 (Sept., 1974): 55–69.

Hannan, M.T. and Freeman, J., "Obstacles to Comparative Studies," in P.S. Goodman and J.M. Pennings (eds.), *New Perspectives on Organizational Effectiveness* (San Francisco: Jossey-Bass, 1977).

Honadle, B.W., "A Capacity-Building Framework: A Search for Concept and Purpose," *Public Administration Review*, v. 41 (Sept.–Oct., 1981): 575–580.

Honadle, B.W., Managing Capacity-Building: Problems and Approaches," *Journal of the Community Development Society*, v. 13 (1982): 65–73.

Hudson, R.B., "A Block Grant to the States for Long-Term Care," *Journal of Health Politics, Policy and Law*, v.6 (Spring, 1981): 9–27.

Hudson, R.B., "Client Politics and Federalism: The Case of the Older Americans Act," paper prepared for delivery at the 1973 annual meeting of the American Political Science Association, New Orleans.

Hudson, R.B., "The 'Graying' of the Federal Budget and Its Consequences for Old-Age Policy," *Gerontologist*, v. 18 (October, 1978): 428–440.

Hudson, R.B. and Veley, M., "Federal Funding and State Planning: The Case of the State Units on Aging," *Gerontologist*, v. 14 (April, 1974): 122–129.

Klemmack, D.L. and Roff, L.L., "Predicting General and Comparative Support for Government's Providing Benefits to Older Persons," *Geontologist*, v. 21 (December, 1981): 592–599.

Lammers, W.W., *Public Policy and the Aging* (Washington, D.C.: Congressional Quarterly Press, 1983).

Lebowitz, B.D., "The Management of Research in Aging: A Case Study in Science Policy," *Gerontologist*, v. 19 (April, 1979): 151–157.

Marmor, T.R. and Kutza, E.A., *Analysis of Federal Regulations Related to Aging: Legislative Barriers to Coordination under Title III* (University of Chicago, School of Social Service Administration, 1975).

Mogulof, M., *Making Social Service Changes at the State Level: Practice and Problems in Four States* (Washington, D.C.: Urban Institute, 1973).

Neugarten, B. (ed.), *Age or Need? Public Policies for Older People* (Beverly Hills, Cal.: Sage Publications, 1982).

Newcomer, R.J., Estes, C.L., Benjamin, A.B., Swan, J.B., and Peguillan-Shea, V., *Funding Practices, Policies, and Performance of State and Area Agencies on Aging: Final Report, Executive Summary* (University of California at San Francisco, School of Nursing, 1982).

Office of the Assistant Secretary for Planning and Evaluation, Department of Health and Human Services, *Exploratory Evaluation of Administration on Aging Programs* (Washington, D.C.: ASPE, 1980).

Samuelson, R.J., "Aging America: Who Will Shoulder the Growing Burden," *National Journal*, v. 10 (1978), 1712–1717.

Sheppard, H., *The Administration on Aging — Or A Successor?* (Washington, D.C.: U.S. Senate Special Committee on Aging, 1971).

U.S. Congressional Budget Office, *Long-Term Care for the Elderly and Disabled* (Washington, D.C.: U.S.G.P.O., 1977).

U.S. General Accounting Office, *The Elderly Should Benefit From Expanded Home Health Care But Increasing These Services Will Not Insure Cost Reductions* (Washington, D.C.: U.S.G.P.O., 1982).

Yuchtman, E. and Seashore, S. E., "A System Resource Approach to Organizational Effectiveness," *American Sociological Review*, v. 32 (1967): 891–903.

Conclusion

ARNOLD M. HOWITT AND BETH WALTER HONADLE

The essays that comprise this book provide a variety of views about both the need for and the practice of building improved management capacity in American local governments. No single point of view dominates the essays presented here, but neither is it true that there are no common themes. In this brief final look at our topic, we wish to call attention to three themes that inform the thinking of a number of the authors represented here: (1) the importance of context in determining the needs for enhanced management capacity, (2) the political dimensions of capacity development, and (3) problems of implementation and institutionalization.

The Importance of Context

Among the themes of this volume, none stands out more clearly than the idea that the need for developing management capacity varies by context. Management needs are not static. They depend on the social, economic, technical, and political demands that government faces at a particular time and in a particular place. To build management capacity, therefore, is not to install a standard package of administrative tools, drill into imployees a prescibed set of skills, or rearrange

334

organizational units into an ideal configuration. It is to develop competence to perform the tasks that a state or local government must be able to accomplish, given the expectations placed upon it by citizens and other levels of government.

Management capacity needs also vary, first, by historical era. In retrospect, we can see clearly the dramatic evolution of state and local governments in the post-World War II period—the explosive increase in the number of employees and funds handled, the broad expansion of government functions, the enhanced specialization and complexity of operations, the increased interdependence of these operations both within government and between government and the private sector, and the wrenching changes necessitated by the sudden end of the long period of fiscal abundance. As Donald Kettl effectively analyzes in this volume, these changes have made many new demands on managers in the state and local sector.

Management capacity needs also vary, as Kettl points out, by type of government function. In the past, state and local governments had to concern themselves mainly with the direct management of service delivery, with relatively little attention to regulatory activity and contract management. Today the latter two functions have become vastly more significant, requiring executives in state and local government to adopt new strategies for dealing with them effectively.

As the papers in this volume by Norman Reid, Mark Schneider, and Joseph Viteritti and Robert Bailey suggest, varying patterns of social and economic development create differing pressures for improving management capacity. The vast intrametropolitan and interregional movement of population and economic activity in recent decades and important demographic changes (such as the effects of the baby-boom generation and the current aging of the population) create many new challenges for state and local governments.

The scale of government makes a difference in the nature of management processes and development needs, too. As Reid notes, small-town governments typically have small numbers of employees, are less likely to employ professionals, and are less structurally differentiated and organizationally sophisticated than those in larger communities. As a result, the stresses imposed by the changing functions of government have pushed many of these governments to take the initial step toward a more bureaucratic style of mangement: the recruitment of employees with more varied skills (or the retraining of the existing labor force); the development of new organizational units; participation in the financial, programmatic, and regulatory systems of

federal and state intergovernmental programs; and the partial trans-
formation of a highly personalized, particularized administrative style
into more routinized and universalistic operating methods.

Many of the suburban governments that Schneider writes about
have already made this transition. Having assimilated new functions
and programs during years of rapid growth—the general post-war
expansion of government coinciding with a period of extraordinary
population growth in many localities—suburban governments are more
oriented toward improving the productivity and effectiveness of their
management systems than to establishing them nearly from scratch.
This frequently involves taking advantage of more specialized methods
developed elsewhere, importing expert assistance, and pushing professionalism more deeply into the government structure.

In many large cities, as Viteritti and Bailey argue, bureaucratized
methods and professionalization took hold at an earlier stage and had
grown far more powerful than in smaller jurisdictions. In the face of
rapid change in the environment of government, the big cities
confronted somewhat different management pressures—the need to
restore the ability of central political authorities and administrators to
"steer" and coordinate government. To do this, it was necessary to
weaken the policy-making and management hold of narrowly based
coalitions of professional administrators, public employee unions (or
less formally organized employee interests), and specialized pressure
groups, by the establishment of stronger central budget, personnel, and
information systems.

The Political Dimensions of Capacity Building

A second major theme of this volume is that capacity building is
intimately entwined with politics. This is true in several senses.

As Timothy Mead argues, judgments about what constitutes an
adequate amount of management capacity are inherently subjective and
thus, in practice, are politically defined. One's perspective on this matter
is likely to depend critically on one's vantage point. Communities are
frequently content with a level of management capacity (at least as that
is represented by professionalism, expertise, and formal procedure) that
many external observers regard as insufficient. To a substantial degree,
these differences of perspective arise because some parties see values at
stake other than instrumental effectiveness or efficiency. Communities
may prefer to maintain a smaller scale of organization, or to forgo

intergovernmental financial assistance, or to continue to employ citizen-bureaucrats rather than professionals, or to pass up "modern" programmatic innovations, even when they are fully conscious of trade-offs in effectiveness or efficiency. They do this not because of small-mindedness but in order to restrict the scope of government and preserve local autonomy. They may also wish to sustain a personalized style of administration that appreciates and respects deeply held community beliefs, the local structure of status and power, and the community's way of life. Thus, what some may label parochialism, others may perceive as an expression of liberty.

We tend to think of such trade-offs most frequently in the context of small-town government, but Viteritti and Bailey make clear that other values may also supersede management capacity in the big-city environment. They point to the experience of the 1960s and early 1970s, when sacrifices of effectiveness and efficiency were made in the name of decentralization and inclusiveness in public employment practices. Some believe that such measures were essential to preserve the fabric of big-city life, to give groups too long excluded from sharing power a sense that government could respond to and represent them, too. More recently, in part as a result of pressure from outside the city, the pendulum has swung hard in the opposite direction, as fiscal troubles in many jurisdictions have forced local officials to make difficult budget-cutting choices and to look for productivity gains in all government programs and services. Viteritti and Bailey, however, wonder whether the contemporary stress on good management has weakened the accountability relationship between public officials and their constituents. Kettl, too, shares this concern with accountability.

The competition between instrumental effectiveness and efficiency, on one hand, and other public values, on the other, is not limited to a tension between community insiders and outsiders from other levels of government. Because there is no consensus in many communities about the appropriate balance among these values, issues of management capacity become major points of political contention. Moreover, factions within the community's political elite, appealing to different constituencies in the community-at-large, may focus their rivalry for status, power, and material advantage on such matters. In the nation's big cities, this was true when ethnic political conflict was acted out through the battle between the "machine" and "reform" political agendas; and, as Viteritti and Bailey note, it has been true more recently when racial minorities have pressed for more power and recognition in city affairs. As another example, in some formerly ex-urban, now suburban communities, seemingly narrow issues of management procudure or philosophy have become the battleground in a power struggle between long-time residents and new arrivals.

Even within the administrative system of a particular community, specific plans for enhancing management capacity may be controversial and hence the focus of intense bureaucratic politics. Management improvements are rarely perceived as neutral instruments in an administrative system. Instead various parties are likely to see potential advantages or disadvantages for their own positions of power or status. Improvements in management capacity frequently strengthen central administrators at the expense of their subordinates. For example, an agency head may regard a city manager's design for a management information system as a thinly veiled attempt to gain more leverage for himself in controlling the agency's operations, appraising the head's performance, and reducing the influence of a constituency with which the head works closely. As a result, the agency head may resist the adoption of the information system. The strengthening of central administration is not the inevitable effect of enhancements in management capacity, however. The development of new technical capabilities, especially if done with the support of an external funding source such as a federal or state grant-in-aid, may increase the autonomy and power of agency personnel in relation to generalist managers or political officeholders. Although the expected outcome may vary depending on features of the situation, there is a substantial likelihood that at least some parties will see any substantial change in management capacity as affecting the stakes of bureaucratic politics.

Implementation and Institutionalization

A third important theme of this book is the problem of implementing and institutionalizing improvements in management capacity. This theme is closely related to the political dimensions of capacity building.

Several of the essays in this book have dealt with the possibilities of promoting improvements in capacity from outside of the community or organization in question. Both Jacobs and Weimer and Howitt and Kobayashi consider this problem in the context of how external proposals affect the incentives—or perceptions of benefits and costs—of officials on both sides of the assistance relationship.

Howitt and Kobayashi are concerned first with the incentives of the aid-giving agency. They assess what interests several types of assistance providers (private consultants, "helping" agencies, "mission" agencies, nonprofit organizations, associations of government, and volunteers) bring to the assistance relationship and how these interests shape their behavior. In a complementary paper, Jacobs and Weimer examine the specific "tools" available to these aid-providers. Their analysis of three generic strategies of assistance (targeted financial subsidies, information provision, and technical assistance) and ten more specific tactics suggests the range of approaches available to those promoting capacity building.

From the other side of the relationship, the authors of both of these essays emphasize how the balance of incentives in the recipient government may cause resistance to the proposed project or management improvement. Both sets of authors argue that the strategic problem for the aid-giver is helping a "client" in the recipient government build a political and bureaucratic coalition strong enough to secure the adoption, implementation, and institutionalization of the proposed innovation.

From these two essays there emerges a strong sense of the limits of external intervention as a capacity-building approach. On the one hand, the "target" government may include a number of key actors who are resistant to, or at best unenthusiastic about, the proposed change; they may be acutely sensitive to a range of costs that outsiders only dimly perceive. On the other hand, the assistance provider may have insufficient motivation, political skills, or other resources to promote change effectively. Thus, the chances for a mismatch between the aid provider/strategy and the aid recipient are substantial, and so are the chances that the proposed innovation will be defeated, side-tracked, implemented incompletely or too slowly, or ultimately tried and abandoned.

Charles and Kathleen Warren and Beverly Cigler have looked closely at federal efforts to encourage capacity development in financial management and energy conservation. In these areas, at least, the results of federal intervention have been modest. Both programs recognized the tendency of local governments to be guarded in their acceptance of federal guidance; the programs therefore described their efforts as "capacity sharing" rather than "capacity building" to suggest the possibility of two-way exchange of information. Given their limited financing and relatively short lifespans, these programs enjoyed modest success. Their reach into the nation's local governments was far from comprehensive; and, because they were largely limited to transferring information about technical and managerial approaches, they had relatively litttle influence on the actual adoption and implementation of innovative practices.

Even given the weight of these theoretical and empirical essays, however, abject pessimism is not required because there is no categorical reason why external assistance initiatives cannot produce positive results in many circumstances. These analyses do suggest, though, the need for greater sophistication in selecting strategies of assistance and in designing the tactics that are to be used in any particular instance.

Another insight into the implementation process—the need to integrate improvements in management capacity into the overall structure of management—is offered by several of the essays in this volume. Jonathan Brock, for example, argues that labor relations should not be thought of as an isolated set of activities connected with episodic contract negotiations with public employee unions. Instead, he believes, labor relations must be part of the general fabric of management practice in the government. Conceptualized as the day-to-day management of human resources, labor relations considerations should be taken into account when major decisions are contemplated, and their relationship with high performance by government agencies should not be forgotten. Richard Higgins makes a similar argument in urging recognition of the interdependence between financial management functions (such as budgeting and accounting) and other central management processes (such as personnel management and program operations). Cigler's study of energy management also supports this point of view. She concludes that progress in energy conservation in local government has been hampered by the tendency to make "energy" a distinct issue with separate organizational structures and personnel. More promising, she feels, would be an approach that sought to make energy efficiency considerations part of a more general productivity improvement program.

In the view of these authors, therefore, the effectiveness of an innovation in mangement capacity can be significantly enhanced if it is well integrated with the overall management structure of the government. Nonetheless, there is a danger in the viewpoint represented by Brock, Higgins, and Cigler. By saying that capacity improvements should be integrated with the most important general management processes, they are demanding, in effect, that the sponsors of innovative practices achieve an even greater level of influence in the government than that required for simple adoption of the practice. It may be the case, therefore, that there is a trade-off between such integration and the probability of achieving any enhancement of management capacity. That need not be a fatal problem. It does suggest, though, that the backing of the government's chief executive is highly important, perhaps crucial, for the success of these more integrated capacity development projects. It also suggests that sometimes taking a foot-in-the-door strategy to establish a management practice, coupled with a later effort to achieve greater integration with general management systems, may be the only available course of action under some circumstances.

A Look to the Future

The task of improving management capacity in local governments is a continuing one. The federal government's role in that endeavor has been reduced in recent years by the Reagan administration's block grants, sharp budget cuts, and philosophy of reducing the federal government's interventions in local affairs. There is little likelihood that it will be expanded in the short run. The federal government's stance, however, puts added pressure on many municipalities to become better managers of the increasingly scarce resources they control. They may receive some assistance from the states, but it is unlikely that state government will have the resources to play a major role. As a result, we are likely to see local governments seeking to learn from each other, through various professional associations and leagues of cities and towns, about innovative management approaches. Federal and state governments may continue to play an information-sharing role, but the burden of promoting better management is likely to fall increasingly on local governments themselves.

Index

Aid *(cont.)*
  of, 131-138; prepackaged, 128-129. *See also* Technical assistance
Aid provision, the politics of, 131-138
American Planning Association, 302
Anthony, Edward, 13
Arab oil embargo, 286
Area Agencies on Aging, 312, 313, 316-320, 323, 324-328; Newcomer on, 319; perceived roles and purposes of, 319-321
Assessing procedures, 167-168
Assessing Department of Boston, 168
Assessment, 191
Associations of governments, 125-126, 131, 132
Associations of municipalities, 122-123, 128-129
Auditing, as a complement to budgeting, 188-189

Bailey, Robert, 102, 335, 336, 337
Bailey, Stephen, 247
Bargaining: and hired negotiators, 221-222; and in-house negotiators, 221-222; and legislative relations, 220-221; organizing for, 219-220; preparation for, 219; strategy, 219
Barnard, Chester, 140
Big-city government: capacity building and, 102-113; capacity versus governance, 103-105; and civil service, 110-111; Integrated Financial Management System, 109; and Ed Koch, 110; management information systems, 108; new capacities for, 106-111; a new crisis of legitimacy for, 111; Newland on, 103, 113; New York City's Health and Hospital Corporation, 110; New York City's Management Plan and Reporting System, 109; New York City's Metropolitan Transportation Authority, 110; New York City's Stabilization Reserve Corporation, 109; New York State Urban Development Corporation, 109; New York City's UDC default, 110; and the Office of Management and

Budget. 107: and public benefit corporations, 109, 110; Viteritti and Bailey on, 102
Block grants, 50, 51, 88
Boston: Assessing Department, 168; CAMA system, 174; a case study of, 166-171; computer-assisted mass appraisal system, 168; computers in assessing, 167-168; Data Processing Division, 166: Department of Health and Hospitals, 166; and the Digital Equipment Corporation, 170; Division of Administrative Services, 166; and the Flynn administration, 168, 171; and IBM, 166, 170; the implications of the experiences, 170-171; MIS Data Processing Center, 170; MIS Department, 166-167, 169-170; Office of Property Equalization, 168; parking ticket collection in, 167; payroll and personnel in, 168-169; and the turnkey personnel/payroll system, 169; and the White administration, 166, 170; and Wang, 169-170; and word processing, 169-170
Broadbanding, 111
Broadnax, Walter, 228
Brock, Jonathan, 209, 340
Brown, Anthony, 12
Bryce, Herrington, 30
Budgeting, 186-188, 202; and accounting, 188-189; and auditing, 188-189; control approach to, 188; management approach to, 188; and performance management, 188; planning approach to, 188; Schick on, 188
Business development, in suburbia, 94-95

California Office of Appropriate Technology, 295
CAMA system, 174, 175, 176
Capacity building: achieving community energy managment through, 292-295; Advisory Committee on Intergovernmental Relations, 272; Anthony on, 13; and appropriate assistance, 20; aging network development and, 315-321; Barnard on,

140; and big-city governance, 102-113; Brown on, 12; and the case of the aging network, 313-329; and civic entrepreneurship, 260; and combined funding, 19; the concept of, 10-13; conclusions concerning management, 334-341; Council of State Community Affairs Agencies, 13; defining and doing, 9-21; Drob on, 11; and empowerment, 10-11; the federal role in, 271-284; Feller on, 13; and financial and energy management programs, 273-283; a framework for, 13-18; funding strategies for inducing, 145-151; General Accounting Office, 12; generic strategies for inducing, 144-145; to govern, 242-262; and governance, 242-262; Graham on, 10; Hawkins on, 11; Hondale on, 9, 313; Howitt on, 11; inducing, 139-157; and inner- versus other- directedness, 12-13; and institutional development, 11; Integrated Financial Management System, 109; in an intergovernmental context, 312-329; is there a federal role in, 271-273; Lindley on, 12; for local energy management (Table 2), 293; and local-level officials, 20; local views on needs for, 66-80; and management information systems, 109; Management Plan and Reporting System, 109; and managing contract services, 55-59; and managing direct services, 53-55; and managing regulation, 59-62; in municipal labor-management relations, 209-226; National Science Foundation, 271; needs in different settings, 47-115; Newland on, 103; the new relevance of, 321-323; Niskanen on, 142; Office of Management and Budget, 271, 272; Office of Personnel Management's Intergovernmental Personnel Program, 271; the organizational concept of, 119-157; the organizational context of, 140-144; in an organizational context, 313-315; and policy for local energy management, 286-304; the political dimensions of, 336-338; and problems of suburban governments, 84-99; and public benefit corporations, 109; and

rewards, 19; and risk alleviation, 20-21; and the role of the external change agent, 139-157; in rural areas, 66-80; and the search for accountability, 62-64; Simon on, 140; steps for the aging network, 323-328; strategies for inducing (Table 1), 146-147; for suburban governments, 84-99; and systems development, 11-12; and survival, 10; and technical assistance relationships, 119-138; Tennessee Municipal League, 11-12; and third party in governance, 257-260; Toft on, 242; and trust, 18-19; and the use of established resources, 21; versus governance, 103-105; Wilson on, 141

Capacity building framework: anticipate change, 15; attract and absorb resources, 16-17; develop programs to implement policy, 16; evaluate current activities to guide future decisions, 17-18; make informed decisions about policy, 15-16; manage resources, 17. *See also* Capacity building

Capacity problems of suburban governments, 84-99

Capacity-sharing principles: Academy for State and Local Government, 281; Conference of Mayors, 280, 281; the Energy Center, 276, 278, 281; FMCS, 276-281; HUD, 280; International City Management Association, 281; and levels of management assistance, 277-278; *Mayor's Handbook on Financial Management*, 280; Municipal Finance Officers' Association, 280; National Association of Counties, 287; National League of Cities, 281; NCEMC, 276-281; a support network, 280-281; and user-defined program priorities, 276-277; and working through assications, 278-280

Capital facilities planning, 194-196
Capital Improvement Program (CIP), 195
Carver, John, 252
Cash management, 197-199, 203
Categorical project grants, 143
CEM. *See* Community energy management
Center for Research on Judgment and

280, 283, 293, 300; Financial
Management Capacity Sharing
Program, 185, 203-204, 273-283;
Office of Policy Development and
Research, 274
Department of Labor, 313
Department of Transportation, 273, 293
Demonstration projects, 130
Digital Equipment Corporation (DEC),
170
Digital Equipment PDP/11, 164
Direct services, the managing of, 53-55
Direct training, 147, 154-155
Diseconomies of scale, 29
Diversification, 184
Division of Administrative Services, of
Boston, 166
Drob, Judah, 11
Drucker, Peter, 242
Dye, Thomas, 40

Economic Research Service, 153
Economies of scale, 28-29, 31, 92
Eisenstadt, 323
Ellis, R. Jeffrey, 264
Empirical research, 295-299
Empowerment, 10-11
Energy capacity-building projects (Table
1), 291
Energy Center, the, 276, 278, 281, 283
Energy management: Academy of State
and Local Governments, 274, 281;
achieving community, through capacity
building, 292-295; Advisory Committee
on Intergovernmental Relations, 272;
American Planning Association, 302;
Arab oil embargo, 286; California
Office of Appropriate Technology, 295;
capacity-building policy for local,
286-304; and capacity-sharing
principles, 276-281; Cigler on, 286;
community, 287-288; and
comprehensive, 292-296;
Comprehensive Community
Management Program, 297; Conference
of Local Energy Officials, 294;
Conference of Mayors, 280;
Department of Energy, 273, 293, 300,

302; Department of Transportation,
273, 293; and empirical research,
295-299; federally funded energy
capacity-building projects (Table 1),
291; the Energy Center, 274, 278, 281,
283; and the evaluation results of
FMCS and NCEMC; FMCS, 273-283;
Government Finance Officers'
Association, 302; Henderson on, 289;
HUD, 273, 280, 283; International City
Management Association, 294, 300; is
there a federal role in municipal
271-273; lessons in financial
management and, 271-284; levels of
assistance in, 277-278; *Linkages:
Improving Financial Management in Local
Government*, 302; and local government
energy roles, 288-291; *Mayor's Handbook
on Financial Management*, 280; National
Association of Counties, 300; National
Academy of Public Administration, 274,
282; National Community Energy
Management Center, 273-282; National
Science Foundation, 271; NCEMC,
293-294, 300; National League of Cities,
294, 300; Office of Personnel
Management's Intergovernmental
Personnel Program, 271; Office of
Policy Development and Research, 274;
OMB, 271, 272; OPEC, 292; and the
Peer Practitioner Network, 281-282;
potential organizing models for,
299-303; *Productivity Improvement
Handbook for State and Local Governments*,
302; program philosophy for, 275-276;
and the Reagan administration, 274,
287, 294, 295; recommendations
concerning local, 303-304; the Shah of
Iran, 292; a support network for,
280-281; Three Mile Island, 286; and
user-defined program priorities,
276-277; and working through
associations, 278-280
Environmental protection regulations, 70
Etizoni, A., 314
Expenditures, the fastest growing state
and local (Table 1), 51
Extension Service, the, 153
External agent. *See* External change agent
External change agent: Barnard on, 140;

Peer Practitioner Network, 281-282; and the program philosophy, 175-176; and the Reagan administration, 274; a support network, 280-281; and user-defined program priorities, 276-277; working through associations, 278-280. *See also* Financial management capacity; Financial management practices
Financial management capacity: and accounting, 188-189; and auditing, 188-189; and budgeting, 186-189; and the control approach to budgeting, 188; developing, 182-205; and fiscal austerity, 183-185; Hays on, 185; HUD's Financial Management Capacity Sharing, 185; and implementation issues, 199-202; integration, 189-192; at the local government level, 182-205; and the management approach to budgeting, 188; and the New Federalism, 184; and new financial management practices, 192-199; and performance management, 188-189; and the planning approach to budgeting, 188; and policy management, 185-186; and program management, 185-186; and resource management, 185-186; Schick on, 188; the state role, 202-203; and traditional practices, 186-189; and where to go for help, 203-204
Financial Management Capacity Sharing (FMCS), 185, 282-283
Financial management functions, 191
Financial management practices: capital facilities planning, 194-196; Capital improvement Program, 195; cash management, 197-199; debt administration, 196-197; new, 192-199; and Proposition 13, 192
Financial reporting, 202-203
Fiscal austerity diversification, 184-185
Fiscal Disparities Act, 95
Fisher, F., 325
Flynn, Raymond, the administration of, 171
FMCS Program. See Financial Management Capacity Sharing Program
Form: ACIR, 36, 38; the issue of, 35-39; the OMB Study Committee, 38; *State*

and Local Roles in the Federal System, 38; Wood on, 37; Zimmerman, on, 36
Fourth Face of Federalism, 91
Fowler, Edmund, 40
Fragmentation, suburban, 85-86
Freeman, J. 314
Friend, J. K., 252
Function: Garcia and Dye on, 40; the issue of, 39-40; Liebert on, 39; Lineberry and Fowler on, 40
Functional unit building, 146, 148-149
Funding strategies, 145-149, 150-151

Gamm, L. 325
GAO. *See* General Accounting Office
Garcia, John, 40
Gargan, John, 25, 27
General Accounting Office, 12, 33, 50
Governance: Bailey on, 247; capacities (Table 1), 245; capacities for implementing policy, 245; capacities for making policy, 245; capacities for networking, 245; capacity building, 242-262; capacity building and big-city, 102-113; Carver on, 252; and civic entrepreneurship capacity building, 260; comparison of organization specific approaches to, 257-258; defined, 244-246; Friend on, 252; Graham on, 248; information systems, 250-252; *In Search of Excellence*, 248; International City Management Association, 242-243; Jessup on, 252; Lipshitz on, 259; key factors for success in strategic, 248-252; Korn/Ferry Study, 243; *The Leader*, 260; and legislative organization and management, 250; Maccoby on, 260; management training approach to, 253; Mansbridge on, 247; Naisbitt on, 261; NLC, 243, 254; Ohmae on, 249; operations research approach to, 256-257; the organizational development approach to, 253-255, 258; policy leadership in, 248-249; Sherwood on, 259; social judgment theory approach to, 255-256, 258; strategic, 246-247; and strategic

Scale *(cont.)*
Management Association, 30; the issue
of, 28-31; OMB Study Committee on
Policy Management Assistance, 29;
Reed on, 30; Rosenthal on, 31;
Whitaker on, 28-31
Schick, Allen, 188
Schneider, Mark, 84, 335, 336
SCOPMA. *See* Study Committee on
Policy Management Assistance
Seashore, S. E., 314
Senior Community Service Employment
Program, 313
Service delivery systems, changing
demands on, 89-91, 104
Services, managing contract, 55-59;
managing direct, 53-55
Shah of Iran, 292
Sherwood, John, 259
Simon, Herbert, 140
Skills seeding, 145-148
Smith, Bruce, 56
Social judgment theory approach, 255-
256, 258
Social Security, 316
Solid state chips, 164
Strategic governance: Bailey on, 247; and
governance information systems, 250-
252; Graham on, 248; *In Search of
Excellence*, 248; Ohmae on, 249; key
factors for success in, 248-252;
Legislative organization and
management factors in, 250;
Mansbridge on, 247; policy leadership
as a factor in, 248-249; strategic
thinking and policy judgment as factors
in, 249-250; Sundquist on, 247; Yates
on, 247. *See also* Governance
State governments: and accounting, 202;
arguments about the capacity of, 49-53;
and block grants, 50; and budgeting,
202; and cash management, 203; and
debt administration, 202-203; and
direct services, 53; and the fastest
growing state expenditures (Table 1),
51; and financial reporting, 202; Gulick
on, 52; Hamilton on, 51-52; initiatives
to improve human resource
development for local governments,

233-234-239; and managing contract
services, 55-59; and managing
regulation, 59-62; the Oregon
Municipal Debt Advisory Board, 203;
and POSDCORB skills, 52; the role of,
in developing financial management
capacity, 202-203; Salamon on, 53; and
the search for accountability, 62-64;
state and local partnerships in human
resource development for local
governments, 234-236, 239; the United
Way, 235
State and local initiatives, in human
resource development, 233-236, 239
State Units on Aging (SUAs), 312, 313
Strategic governance, and policy
leadership, 248-249
Strategic thinking, and policy judgment,
249-250
Strategy development approach, 255, 257,
258
*Strengthening Public Management in the
Intergovernmental System*, 26, 29
Study Committee on Policy Management
Assistance, 26, 29
Suburban diversity, 86-87
Suburban environment: and the changing
demands on service delivery systems,
89-91; and the changing economy,
87-88; and the changing government
structure, 91-93; and the changing
intergovernmental milieu, 88-89; and
fragmentation, 85-86; Kettl on, 91; and
population changes, 86-87
Suburban fragmentation, 85-86
Suburban government: A-95 Review, 93,
98; and business and commercial
development, 94-95; and capacity
issues, 93-98; capacity problems of,
84-99; and the changing demands on
service delivery systems, 89-91; and the
changing economy, 87-88; and the
changing governmental milieu, 88-89;
and the changing suburban
environment, 85-93; and the changing
structure of, 91-93; Community
Development Act, 89-90; and
contracting, 96-97; and demographic
changes, 93-94; and the emerging

United Way, the, 235
Urban Development Action Grants, 90
Urban Outcomes, 34

Visiting Nurses Associations, 320, 324
Viteritti, Joseph, 102, 335, 336, 337
Volunteers, 123, 127, 131, 132. *See also*
   Human resources

Wang Laboratories, 169-170; Wang 2200,
   164
Warren, Charles and Kathleen, 271, 339
Weimer, David Leo, 139, 338
White, Kevin, the administration of, 166,
   170

White, Theodore, 260
White House Conference on Aging, 316
Wilson, James, 141
Wolensky, Robert, 27
Wood, Robert, 37
Word processing systems, 64; in Boston,
   169-170; Digital Equipment
   Corporation, 170; IBM, 170; MIS Data
   Processing Center in Boston, 170; MIS
   Department in Boston, 169-170; Wang
   systems, 169-170

Yates, Douglas, 54, 247
Yuchtman, E., 314

Zimmerman, Joseph, 36